Computer Accounting Essentials
with
QuickBooks® 2018

Desktop Versions Pro, Premier & Accountant

Ninth Edition

Carol Yacht, MA
Software Consultant

Matthew Lowenkron, BSBA, EA
Glendale Community College

Mc
Graw
Hill
Education

YACHT/LOWENKRON: COMPUTER ACCOUNTING ESSENTIALS USING QUICKBOOKS® 2018, NINTH EDITION

ISBN 978-1-259-54589-4 (bound edition)
MHID 1-259-54589-X (bound edition)

Executive Portfolio Manager: *Steve Schuetz*
Product Developer: *Allie Kukla*
Marketing Manager: *Michelle Williams*
Lead Content Project Manager: *Dana M. Pauley*
Senior Buyer: *Susan K. Culbertson*
Design: *Egzon Shaqiri*
Content Licensing Specialist: *Melissa Homer*
Cover Image: © *f11photo/Shutterstock*
Compositor: *SPi Global*

mheducation.com/highered

About the Authors

Carol Yacht is an educator and author of technology-based accounting textbooks. Carol authors QuickBooks Online (2/e), QuickBooks Desktop (9/e), and Sage Peachtree (20/e), textbooks. Carol taught on the faculties of California State University-Los Angeles, West Los Angeles College, Yavapai College, and Beverly Hills High School. She started using accounting software in her classes in 1980. Carol's teaching career includes first and second year accounting courses, accounting information systems, and computer accounting.

Since 1989, Carol's textbooks have been published by McGraw-Hill. She contributes regularly to professional journals and is the Editor of the American Accounting Association's Teaching, Learning, and Curriculum section's *The Accounting Educator.*

Carol Yacht was an officer of AAA's Two-Year College section and recipient of its Lifetime Achievement Award. She is a board member of the Microsoft Dynamics Academic Alliance; worked for IBM Corporation as an education instruction specialist; serves on AAA's Teaching, Learning, and Curriculum section's research, instructional, and hall of honor award committees; and works for Intuit and Sage as a consultant. Carol earned her MA degree from California State University-Los Angeles, BS degree from the University of New Mexico, and AS degree from Temple University.

Matthew Lowenkron teaches Financial Accounting, Managerial Accounting, Uses of Accounting Information, and Business Communications at Glendale Community College in Arizona. Previous to teaching Matt worked as a tax accountant. He is an Enrolled Agent. Matt earned his BSBA degree in Management at Northern Arizona University, and completed his post-baccalaureate in Accounting at Arizona State University.

Preface

Computer Accounting Essentials with QuickBooks 2018, 9th Edition, teaches you how to use QuickBooks (QB) 2018 ***desktop software***[1] QuickBooks 2018 is a financial management program created for small businesses.

QuickBooks 2018 is a comprehensive accounting program that includes customer and vendor processing, banking, inventory management, and payroll. You can also share information with Office programs, such as Word, Excel, and Outlook.

Additional resources are available on the Online Learning Center (OLC) at www.mhhe.com/qbd2018. QBD is an abbreviation for QuickBooks Desktop. Desktop software is installed locally on your computer's hard drive. The OLC includes additional chapter resources, including troubleshooting tips, narrated PowerPoints, online quizzes, and QA templates with multiple-choice and true/false questions.

QUICKBOOKS 2018

Each textbook includes a license number and product number used for the download of QuickBooks 2018 software. QuickBooks 2018 desktop software can be used for 5 months. For more information, go to Online Learning Center at www.mhhe.com/qbd2018 > Access Codes. *Computer Accounting Essentials with QuickBooks 2018, 9e,* shows how to set up and operate a merchandising business. After completing the textbook, you will have a working familiarity with QuickBooks desktop software.

---

[1]Words that are boldfaced and italicized are defined in the glossary, Appendix C.

TEXTBOOK ORGANIZATION BY CHAPTER

1: Software Installation and Creating a New Company

After verifying your computer meets or exceeds the system requirements, install QB 2018. Following the Express Start interview, you create a new company and then back up.

2: Exploring QuickBooks

There are numerous sample companies included with the software. To learn about QB 2018's user interface, internal controls, and help resources, you explore a sample product company and a sample service company. In addition, you review user roles, customize the privileges of a user, and e-mail a company backup to your professor.

3: New Company Setup for a Merchandising Business

In Chapter 3, you begin operating a retail business called Your Name Retailers Inc. You enter beginning balances for October 1 of the current year, edit the chart of accounts, record and post bank transactions, complete bank reconciliation, and print reports. Detailed steps and numerous screen images help you learn how to use QB 2018.

4: Working with Inventory, Vendors, and Customers

In Chapter 4, to learn basic business processes you complete two months of transactions. You set up vendor preferences, defaults and inventory items, record vendor transactions, make vendor payments, record sales transactions, and collect customer payments. You also complete bank reconciliation, display various reports, and prepare financial statements.

5: Accounting Cycle and Year End

In Chapter 5, you review the accounting cycle and complete end-of-year adjusting entries, print financial statements, and close the fiscal year.

6: First Month of the New Year

In Chapter 6, you begin the new fiscal year, record one month of transactions for your business, make adjusting entries, and print reports.

Project 1: Your Name Hardware Store is a comprehensive project that incorporates what you have learned in Chapters 1 through 6. In Project 1, you analyze typical source documents used by a merchandising business and complete the accounting cycle.

Project 2: Student-Designed Merchandising Business asks you to create a merchandising business from scratch.

Appendix A: Review of Accounting Principles. Appendix A is a review of basic accounting principles and procedures.

Appendix B: Troubleshooting. Refer to this window for additional troubleshooting tips.

Appendix C: Glossary. Appendix C is a glossary of terms.

Index: The textbook ends with an index.

Online Learning Center: www.mhhe.com/qbd2018. Each chapter includes additional resources online.

Practice Sets: The Online Learning Center at www.mhhe.com/qbd2018 includes two additional projects: Practice Set 1, Your Name Accounting; and Practice Set 2, Your Name Sports.

BACKING UP OR SAVING QUICKBOOKS 2018 FILES

QuickBooks can store your data several different ways. In this text, you save or backup work using either QuickBooks backup files (.QBB extensions) or QuickBooks portable company files (.QBM extensions).

Local backup: .QBB

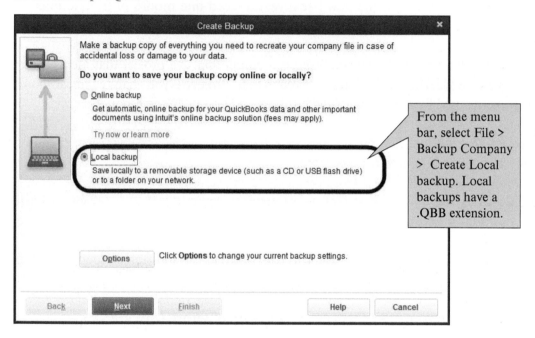

From the menu bar, select File > Backup Company > Create Local backup. Local backups have a .QBB extension.

Portable company file: .QBM

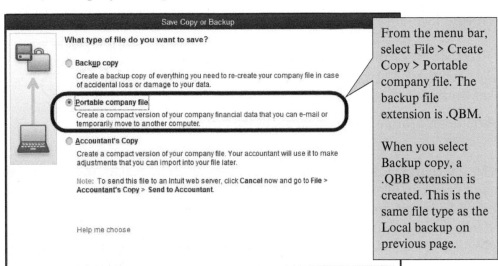

From the menu bar, select File > Create Copy > Portable company file. The backup file extension is .QBM.

When you select Backup copy, a .QBB extension is created. This is the same file type as the Local backup on previous page.

CONVENTIONS USED IN TEXTBOOK

As you work through the chapters, read and follow the step-by-step instructions. Numerous screen illustrations help you check work.

1. Information that you type appears in **boldface;** for example, Type **Melody Harmony** in the Customer name field.

2. Step sequences are separated by a greater-than sign; for example, www.mhhe.com/qbd2018 > Student Edition > choose Chapter > Multiple Choice.

3. Keys on the keyboard that are pressed appear like this: <Tab>; <Enter>.

4. QuickBooks selections are also shown with brackets; for example, <Save and Close>, <OK>, etc.

5. Dates are shown with Xs; for example, 10/1/20XX. For the Xs, substitute the current year.

6. Icons are shown as they appear on the QuickBooks' interface; for example, Home, Check Register, etc.

7. Read Me boxes go into more detail about a QB feature. Whenever you see a Read Me box, read this information.

8. Footnotes provide information about the task you are completing.

Refer to the chart below and on the next page for chapter, backup file names, file sizes and page numbers where files were backed up. The chart shows the backups made in Chapters 1 through 6, Project 1, and Practice Sets 1 and 2. The chart includes the page number where the backup is made and the file size. The authors recommend that you back up to a USB flash drive. Backups can also be made to the desktop, network drive, or hard drive location.

Chapter, Project, PS	Backups (.QBB and .QBM extensions)	File Size	Page No.
1	Your Name Retailers Inc.(Backup date-time).QBB	6,168 KB	15–20
	Your Name Hardware Store.QBB	6,180 KB	27
2	sample_product-based business.QBM	2,9935 KB	33–36
	Your Name Chapter 2 End.QBM	2,944 KB	72–74
	Your Name sample_service-based business. QBM	5,103 KB	81
	Your Name Chapter 3 October 1.QBB	6,332 KB	103
3	Your Name Chapter 3 October Check Register.QBB	6,408 KB	115
	Your Name Chapter 3 October End.QBB	6,540 KB	126
	Your Name Retailers Inc. Chapter 3 (Backup date-time).QBB	6,168 KB	126–127

Chapter, Project, PS	Backups (.QBB and .QBM extensions)	File Size	Page No.
4	Your Name Chapter 4 Vendors and Inventory.QBB	6,656 KB	150
	Your Name Chapter 4 Vendors.QBB	6,760 KB	166
	Your Name Chapter 4 November.QBB	6,904 KB	188
	Your Name Chapter 4 End.QBB	7,036 KB	198
	Your Name Exercise 4-2 December.QBB	7,072 KB	204
5	Your Name Chapter 5 December UTB.QBB	7,212 KB	217
	Your Name Chapter 5 December Financial Statements.QBB	7,216 KB	226
	Your Name Chapter 5 EOY (Portable).QBM	998 KB	230
6	Your Name Chapter 6 January Check Register.QBB	7,376 KB	244
	Your Name Chapter 6 UTB.QBB	7,508 KB	248
	Your Name Chapter 6 January Financial Statements.QBB	7,508 KB	252
	Your Name Exercise 6-1 (Portable).QBM	1,110 KB	256
Project 1	Your Name Hardware Store Chart of Accounts (Portable).QBM	623 KB	264
	Your Name Hardware Store Beginning Balances (Portable).QBM	628 KB	266
	Your Name Hardware Store Vendors Inventory Customers (Portable).QBM	651 KB	272
	Your Name Hardware Store January (Portable).QBM	665 KB	284
	Your Name Hardware Store Complete (Portable).QBM	751 KB	286
Practice Set 1	Your Name Accounting	OLC**	OLC
Practice Set 2	Your Name Sports	OLC	OLC

File sizes may differ.

There are two practice sets on the Online Learning Center at www.mhhe.com/qbd2018 > Student Edition. They include additional practice with a service business, Your Name Accounting, and a merchandising business, Your Name Sports. Both practice sets include reminders to back up portable company files.

Table of Contents

Comment:

The Timetable for Completion is meant as a guideline for hands-on work. Work can be completed in class or as an outside-of-class project. Work not completed in class is homework. In most Accounting classes, students can expect to spend approximately two hours outside of class for every hour in class.

TIMETABLE FOR COMPLETION		Hours
Chapter 1	Software Installation and Creating a New Company	2.0
Chapter 2	Exploring QuickBooks	3.0
Chapter 3	New Company Setup for a Merchandising Business	3.0
Chapter 4	Working With Inventory, Vendors, and Customers	3.0
Chapter 5	Accounting Cycle and Year End	1.0
Chapter 6	First Month of the New Year	2.0
Project 1*	Your Name Hardware Store	2.0
Project 2	Student-Designed Merchandising Business	2.0
Practice Set 1	Service Business (Online Learning Center)	3.0
Practice Set 2	Merchandising Business (OLC)	4.0
	TOTAL HOURS:	**25.0**

*In Project 1, typical source documents are used for transaction analysis, including accounts payable, inventory, accounts receivable, cash, and bank reconciliation. The accounting cycle is completed for one month. An audit trail report is also completed.

Chapter 1

Software Installation and Creating a New Company

OBJECTIVES

1. System Requirements.
2. Download QuickBooks Desktop 2018.
3. Create a New Company.
4. Activate QuickBooks Desktop 2018.
5. Backing up Company Data.
6. Go to QuickBooks Learn & Support page.

> **IMPORTANT MESSAGE: QuickBooks Desktop 2018**
>
> For 5 months (or 160 days) of QuickBooks Desktop 2018 use on a single computer, the software must be activated. Refer to Activate QuickBooks Desktop, pages 13–15. If the software is <u>not</u> activated, you have 30 days of use (or 15 startups). QuickBooks 2018 cannot be networked in computer labs. QB Desktop 2018 Student Trial Edition will operate for 160 days **after** activation.

DESKTOP SYSTEM REQUIREMENTS

The following systems requirements are online at
https://quickbooks.intuit.com/desktop/premier/ > select Tech Specs.

- Windows 7 SP1, 8.1 Update 1, or Windows 10 (all 32-bit & 64-bit)
- Windows Server 2008 R2 SP1, 2012 R2 or 2016
- 2.4 GHz processor
- 4 GB of RAM (8GB recommended)

- 2.5 GB disk space recommended (additional space required for data files)
- Payroll and online features require Internet access (1 Mbps recommended speed)
- Product activation is required. Refer to pages 13–15.
- Optimized for 12080 × 1024 screen resolution or higher. Supports one Workstation Monitor, plus up to 2 extended monitors. Optimized for Default DPI settings.
- 2GB or higher *USB drive* for backups

Integration with Other Software

- Microsoft Word and Excel integration requires Office 2010, 2013, 2016, or Office 365 (32 and 64 bit)
- E-mail Estimated, Invoices and other forms with Microsoft Outlook 2010–2016, Microsoft Outlook with Office 365, Gmail, Yahoo Mail, and Outlook.com, other SMTP-supporting e-mail clients.
- Adobe Acrobat Reader DC–free download at https://get.adobe.com/reader/.

Browser Requirement

- Internet Explorer 11 (32-bit)

DOWNLOAD QUICKBOOKS 2018

This section includes steps for installing QuickBooks 2018 desktop software on a single computer. Instructions for uninstalling lower versions of QuickBooks are included in Appendix B, page 311.

Note to instructors: For classroom site license information, go to www.mhhe.com/qbd2018 > Site License. Educators can sign up for free QuickBooks Desktop software for the classroom at http://education.intuit.com/signup/desktop/.

Windows 10 and Microsoft Edge was used to download QB Desktop 2018. Some steps and screen illustrations may differ for other versions of Windows or browsers.

1. To download QuickBooks Desktop Accountant 2018, go to https://support.quickbooks.intuit.com/Support/ProductUpdates.aspx. The Downloads & Updates page appears for QuickBooks Desktop Accountant 2018 > click Download.

If QuickBooks Desktop Accountant **2018** does not appear, link to [Change] > select QuickBooks Desktop Accountant > Accountant 2018.

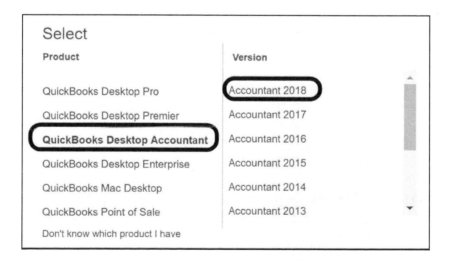

2. After selecting <Download>, a Setup_QuickBooks. . . exe prompt
    appears on the taskbar 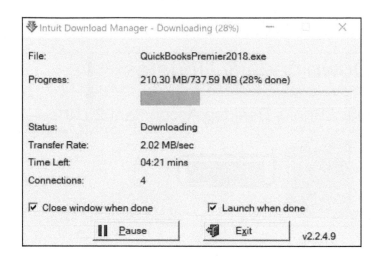 > double click on it.
    When the User Account Control pop-up appears, click <Yes>. The Intuit
    Download Manager shows the percent of progress.

3. When the download manager is finished, the Welcome to the InstallShield
    Wizard for QuickBooks Financial Software 2018 R1 appears > click <Next>.
    Your release number (R) may differ.

4. After clicking <Next>, QuickBooks 2018 starts to extract files. After a little while, the Welcome to QuickBooks Desktop! window appears. This wizard will guide you through your installation. Close any open programs, especially virus protection program, before continuing. Click <Next> to continue.

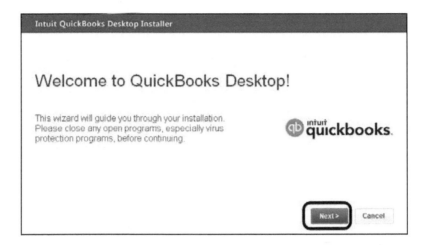

5. After clicking <Next>, the License Agreement appears. Click on the box next to I accept the terms of the license agreement to place a checkmark in it > click <Next>.

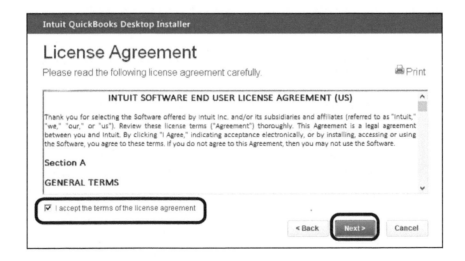

6. After accepting the License Agreement, the License and Product Numbers window appears. Type the License and Product Numbers that came with your textbook. The License and Product numbers can be used once on a PC computer.

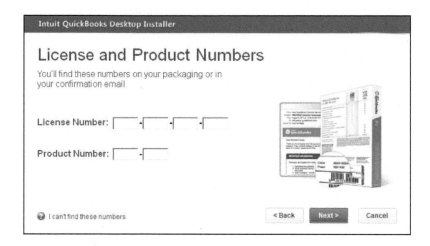

7. Make sure you typed the correct License and Product Numbers > click <Next>.

8. The Choose your installation type window appears. Accept the default for Express > click <Next>.

9. The Ready to install window appears > click <Install>. The Installing QuickBooks Desktop 2018 window shows the progress of installation. This will take a few minutes.

10. When the Congratulations! window appears, click <Open QuickBooks>.

11. The Let's get your business set up quickly! Window appears. (*Hint:* You may need to select File > New Company.)

Create a New Company

12. Select . The Glad you're here window appears. Type **Your Name Retailers Inc.** (use *your first and last name*) in the Business Name field. Red asterisks (*) indicate fields that must be completed.

Glad you're here!

Tell us about your business so we can give you the right tools for what you do.

* Business Name   Your Name Retailers Inc.

13. For Industry, link to Help me choose. The Select Your Industry window appears. Scroll down the list and highlight Retail Shop or Online Commerce.

14. After clicking <OK>, link to Help me choose in the Business Type field. Select Corporation.

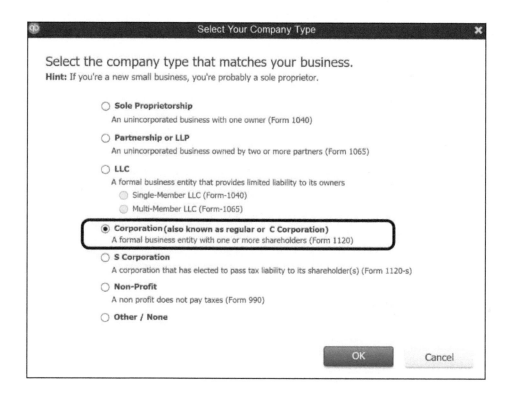

15. After selecting Corporation, then <OK>, you are returned to the Glad you're here! window. Leave the Employer Identification Number (EIN) field blank. Complete these fields.

Business Address:	type your address
City:	**Reno**
State:	**NV**
ZIP:	**89557**

16. Compare the Glad you're here! window to the one shown. *Your first and last name* Retailers Inc should be shown for the Business Name.

17. After selecting 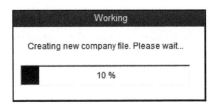, a working window appears. Wait while QB creates your company.

Working

Creating new company file. Please wait...

10 %

18. When the Get all the details into QuickBooks Desktop window appears, read the information.

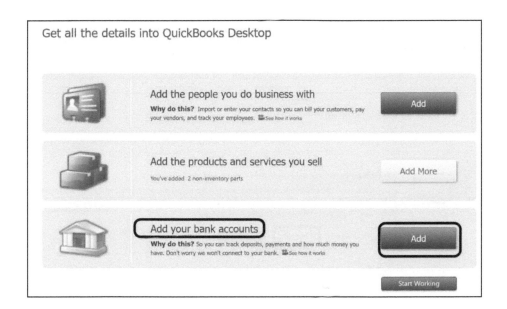

19. In the Add your bank accounts section, click [Add]. The Add your bank accounts window appears. In the Account name field, type **Home State Bank.**

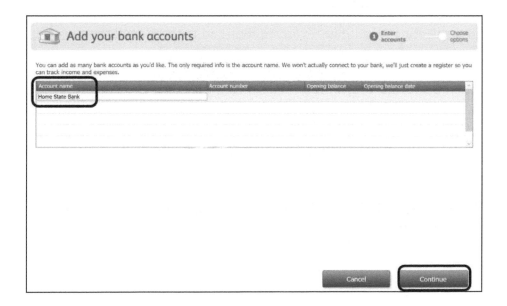

20. After selecting <Continue>, click on the radio button for No Thanks for ordering checks from Intuit.

21. After selecting <Continue>, you are returned to the Get all the details into QuickBooks Desktop window. Select Start Working .

22. If a New Feature Tour window opens, read the information > click <X> on its title bar to close.

23. Read the Accountant Center information. Click on the <X> on the Accountant Center window's title bar to close it. Click <OK>.

24. The QuickBooks Home Page appears. The title bar shows Your first and last name Retailers Inc. – QuickBooks Accountant Desktop 2018. A partial **Home Page** is shown on the next page.

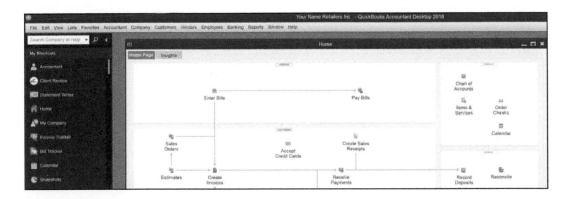

Activate QuickBooks Desktop

25. Check QuickBooks Desktop registration. Press the function key F2 on your keyboard. The Product Information window displays. Look for the registration status to the right of the license number. If QuickBooks says **ACTIVATED,** then you are all set. To close the Product Information window, click <OK>.

26. If QuickBooks is **NOT ACTIVATED** click <OK> to close the Product Information window.

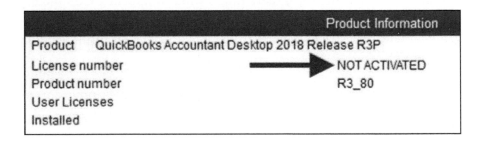

27. From the menu bar, select Help > Activate QuickBooks Desktop. The Activate QuickBooks Premier: Accountant Edition 2018 window appears. Read the information. You must activate to have access to QB 2018 for 5 months. If you do <u>not</u> activate, the software will stop working after 30 days. Compare your Activate window to the one shown on the next page.

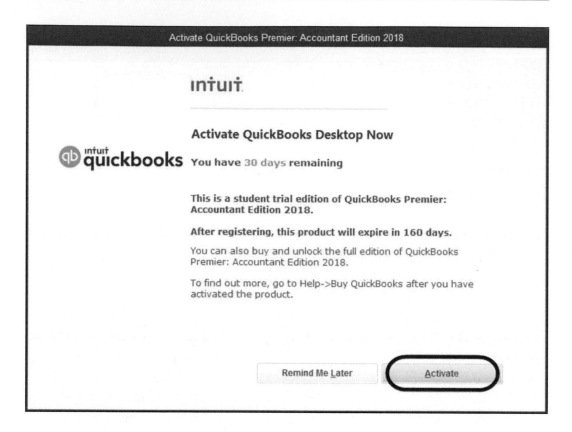

28. After selecting Activate, the Create Login window appears. Complete these fields: Email address, First Name, Last Name, and Password (6-32 characters no spaces). **Note:** If you already have an Intuit account, select Sign In.

29. A Confirmation window appears showing that your activation is complete. Select <No Thanks, Start QuickBooks>. The Home page appears.

30. To view activation information, from the Home Page press the `F2` function key. **You have 5 months of use. After that time, the software is not accessible.** The Product Information window shows ACTIVATED. Your license and product numbers are shown and the date QB was installed. (*Hint:* If NOT ACTIVATED is shown, refer to pages 13–15.)

```
                                          Product Information
Product      QuickBooks Accountant Desktop 2018 Release R1P
License number                               ACTIVATED
Product number                               R1_38
User Licenses
Installed
```

31. Your Release number may differ. To close the Product Information window, click <OK>. If necessary, close your browser.

BACKING UP COMPANY DATA

Frequent saving or **backing up** of company data is a good business practice. In this textbook, you are shown how to back up to the desktop or external media. Backing up to a drive other than the computer's hard drive or network drive is called backing up to **external media.** (Words that are boldfaced and italicized are defined in Appendix C, Glossary.) Authors suggest you backup to a USB flash drive.

When you back up, you are saving to the current point in QuickBooks. Each time you save or make a backup, the file name and date and time of the backup will distinguish between them. In this way, if you need to **restore** an earlier backup (for example, you make a mistake), you have the data for that purpose. See Preface, pages x-xi, for a list of backups that are made in this text and their file sizes.

In the business world, backups are unique for each business day. Daily backups are necessary. If you are working in a computer lab, *never leave the computer lab without first backing up your data to external media, for example, your USB flash drive.*

Follow these steps to back up Your Name Retailers Inc. company data.

1. From the menu bar, click File > Back Up Company, Create Local Backup.

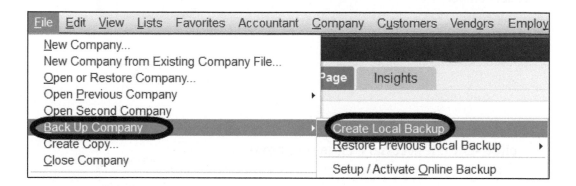

2. The Create Backup window appears. Local backup is selected. Insert a USB flash drive.

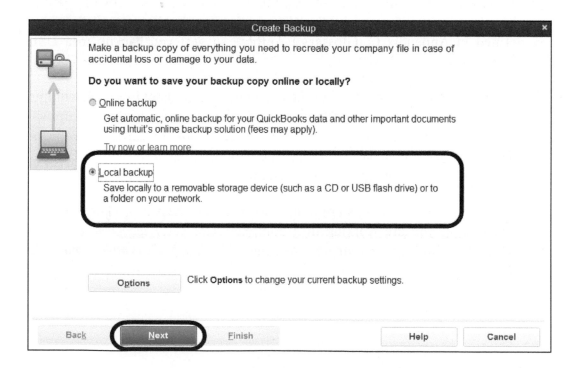

3. After selecting <Next>, the Backup Options window appears. Click <Browse>. Go to the location of your USB drive, click <OK>. In the illustration, drive F:\ is shown on the Browse for Folder window. (Your drive letter may differ.) You can back up to a USB drive, other external media, or the desktop.

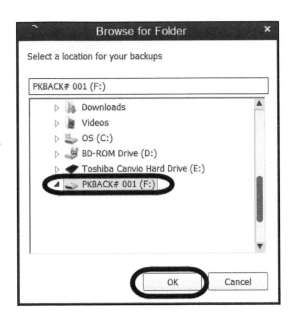

4. After clicking <OK>, you are returned to the Backup Options window. Your USB drive letter is shown in the <Browse> field. (The author's USB drive is F:\.) The number 4 is shown in the Remind me to backup up when I close my company.

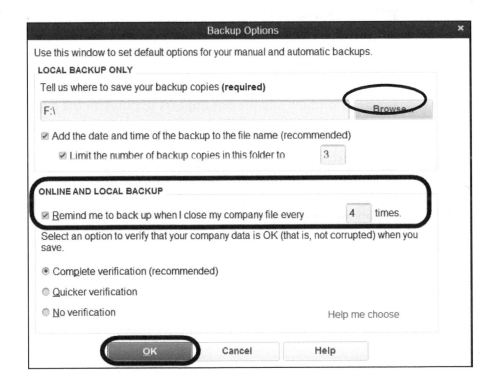

5. After selecting <OK>, the screen prompts When do you want to save your backup copy? The default is Save it now.

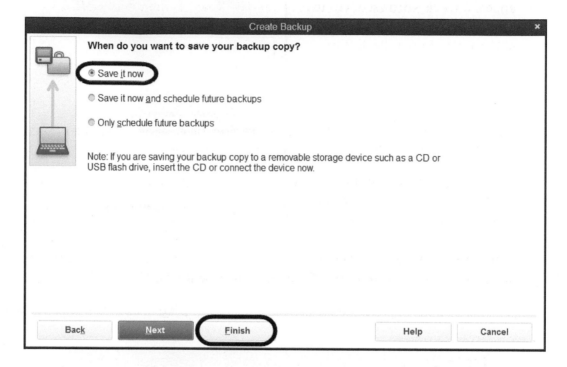

6. After selecting <Finish>, a Verifying data integrity window appears. Then, the Working window appears while your file is being backed up. When the backup is complete, a window like the one appears to confirm the date, time, and location of the saved company data. Your date and time differs.

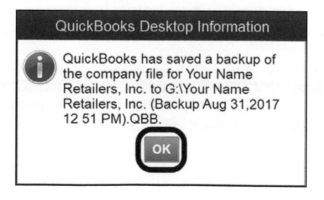

7. After selecting <OK>, you are returned to the QuickBooks Home
    Page. Exit or continue working on the next section. If you exit QB,
    an Automatic Backup window may appear. Read it, then click <No>.
    If the QuickBooks Web Connector window appears read it > click
    <Exit>.

QUICKBOOKS LEARN & SUPPORT

QuickBooks includes a Help Hub, Ask a question field, topics, and additional
resources. Let's take a look at how QuickBooks coaches you.

1. If a Set Up an External Accountant User window appears, read the
    information. Click on the box next to Don't show this again. Then
    select <No>.

2. From the menu bar, select Help > Support. A QuickBooks Learn & Support
    window appears. Review the information on these sections.

    *   QuickBooks Accountant Help Hub includes the Ask a question field.
    *   Browse Topics
    *   Top FAQs
    *   Announcements
    *   Additional resources
    *   Other Options

3. In the Browse Topics area, select Getting Started > in the QuickBooks
    Desktop FAQs list > link Windows 10 FAQ. If necessary, enlarge the page
    and read the information. Close the Window 10 FAQ page.

4. Click on the left-arrow to go back to QuickBooks Learn & Support
    Home. Explore other links, for example, Account and billing,
    Employees and payroll, Reports, Bank feeds, Accountant's copy, Money
    in/out, QuickBooks Self Employed, ProConnect Tax Online. Close all
    windows.

5. To close all windows, from the menu bar, select Window, Close All. To see the Home Page, on the Icon bar, click [Home].

SUMMARY AND REVIEW

Additional resources are on the textbook's Online Learning Center (OLC) at www.mhhe.com/qbd2018. The OLC includes Student Edition links and Information Center links. When you link to the Student Edition, choose a chapter to populate more resources.

Student Edition

Glossary	Multiple Choice Quiz
Practice Set 1	Narrated PowerPoints
Practice Set 2	QA Templates

Information Center

About the Authors	Sage 50 2017 20e
Access Codes	Sample Chapter
Book Preface	Site License
Feature Summary	Support
QuickBooks Online 2e	Table of Contents
	Troubleshooting

RESOURCEFUL QUICKBOOKS

Go to the QuickBooks website at http://quickbooks.intuit.com/premier/. Explore the website. To answer the questions, select these tabs: Pricing, Overview, Features, and Tech Specs.

1. What prices are shown?
2. How does QB Premier organize your finances?
3. List each industry. What tasks are unique to each industry.
4. What are the technical specification?

Multiple Choice Questions: The Online Learning Center includes the multiple-choice questions at www.mhhe.com/qbd2018 > select Student Edition > Chapter 1 > Multiple Choice.

_____ 1. After activation, how long will QuickBooks be accessible?

       a. Only 30 days.

       b. Not more than 60 days.

       c. Up to 120 days.

       d. 5 months.

_____ 2. Once QuickBooks is installed, which of the following icons appear on the desktop:

       a. Support for QuickBooks.

       b. QuickBooks Library.

       c. QuickBooks 2018.

       d. Payroll for QuickBooks.

_____ 3. The Welcome to QuickBooks window allows users to:

       a. Explore QuickBooks.

       b. Open an existing company file.

       c. Create a new company.

       d. All of the above.

_____ 4. The name of the company created in Chapter 1 is:

    a.   Your Name Retailers Inc.

    b.   Your Name Merchandisers.

    c.   Sample product-based business.

    d.   Sample service-based business.

_____ 5. The type of business created in Chapter 1 is:

    a.   Nonprofit.

    b.   Repair and maintenance.

    c.   Retail shop or online commerce.

    d.   Sales-independent contractor.

_____ 6. The business created in Chapter 1 will operate as a:

    a.   Sole proprietorship.

    b.   Corporation.

    c.   LLP.

    d.   LLC.

_____ 7. The business created in Chapter 1 does:

    a.   Accept credit cards.

    b.   Print checks.

    c.   Employ many employees.

    d.   Accept cash and checks.

_____ 8. Software activation with Intuit must be completed within how many days of installation?

    a.   30 days.

    b.   60 days.

    c.   120 days.

    d.   160 days.

_____ 9. Account activation information can be viewed from the QuickBooks desktop by selecting which function key?

    a. <F1>.

    b. <F2>.

    c. <F3>.

    d. <F4>.

_____ 10. The cash balance at Home State Bank is:

    a. $0.

    b. $50,000.

    c. $80,000.

    d. $100,000.

True/Make True: To answer these questions, go online to www.mhhe.com/qbd2018 > Student Edition > Chapter 1 > QA Templates. The analysis question on page 27 is also included.

1. QuickBooks 2018 can only run on personal computers with the Windows Vista operating system.

2. QuickBooks 2018 can be installed on both individual and computer lab computers.

3. If QuickBooks is activated, the Help menu shows Activate QuickBooks Desktop.

4. Creating a new company in QuickBooks is easy with the Express screens.

5. You can close the application you are working with if you single click with your mouse on the close button (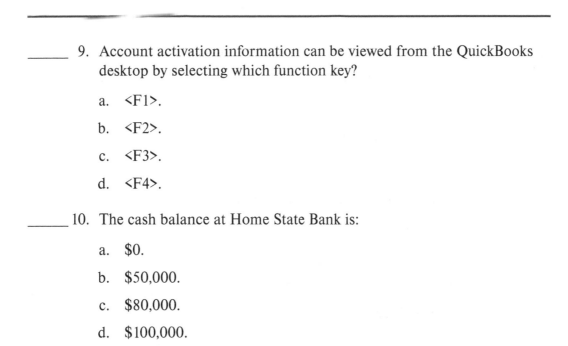).

6. It is a good idea to regularly back up or save to the hard drive instead of external media such as a USB drive.

7. The new company that you created is a sole proprietorship.

8. A new company can be set up from the File menu's Create Copy selection.

9. The new company that you created orders checks from Intuit.

10. The software included with the book does not have a time limit.

Exercise 1-1: Follow the instructions below to complete Exercise 1-1:

1. Start QuickBooks. If an Update Company window appears, refer to pages 84–85 or Appendix B, pages 313–316. The authors recommend installing the update.

2. From the menu bar, select File > New Company from Existing Company File.

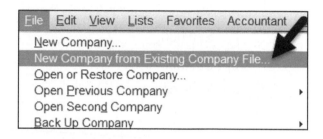

3. The Create From Existing File window appears. The Select a company to copy from field shows the location of Your Name Retailers.qbw. In QB, files that end in a .qbw extension are known as *company files or QuickBooks working files.*

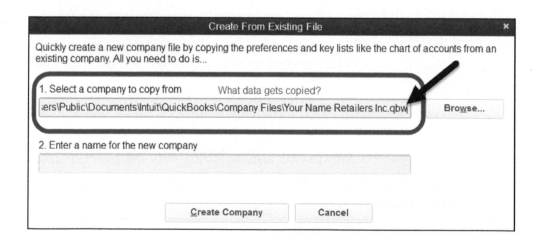

4. In the Enter a name for the new company field, type **Your Name Hardware Store** (use your first and last name). This is the business you will use to complete Project 1.

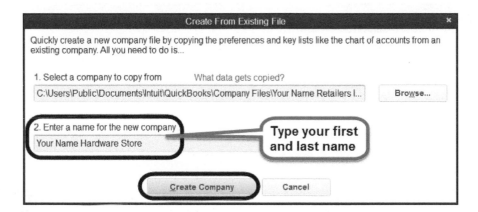

5. After selecting <Create Company>, the Filename for New Company window appears. The Save in field automatically defaults to the Company Files folder. Observe that the File name field shows Your Name Hardware Store. QBW. The Save as type field shows QuickBooks Files (*.QBW). Observe that the company set up in Chapter 1, Your Name Retailers Inc.qbw, is also shown in the Company Files list.

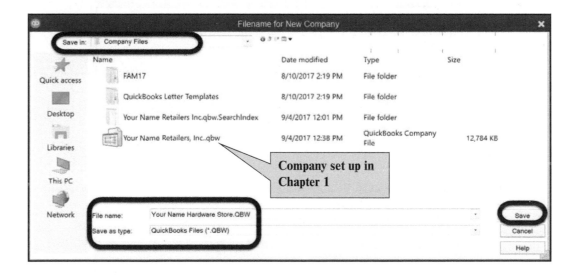

6. After selecting <Save>, the Filename for New Company window appears. Select <Save>.

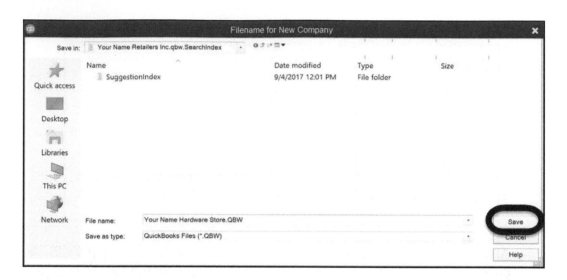

7. After selecting <Save>, the Verify window then the Working window appears while your company file is being set up.

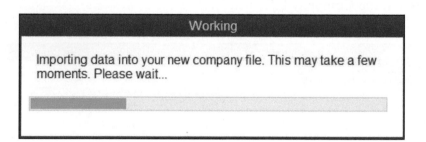

8. When the QuickBooks Information window appears with this message, "QuickBooks has successfully created your new company file. The original file is unchanged," click <OK>.

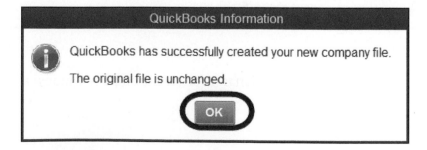

9. After selecting <OK>, you are returned to the QB desktop. Close the Accountant Center. Continue with Exercise 1-2. Close any pop-up windows.

Exercise 1-2

1. Back up. The suggested file name is **Your Name Hardware Store.** Detailed steps for backing up are shown on pages 16–19, steps 1-7.

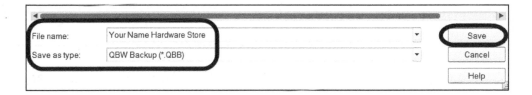

2. Exit QuickBooks 2018.

Analysis Questions:

1. How do you locate information about whether or not your software is activated?

2. How long do you have to activate the software?

3. After activating the software, what is the time period for accessing the QuickBooks Accountant Desktop 2018 software included with the textbook?

Chapter 2

Exploring QuickBooks

OBJECTIVES

1. Start QuickBooks 2018 (QB).

2. Open the sample product-based business.

3. Backup and restore the sample business.

4. Learn about the User Interface.

5. Icon Bar and menu bar.

6. Help, Preferences, and Product Information.

7. Internal Control features.

8. Using File Explorer.

In Chapter 2, you become familiar with some of the QB features. There are two sample businesses included with the software: a product company and a service company. You explore the sample product business to learn about the QB *user interface* or general look of the program. Internal controls and help resources are also included in Chapter 2. In addition, you review procedures to backup and restore company data, use File Explorer, and e-mail a company backup to your professor.

GETTING STARTED

1. Start QuickBooks 2018 by clicking on the QuickBooks icon on the computer's desktop. If you do not want the Accountant Center to open, uncheck the box next to Show Accountant Center when opening a company file. Then, close the Accountant Center.

2. If a Register or Activate QuickBooks Now window appears, you have not activated the software. If QB 2018 is not activated, you have 30 days or 15 startups to use the software. Refer to pages 7 and 8.

OPEN SAMPLE COMPANY

Sample company data files for a sample product-based business and a sample service-based business are included with the software. Follow the steps below to open starting data for the sample product-based company, Sample Rock Castle Construction. Similar steps can be followed to open data from the sample service-based company, Sample Larry's Landscaping and Garden Supply.

1. From the QuickBooks 2018 menu bar, select File > Close Company.

2. A No Company Open window appears. Select the down arrow next to Open a sample file. Then select Sample product-based business.

3. A QuickBooks Desktop Information window says "You're opening a QuickBooks Desktop sample file." Read the information.

4. After clicking <OK>, the title bar shows Sample Rock Castle Construction–QuickBooks Accountant Desktop 2018.

    A product-based business purchases merchandise from vendors, and then sells that merchandise to customers. Products fall into two categories: inventory and non-inventory items. Another way to describe a product-based company is to call it a merchandising or retail business. The sample company that you are going to use, Sample Rock Castle Construction, is a product-based business.

5. Select the Insights tab. It is next to the Home page tab. Compare yours with the one shown. In Chapter 2, the various parts of the Insights page are explained.

BACK UP AND RESTORE SAMPLE COMPANY

When using QB, information is automatically saved to the hard drive of the computer. In a classroom setting, a number of students may be using the same computer. This means that when you return to the computer lab or classroom, your data is gone. Backing up your data means saving it to a hard drive, network drive, or external media. Backing up ensures that you can start where you left off the last time you used QuickBooks.

Back Up Sample Company

In this section, you create a backup of the original starting data for the sample product-based business and then restore the backup. This backup is made *before* any data is added to the sample company so if you want to start with fresh, beginning data again, you can restore from this backup of the starting data.

Comment

In this textbook, you are shown how to backup to external media, a USB drive location. Backing up to a drive other than the hard drive or network drive is called backing up to external media. The instructions that follow assume you are backing up to external media. Authors recommend backing up to at least a **2 GB USB flash drive *OR* if you are working on your own computer, your desktop.**

When you back up, you are saving to the current point in QB. Each time you make a backup, you should type a different backup name (file name) to distinguish between them. In this way, if you need to restore an earlier backup, you have the data for that purpose. See Preface for the list of backups made in this text and their file size.

In the business world, backups are unique for each business day. Daily backups are necessary. If you are working in a computer lab, *never leave the computer lab without first backing up your data to external media, for example, your USB flash drive.*

The text directions assume that you are backing up to *an external media* location. QB includes a couple different backup types. In Chapter 1, you backed up using the .QBB extension. In the steps that follow, a portable backup file is used. ***Portable backups*** have a .QBM extension. QBB (or ***QuickBooks backups***) are larger than QBM, portable backups.

Before backing up, create a folder on your USB drive labeled Your Name QB Backups (use your first and last name). This is where you will save backups.

1. If necessary, select the <Home Page> tab *or* click [Home]. From the menu bar, select File > Create Copy.

2. The Save Copy or Backup window appears. Select Portable company file for the type of file you want to save.

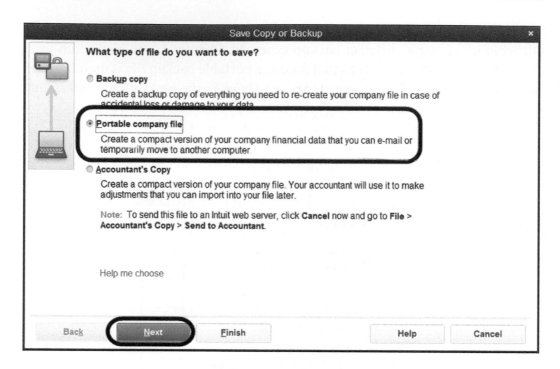

3. After selecting <Next>, the Save Portable Company File window appears. Go to the location of your USB drive. Open the folder.

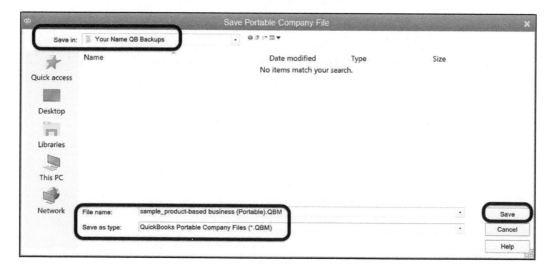

4. After clicking <Save>, the Close and reopen window appears.

5. After clicking <OK>, the screen prompts "You're opening a QuickBooks Desktop sample file."

6. After clicking <OK>, the Creating Portable Company File window appears. When the QuickBooks Desktop Information window says QuickBooks has saved a portable file version for Rock Castle Construction, your file is backed up.

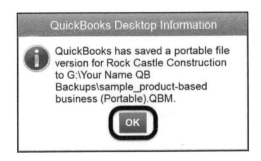

7. After clicking <OK>, the You're opening a QuickBooks Desktop sample file appears again. Click <OK>. You are returned to the Sample Rock Castle Construction desktop. Click . Click on the Insights tab.

 **Read me: Data Files**

Refer to the Preface, to review information about the several types of QB files. The Preface also lists the names of all the backups you will make in this text.

Locate the Backup File

The steps that follow assume that the backup was saved to external media. These steps are consistent with Windows 10. Follow these steps to locate the backup file.

1. To locate your backup file, open File Explorer —[file explorer icon].

2. Select your USB drive. In this example PKBACK# 001 (F:) identifies the USB drive. Click on the drive letter.

    ☑ USB DISK (F:)
    7.18 GB free of 7.20 GB

3. Open the Your Name QB Backups folder 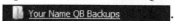.

4. Observe the Name, Type and Size of your backup file. Your file size may differ.

Name	Type	Size
📄 sample_product-based business (Portable).QBM	QuickBooks Portable Company File	2,934 KB

Portable files automatically add a .QBM extension to the file name. If your file extension does <u>not</u> appear, do this:

a. From File Explorer's menu bar, select the View. File name extensions should be checked.

☑ Item check boxes
☑ File name extensions
☑ Hidden items
        Show/hide

b. Close File Explorer.

5. File > Exit QuickBooks.

Restore Sample Company

1. Start QuickBooks 2018. If a QuickBooks update window appears, close it. The authors recommend installing the update. To update, follow the screen prompts.

2. The QuickBooks 2018 desktop appears. If a company opens, from the menu bar, select File > Close Company.

3. The No Company Open window appears > click [Open or restore an existing company].

4. The Open or Restore Company window appears. Select Restore a portable file.

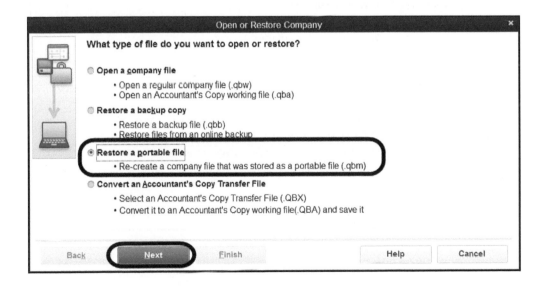

5. After selecting <Next>, the Open Portable Company File window appears.
    Go to the location of your USB drive and open the Your Name QB
    Backups folder. Select the sample_product-based business (portable).
    QBM file.

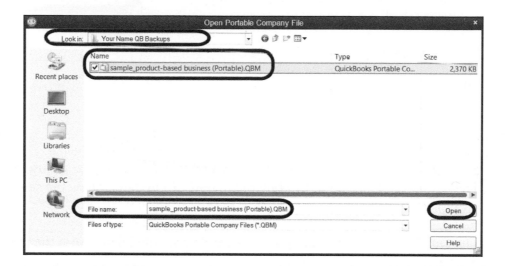

6. After selecting <Open>, the Open or Restore Company window appears.
    Read the information on the Where do you want to restore the file
    window.

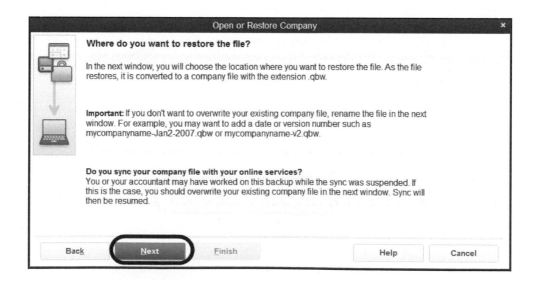

7. After selecting <Next>, the Save Company File as window appears. Type your first and last name in front of the File name.

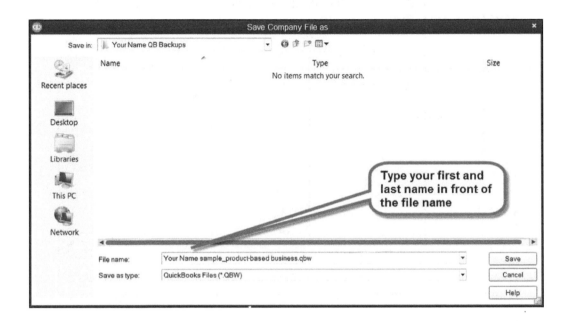

8. After selecting <Save>, the Working window appears. Be patient. Opening a portable company file takes several minutes.

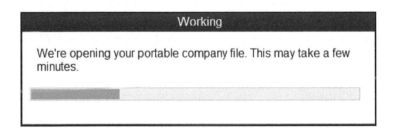

9. When the QuickBooks Desktop Information window appears, read the information.

10. After selecting <OK>, a window prompts "The QuickBooks portable company file has been opened successfully," your file is restored.

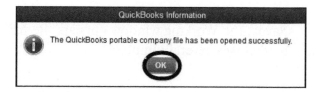

11. After selecting <OK>, you are restored to the Sample Rock Castle Construction – QuickBooks Accountant Desktop 2018 Home page.

12. Exit QB or continue.

USER INTERFACE (UI)

If you exited QuickBooks, follow these steps to open Sample Rock Castle Construction.

1. Start QuickBooks. If an Update Company window displays, the authors recommend installing the update.

2. From the menu bar, select File > Open Previous Company. The author's file is located at G:\Your Name QB Backups\Your Name sample_product-based business.qbw. Your file location will differ. Observe that the file extension is .qbw which indicates the company file or QuickBooks working file.

3. When the QuickBooks Desktop Information window appears, click <OK>. If necessary, click on the Home Page tab — Home Page .

 Read me: Open a Previous Company or Restore a Backup File?

Opening a previous company (.qbw extension) is an alternative to restoring a file. This works well on your own individual computer. If you are working in the computer lab, restoring the portable company backup file (.QBM extension) is best.

The general look of a program is called its user interface. As you know, most programs include the mouse pointer, icons, toolbars, menus, and an Icon Bar. QuickBooks' UI is shown below.

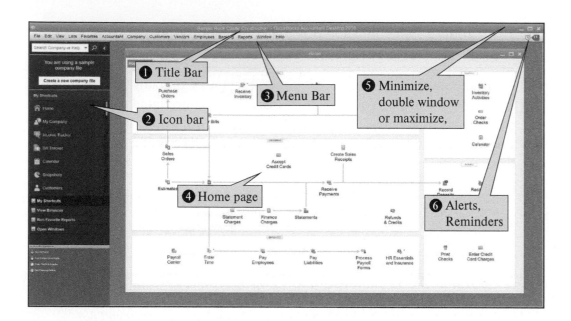

In this textbook, you will use the Icon bar, menu bar, and Home page selections.

For now, let's study the parts of the window. Some features are common to all software programs using Windows. For example, in the upper right corner is the Minimize ▬ button, Double Window ⧉ button, and the Close ✕ button. The title bar, window border, and mouse pointer are also common to Windows programs. Other features are specific to QB: Icon Bar, menu bar, and Home page selections. The contents of these menus differ depending on the application.

① *Title Bar:* Contains the company name and the software version.

Sample Rock Castle Construction – QuickBooks Accountant Desktop 2015

② *Icon Bar:* The Icon Bar contains shortcuts to the tasks and reports you use most. You can place the Icon Bar to the left of the QB desktop, above it, or hide it.

3   *Menu Bar:* Contains the menus for File, Edit, View, Lists, Favorites, Accountant, Company, Customers, Vendors, Employees, Banking, Reports, Window and Help. You can click with your left-mouse button on the menu bar headings to see the selections.

File	Edit	View	Lists	Favorites	Accountant	Company	Customers	Vendors	Employees	Banking	Reports	Window	Help

4   *Home Page* **or** *Desktop:* Displays information about the company. The following content appears when the Company opens: Vendors, Customers, Employees, Company, and Banking. Each section of the Home page shows workflow diagrams or processes.

5   Minimize ▬, Double Window ⧉, or Maximize ▢, and Close or Exit ✕ buttons: Clicking once on Minimize ▬ reduces the window to a button on the *taskbar.* In Windows, the Start ⊞ (Windows 10) button and taskbar are located at the bottom of your window. Clicking once on Double Window ⧉ returns the window to its previous size. This button appears when you maximize the window. After clicking on the Double Window ⧉ button, the symbol changes to the Maximize ▢ button. Click once on the Maximize ▢ button to enlarge the window. Click once on the Exit or Close ✕ button to close the window, or exit the program.

6   Alerts and Reminders: In the upper right corner of the window, QB gives you instant access to important alerts and reminders.

Insights

Select the Insights tab to see how your business is doing at a glance.

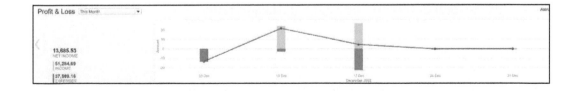

The *Insights page* is divided into 3 sections: Profit & Loss, Income, and Expenses. In the Profit & Loss section, use the left and right arrows to scroll through company information.

1. *Profit & Loss:* This pane summarizes your income and expenses for the time period you choose, so you can tell whether you're operating at a profit or a loss. This pane includes Profit & Loss trend lines. To change the time period, click on the down arrow in the Profit & Loss field. Today is the default. The author selected This Month. Your graph may differ.

a. Click on the <left-arrow> in the Profit & Loss area to go to Prev Year Expense Comparison. All and Yearly are the defaults. Be flexible. Depending on defaults selected your graphs may differ.

b. Click on the <right-arrow> to return to the Profit & Loss pane.

2. **Income:** The Income section bar graph shows invoices that are unpaid, paid, and open, overdue, and paid in the last 30 days invoices.

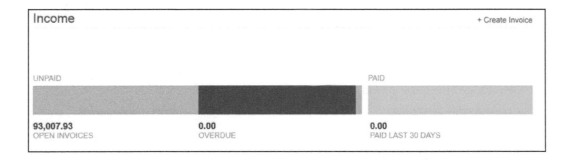

▶ You can place the cursor over the colored bars to see the total number of open, overdue, or paid invoices.

▶ Click any colored filter to open the Income Tracker and see more detailed information. Close the Income Tracker.

3. **Expenses:** The Expenses section shows your expenses over a period of time. Each expense account is color coded. The legend on the left lists individual account balances. The wheel graph on the right lets you see how each expense fits into the big picture.

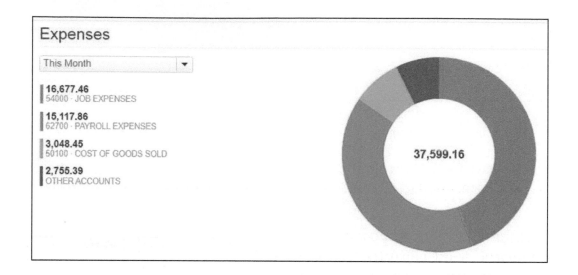

► Place the cursor over the colored sections of the wheel to see the total for that account.

► Click any colored section of the wheel to run a custom transaction detail report that shows every transaction that makes up the total expense for the specified time period.

Typical QuickBooks 2018 Windows

The Icon Bar contains shortcuts to quickly access information about the company; for example, Home, My Company, Income Tracker, Bill Tracker, Calendar, Snapshots, Customers, Vendors, Employees, etc.

When one of the Icon Bar's buttons is selected, an information-rich page appears. For example, click [Customers], and the Customer Information page is shown.

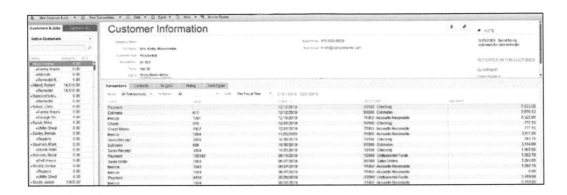

Click on the down-arrow next to Active
Customers. A list populates that includes
All Customers, Active Customers,
Customers with Open Balances, Customers
with Overdue Invoices, Customers with
Almost Due Invoices, Custom Filter. Active
Customers is the default.

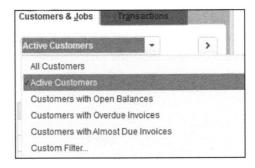

The Customers & Jobs tab and the
Transactions tab both show customer data.
To see the same customer data presented in different ways, select a customer with
the Customers & Jobs tab selected. After looking at the Customers & Job tab information, select the Transactions tab.

From the Customers & Jobs tab, the following selections appear: New Customer
& Job, New Transactions, Print, Excel, Word, and Income Tracker. Explore these
selections. Observe that both Excel and Word are included, along with an Income
Tracker, entering new transactions or new customers.

Select the Transactions tab—⟦ Transactions ⟧. It includes selections for New Customer,
New Transactions, Print, Customer & Job Info, and Export.

Explore these selections; for example, click  Export....
To close the Customer Center, click <X> on its title bar.

ICON BAR AND MENU BAR

To access tasks, use the Icon Bar or menu bar. The Icon Bar contains shortcuts to the tasks and reports used the most. Using the Icon Bar on the left side offers the quickest access but it can also be placed on the top or hidden. Some of the most frequently used Icon Bar selections are Home, Accountant (added below), Customers, Vendors, Reports.

Icon Bar

1. The Icon Bar is usually on the left side of your desktop. (Refer to Icon Bar Location, Appendix B, page 310.)

2. If necessary, add Accountant to the Icon Bar.

    From the menu bar, select View > Customize Icon

    Bar > 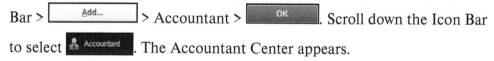 > Accountant > OK. Scroll down the Icon Bar

    to select Accountant. The Accountant Center appears.

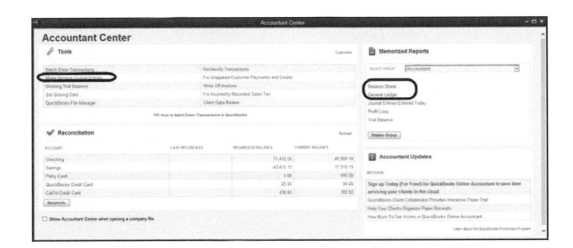

The Accountant Center includes access to the QuickBooks features that accountants use most; for example, Make General Journal Entries, Balance Sheet, General Ledger, etc.

3. Select  (if necessary, scroll up). The Customer Center's Customer Information window appears. The Customers & Jobs list shows information about the people and companies to whom you sell products and services. If you set up jobs for a customer, they appear indented under the customer's name. (*Hint:* If the All Customers page appears with the list of customers, click on the left-arrow, [<], to return to the Customer Center's Customer Information page.) The screen image shows the customer, Babcock's Music Shop.

The Customer Center can be accessed from 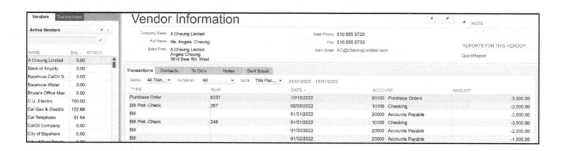 Customers on the Icon Bar or the menu bar's Customers selection — Customers .

4. Select Vendors . The Vendor Center appears. QuickBooks uses the Vendors list to hold information about the people and companies they do business with. For example, the list includes the company name, balance total, phone numbers, email, reports, a list of transactions, etc. The Vendor Center can be accessed from Vendors on the Icon Bar, or the menu bar's Vendors selection.

5. Click Reports . Run detailed reports from the Report Center. Observe that numerous types of reports are listed: Company & Financial, Customers & Receivables, Sales, Jobs, Time & Mileage, Vendors & Payables, Purchases, Inventory, etc. The default window is Company & Financial. Reports can also be accessed from the menu bar.

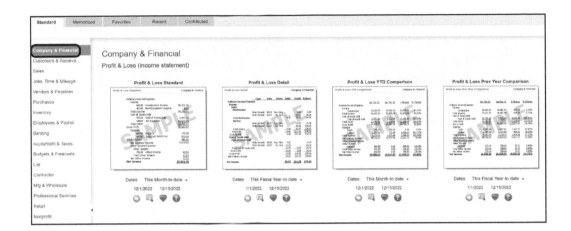

6. Close open windows. (*Hint:* From the menu bar, Window, Close All. To see the Home page, click 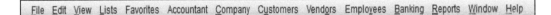 Home .

Menu Bar

Now that you've looked at the Icon Bar, let's explore some menu bar selections. When you want to go to tasks or reports, you can use either the Icon Bar or menu bar. The menu bar selections shown are from Sample Rock Castle Construction.

The horizontal menu bar is another way to access tasks and reports. The Sample Rock Castle Construction menu bar has 14 selections: File, Edit, View, Lists, Favorites, Accountant, Company, Customers, Vendors, Employees, Banking, Reports, Window, and Help.

File Edit View Lists Favorites Accountant Company Customers Vendors Employees Banking Reports Window Help

1. From the menu bar, click File to see the file menu options. The file menu includes selections for New Company, New Company from Existing Company File, Open or Restore Company, Open Previous Company, Open Second Company, Back Up Company, Create Copy, Close Company, Switch to Multi-user Mode, Utilities, Set Up Intuit Sync Manager, Send Company File, Print, Save as PDF, Print Forms, Printer Setup, Send Forms, Shipping, Update Web Services, Toggle to Another Edition, and Exit. If any of the items are gray, they are inactive. An arrow (►) next to a menu item (for example, Utilities)

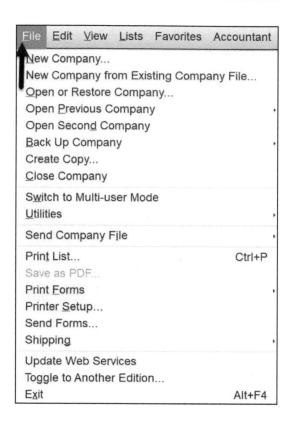

indicates that there are additional selections. Ctrl+P or Alt+F4 means you can press those keys together for the same result.

2. To see the Edit menu, make a selection from the Home page; for example, click

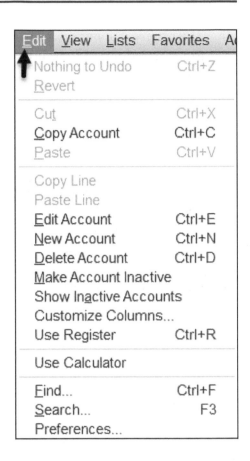

[Chart of Accounts]. (*Hint:* Select Home Page tab.) From the menu bar, select Edit. The edit menu includes selections for Nothing to Undo (inactive), Revert (inactive), Cut (inactive), Copy Account, Paste (inactive), Copy Line (inactive), Paste Line (inactive), Edit Account, New Account, Delete Account, Make Account Inactive, Show Inactive Accounts, Customize Columns, Use Register, Use Calculator, Find, Search, Preferences. Edit menu choices vary depending on what window is selected. The edit menu illustrated shows Chart of Accounts selections. (*Hint:* If the Chart of Accounts is open, close it.)

3. From the menu bar, click View. When the Chart of Accounts is open, the View menu includes more selections. The View menu allows you to Open Window List; place the Icon Bar on the top, left or hide it; Search Box (inactive); Customize Icon Bar; Add "Chart of Accounts" or "Home" to Icon Bar; Favorites Menu; Re-sort List,

McGraw-Hill Education, *Computer Accounting Essentials with QuickBooks 2018, 9e*

Customize Columns, One Window, Multiple Windows. The checkmark shows selections. (*Hint:* If the Chart of Accounts is not open, there are fewer View menu selections.)

4. From the menu bar, click Lists. The Lists menu includes selections for Chart of Accounts, Item List, Fixed Asset Item List, U/M Set List, Price Level List, Billing Rate Level List, Sales Tax Code List, Payroll Item List, Payroll Schedule List, Class List, Workers Comp List, Other Names List, Customer & Vendor Profile Lists, Templates, Memorized Transaction List, and Add/ Edit Multiple List Entries.

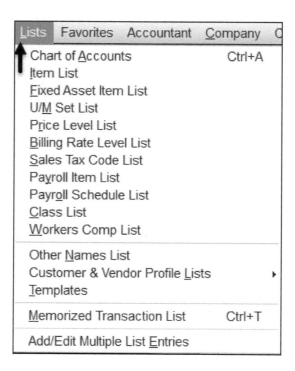

5. From the menu bar, click Favorites. The Favorites menu allows you to customize menus.

6. From the menu bar, select Accountant. The selections include Accountant Center, Chart of Accounts, Fixed Asset Item List, Batch Enter Transactions, Batch Delete/Void Transactions, Client Data Review, Make General Journal Entries, Send General Journal Entries, Reconcile, Working Trial Balance, Set Closing Date, Condense Data, Manage Fixed Assets, QuickBooks Desktop Statement Writer, ProAdvisor Program, and Online Accountant Resources.

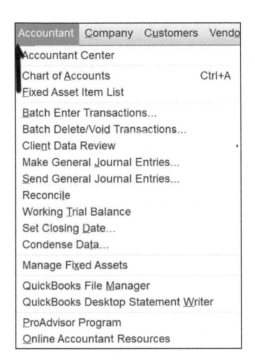

7. From the menu bar, click Company. Selections include Home Page, Company Snapshot, Calendar, Documents, Lead Center, My Company, Set Up Users and Passwords, Customer Credit Card Protection, Set Closing Date, Bulk Enter Business Details, Planning & Budgeting, To Do List, Reminders, Alerts Manager, Chart of Accounts, Make General Journal Entries, Manage Currency, Enter Vehicle Mileage, Prepare Letters with Envelopes, and Export Company File to QuickBooks Online.

8. Click on Customers to see its menu. This selection includes Customer Center, Create Estimates, Create Sales Orders, Sales Order Fulfillment Worksheet, Create Invoices, Create Batch Invoices, Enter Sales Receipts, Enter Statement Charges, Create Statements, Assess Finance Charges, Receive Payments, Create Credit Memos/Refunds, Income Tracker, Lead Center, Add Credit Card Processing, Link Payment Service to Company File, Enter Time, Item List, and Change Item Prices.

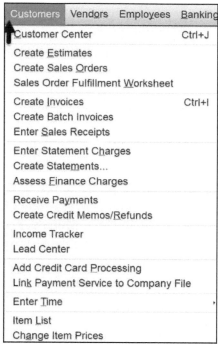

9. Click on Vendors to see its menu. This selection includes Vendor Center, Bill Tracker, Enter Bills, Pay Bills, Sales Tax, Create Purchase Orders, Receive Items and Enter Bill, Receive Items, Enter Bill for Received Items, Inventory Activities, Print/E-file 1099s, and Item List.

10. Click Employees. This selection includes Employee Center, Payroll Center, Enter Time, Pay Employees, Payroll done for you, After-the-Fact Payroll, Add or Edit Payroll Schedules, Edit/Void Paychecks, Payroll Taxes and Liabilities, Payroll Tax Forms & W-2s, Labor Law Posters, Workers Compensation, My Payroll Service, Pay with Direct Deposit, Payroll Setup, Manage Payroll Items, Get Payroll Updates, and Billing Rate Level List.

11. Click Banking. This selection includes Write Checks, Order Checks & Envelopes, Enter Credit Card Charges, Use Register, Make Deposits, Transfer Funds, Reconcile, Bank Feeds, Loan Manager, and Other Names List.

12. Click Reports. This selection includes Report Center, Memorized
    Reports, Commented Reports, Company Snapshot, Process Multiple
    Reports, QuickBooks Desktop Statement Writer, Company & Financial,
    Customers & Receivables, Sales, Jobs, Time & Mileage, Vendors
    & Payables, Purchase,; Inventory, Employees & Payroll, Banking,
    Accountant & Taxes, Budgets & Forecasts, List, Industry Specific,
    Contributed Reports, Custom Reports, QuickReport (inactive if Chart
    of Accounts window is closed), Transaction History, and Transaction
    Journal.

13. Click Window. This selection includes Arrange Icons, Close All, Tile Vertically, Tile Horizontally, Cascade, and Home which has a checkmark next to it. (*Hint:* If other windows are open, they are listed after Home.)

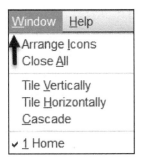

14. Click Help. This selection includes QuickBooks Desktop Help, Ask Intuit, New Features, Support, Find A Local QuickBooks Desktop Expert, Send Feedback Online, Internet Connection Setup, New Business Checklist, Year-End Guide, Add QuickBooks Services, App Center:Find More Business Solutions, Update QuickBooks Desktop, Manage My License, Reset Intuit ID Settings, QuickBooks Desktop Privacy Statement, About Automatic Update, QuickBooks Desktop Usage & Analytics Study, and About QuickBooks Accountant Desktop 2018.

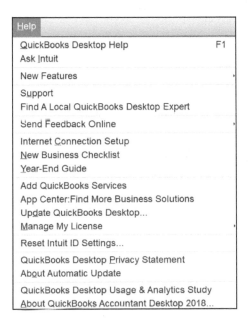

HELP, PREFERENCES, AND PRODUCT INFORMATION

QuickBooks 2018 includes user support or help. The instructions that follow demonstrate Help files.

1. From the menu bar, click Help > QuickBooks Desktop Help.

2. The Have a Question? window appears. Notice you can type in a question, then click the Search icon [🔍] to learn more. Also, notice that a question mark icon appears at the bottom of your screen on the taskbar - [?].

3. From the Have a Question? window you have choices, you can type a question, or link to various parts of the screen.

4. For example, link to How to get help. (*Hint:* You may need click Show more answers.) A How to get help list appears. To get help using QuickBooks, you can:

   - Press F1 in any window to access Help.
   - Download the office Intuit guide to QuickBooks. (Blue font indicates a link to an internet site.)
   - Connect with other QuickBooks users and small business owners in the Intuit Community.
   - Get expert training.
   - Find a local QuickBooks expert.
   - Visit the QuickBooks support site to read in-depth support articles or get help from a QuickBooks Support Representative.

5. You may want to link to the Intuit Community and the QuickBooks support site. When through, close the Have a Question? window.

Company Preferences

Follow these steps to look at the User and Company Preferences for Rock Castle Construction, the product-based sample company.

1. From the menu bar, select Edit > Preferences. The Preferences window appears. If necessary, click on the Company Preferences tab. Select a variety of topics on the left side of the screen to view or change preferences. For example, view General preferences. Read the information on the Company Preferences window. Observe the radio button selection (●) and where the checkmarks (✓) are placed.

2. Click on My Preferences tab to see user preferences. Select a variety of topics on the left side of the screen to view or change preferences. For example, view General preferences. Read the information on the Company Preferences window. Observe the radio button selections and where the checkmarks are placed. The Default Date to use for New Transactions area shows Use today's date as the default. Depending on your instructor's preference, this default can be changed now or later.

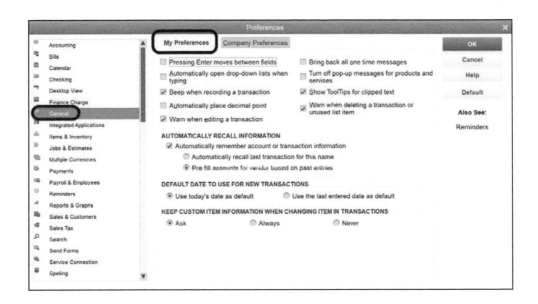

3. To close the window, click <X> on the Preferences title bar.

Displaying Product Information

1. From the menu bar, click on Help > About QuickBooks Accountant
    Desktop 2018. Your License Number, Product Number, and User Licenses
    number is shown.

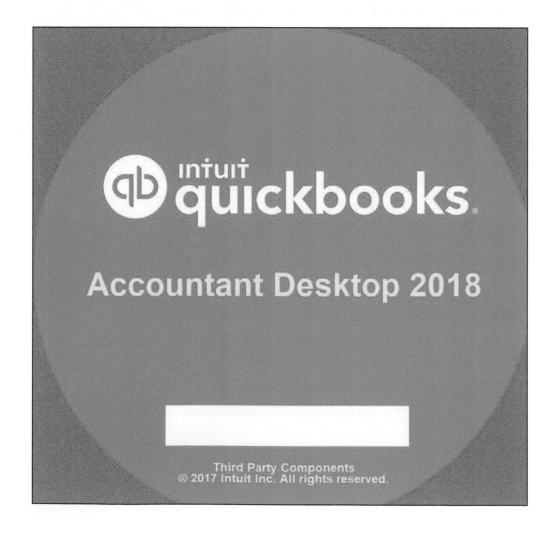

2. After reviewing the window, press <Esc> to close.

INTERNAL CONTROL FEATURES

Security Roles and Permissions

Having user roles with defined permissions allows QB to keep sensitive financial data secure and maintain good company internal controls. Good internal controls reduce a business' risk for wrongdoing and fraud by limiting what users can do or view. Users with administrative rights have full access to all aspects of the software including setting up what other users can view or do in QB. Each user can be permitted different authorized access to QB by the administrator. In this text, since you are the administrator, you can set up users and grant them permissions.

The QB Administrator can give a user access to any or all of these areas when a user's password is set up: sales and accounts receivable, purchases and accounts payable, checking and credit cards, inventory, time tracking, payroll, sensitive accounting activities, and sensitive financial reports. (*Hint:* Using QB Help, type **roles** in the search field. Then, link to Access permissions in QuickBooks.)

Add User Roles

To add a role, follow these steps.

1. From the Sample Rock Castle Construction menu bar, select Company > Set Up Users and Passwords > Set Up Users.

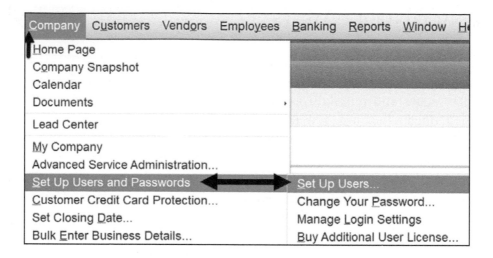

2. The User List window appears.

3. After selecting <Add User>, the Set up user password and access window appears. You are going to add the Cashier role. A cashier enters customer purchases and collects cash payments or credit card payments from customers. For example, a grocery store cashier, store sales clerk, or restaurant wait staff. In the User Name type **Cashier.**

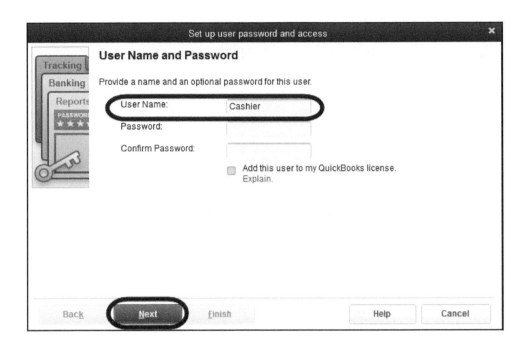

4. After clicking <Next>, the No Password Entered window appears. Read the information. (*Hint:* If you type a password, you will need to enter it every time you restore a backup file. Do *not* type a password.)

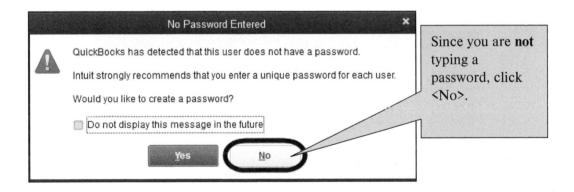

5. After clicking <No>, the Access for user: Cashier information appears. If needed, choose Selected areas of QuickBooks.

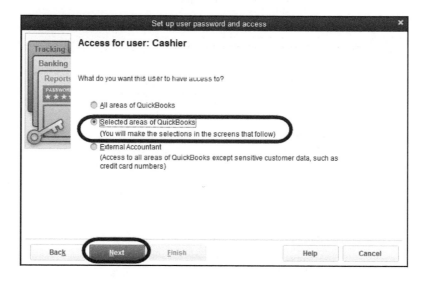

6. After clicking <Next>, the Sales and Accounts Receivable information appears. Since cashiers process customer payments and give customers receipts, the cashier must have selective access to create and print transactions. Choose Selective Access, Create and print transactions.

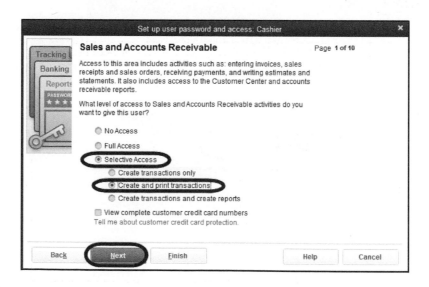

7. After clicking <Next>, the Purchases and Accounts Payable information appears. If necessary, select No Access. Good internal control separates the duties of cash collection from cash payments.

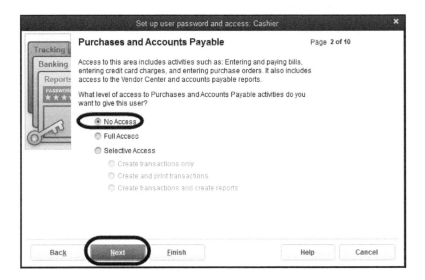

8. After clicking <Next>, the Checking and Credit Cards information appears. If necessary, select No Access. Good internal control assigns different employees the task of making bank deposits versus processing customer payments.

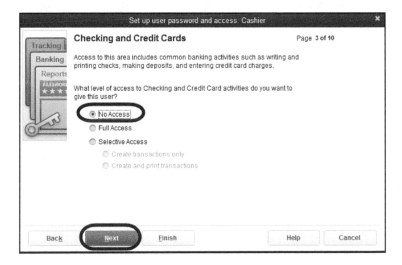

9. After clicking <Next>, Inventory information appears. If necessary, select No Access. If needed, select No Access for Time Tracking, Payroll and Employees, Sensitive Accounting Activities, and Sensitive Financial Reporting. Click <Next> between each window.

10. For Changing or Deleting Transactions, select <No> for both questions since good internal control generally requires supervisor authorization of any changes.

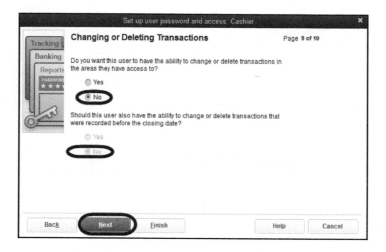

11. After clicking <Next>, review Access for user: Cashier. Make any changes by clicking <Back>. Observe that you are on Page 10 of 10. Scroll down to see all the selections.

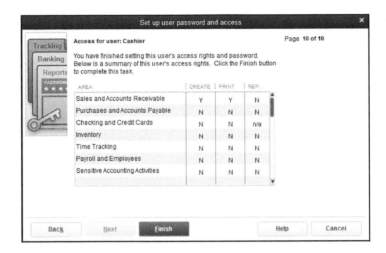

12. Click <Finish>. The User List now contains two user roles, Admin and Cashier.

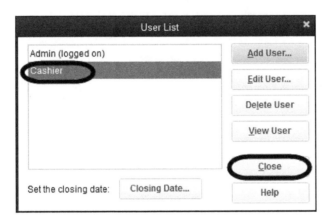

13. Click <Close> to return to the QuickBooks desktop.

EXTERNAL ACCOUNTANT REVIEWS

When a company wants their external accountant to review accounting records, the accountant generally must physically visit the business. With QB Accountant features, a physical visit is no longer necessary and both the company and the accountant can continue to work simultaneously with the data. Company data can be shared with the accountant in various ways. It can be shared using a CD or USB flash drive, or sent via e-mail as an attachment, or uploaded to a shared secure website. In this text, your Accountant is your professor. Periodically throughout the text, you will be sending your company files via e-mail to your professor. In other words, you will be submitting your work for grading purposes. For example, in Exercise 2-1 you will send an e-mail attachment to your professor.

AUDIT TRAIL

Software programs generally have an audit trail feature to keep track of users accessing the software, when they are using it, and what they are doing in the software. An audit trail is another internal control feature of QuickBooks which documents all business activities to keep company data safe. Periodically in this text, you will be printing your audit trail and submitting it to your professor to document your work. To create and view the audit trail of the sample product company, follow these steps.

1. From the Icon Bar, select [Reports] > Accountant & Taxes. If necessary, scroll down the Accountant & Taxes window. In the Account Activity area, select Audit Trail.

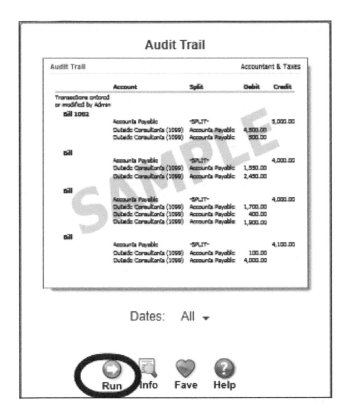

2. Click [Run]. If the Date Entered/Last Modified field shows Today, press [A] on the keyboard to see all of the information on the report

    | Date Entered/Last Modified | All ▾ |. A Building Report window appears, and the Audit Trail is shown. A partial Audit Trail is shown below. Your Date column may differ. Review the type of information the audit trail provides and how the report can be customized.

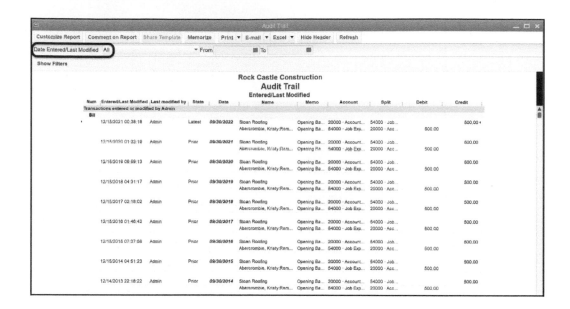

The Audit Trail report lists each accounting transaction and any additions, deletions, or modifications that affect that transaction. Any information about the transactions that has been changed is highlighted in ***Bold Italic type*** in the report. If there are multiple versions of a transaction, the earliest version will have no highlighting, but subsequent versions will highlight each value that differs from the previous version's value in that field by displaying the value in bold italics. If a line item was added to the transaction, that entire line of the report is highlighted.

3. To close the Audit Trail, click <X> on its title bar. Close the Report Center.

CHAPTER 2 DATA BACK UP

At the end of each chapter, the authors recommend that you backup. Backing up insures that you have data to restore if you make a mistake or are transporting your work between computer labs. For example, let's say you would like to start

Sample Rock Castle Construction from the beginning. The backup made earlier in the chapter, sample_product-based business (Portable).QBM, contains fresh, starting data. If you back up your work now and restore the backup file made below (Your Name Chapter 2 End (Portable).QBM), you can start the sample company from the end of this chapter.

1. From the menu bar, select File > Create Copy.

2. When the Save Copy or Backup window appears, select Portable company file.

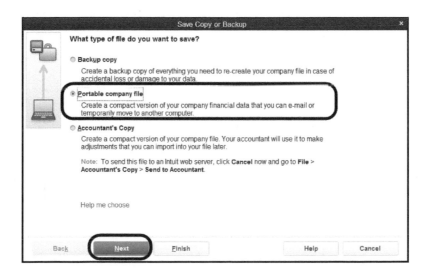

3. After clicking <Next>, go to the location of your USB drive's Your Name QB Backups folder. Type **Your Name Chapter 2 End (Portable)** in the File name field, for example, your First and Last Name Chapter 2 End.

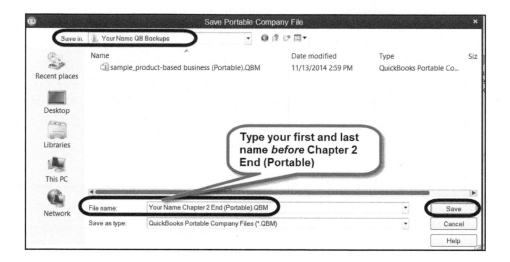

4. Click <Save>. Follow the screen prompts to back up. To return to Rock Castle's desktop, click 🏠 Home .

USING FILE EXPLORER

The instructions that follow show how to identify the QB program path, directories, and subdirectories on the hard drive of your computer. You also see the size of QB and its associated files and folders.

Follow these steps to use File Explorer to identify the QB location on your computer system.

1. If necessary, minimize QuickBooks 2018. Your Windows desktop should be displayed.

2. There are different ways to go to File Explorer. If your desktop has a File

    Explorer folder ![icon], click on it. *Or,* right click on the <Start> button, left-click File Explorer.

3. Select drive C, then double-click on the Program Files (x86) folder to open it. (If you are using Vista, open the Program Files folder.) The address field shows This PC > OS (C:) > Program Files (x86). (*Hint:* Windows 10 is used. If you are using Windows 7 or Vista, your file path will differ.) Now open the Intuit folder so that the Address field shows This PC > OS (C:) > Program Files (x86) > Intuit. This is the location (program path) of QuickBooks 2018 on your computer.

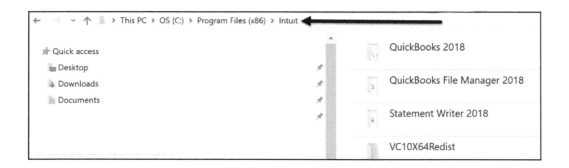

4. Right-click on the QuickBooks 2018 folder. A drop-down list appears. Left-click on Properties. The QuickBooks 2018 Properties window appears. Compare your QuickBooks 2018 Properties window to the one shown. Your files size may differ. The date shown in the Created field will also differ.

5. Click <OK> to close the QuickBooks 2018 Properties window. Close File Explorer.

6. Exit Sample Rock Castle Construction.

Read me: QuickBooks Login window requires password

After exiting Sample Rock Castle Construction, I started QB and opened the company again. Why am I getting a QuickBooks Login window?

1. Start QuickBooks. From the menu bar, select File, Open Previous Company, C:\Users\...\....\Your Name sample_product-based buisness.qbw. The QuickBooks Login window appears. *OR,* restore the Your Name Chapter 2 End (Portable).qbm file.

2. Click <OK> and Sample Rock Castle Construction opens.

    The authors suggest that you do <u>not</u> set up a password. Since you did set up a cashier role, the QuickBooks Login window may appear. (*Hint:* Refer to Add User Roles, pages 63-65.)

SUMMARY AND REVIEW

Additional resources are on the textbook's Online Learning Center (OLC) at www.mhhe.com/qbd2018. The OLC includes Student Edition links and Information Center links. When you link to the Student Edition, choose a chapter to populate more resources.

RESOURCEFUL QUICKBOOKS

Go to this website https://quickbooks.intuit.com/desktop/premier/ > scroll down the page > link to QuickBooks Premier. Go to the FAQs area at the bottom of the page and answer this question - What's the difference between QuickBooks Desktop and QuickBooks Online?"

To watch a QuickBooks Online video, See Your Business' Heath in QuickBooks, go to https://www.youtube.com/watch?time_continue=39&v=8q892InmlAc/

Multiple Choice Questions: The Online Learning Center includes the multiple-choice questions at www.mhhe.com/qbd2018 > Student Edition > Chapter 2 > Multiple Choice.

_____ 1. How do you check your software activation or registration status?

    a.   Select File > Restore previous backup.

    b.   Select Edit > Preferences.

    c.   Software is automatically registered.

    d.   With company open, press <F2>.

_____ 2. What happens to QuickBooks when the 5-month access for students expires?

    a.   Becomes QuickBooks Online Edition.

    b.   Becomes QuickBooks Basic Edition.

    c.   Becomes QuickBooks Premier Edition.

    d.   Becomes inoperable.

_____ 3. When using the sample company today's date is set to:

    a.   12/15/2017.

    b.   12/15/2019.

    c.   12/15/2020.

    d.   12/15/2022.

_____ 4. QuickBooks can be backed up to:

    a. Hard drive.

    b. Network drive.

    c. External media.

    d. All of the above.

_____ 5. Back up files may be saved as:

    a. Back up copy.

    b. Portable company file.

    c. Accountant copy.

    d. All of the above.

_____ 6. Which of the following appears on the Menu Bar:

    a. Help.

    b. Find.

    c. Search.

    d. Feedback.

_____ 7. All of the following Centers appear on the Icon Bar except:

    a. Customer Center.

    b. Employee Center.

    c. Help Center.

    d. Vendor Center.

_____ 8. The File menu contains all the following except:

    a. Exit.

    b. Preferences.

    c. Utilities.

    d. All of the above.

_____ 9. The Edit menu contains all the following except:

    a.   Use Register.

    b.   Preferences.

    c.   Use Calculator.

    d.   List.

_____ 10. The Reports Center lists the following *except:*

    a.   Loans.

    b.   Purchases.

    c.   Inventory.

    d.   Budgets & Forecasts

Short-answer questions: To answer these questions, go online to www.mhhe.com/qbd2018 > Student Edition > Chapter 2 > QA Templates. The analysis question on the next page is also included.

1. What is the name of the sample product-based business?

2. What is the purpose of Backup and Restore?

3. List eight Icon Bar selections for Sample Rock Castle Construction.

4. How can a user access QuickBooks Help?

5. Preferences can be customized two ways, list them.

6. List steps to display QuickBooks product information.

7. What rights and permissions does a QuickBooks Administrator have?

8. When a user is set up, list some of the access rights that can be granted.

9. Why is an audit trail important for good internal control?

10. What Windows program is used to view QuickBooks 2018 properties?

Exercise 2-1: Follow the instructions below to complete Exercise 2-1:

1. Start QB.[1] (*Hint:* If a company opens, select File > Close Company).

2. Open the sample service-based business.

3. The QuickBooks Desktop Information window appears. Read it, then click <OK>. The title bar shows Sample Larry's Landscaping & Garden Supply–QuickBooks Accountant Desktop 2018.

4. Backup the sample service-based business to the USB drive folder named Your Name QB Backups. Select File > Create Copy.
   On the Save Copy or Backup window, select Portable company file. The suggested file name is **Your Name sample_service-based business (Portable).** Use your first and last name.

5. Exit or continue.

Exercise 2-2: Follow the instructions below to complete Exercise 2-2.

1. Start your e-mail program.

2. Create an e-mail message to your professor. Type **Your Name Chapter 2 End** for the Subject. (Use your first and last name.)

3. Attach the file you backed up on pages 73–74, **Your Name Chapter 2 End (Portable).** It is probably located on your USB drive. (*Hint:* If you created a password, remember to send to instructor. If you did <u>not</u> create a password, when the file is restored a QuickBooks Login window appears. Select <OK> to restore the file. Refer to the Read Me box on page 77.)

---

[1] If an Update Company window appears, refer to pages 84–85 and Appendix B, pages 313–316. The authors recommend installing the update. To update, follow the screen prompts.

4. CC yourself on the message to be sure the message sends.

5. Send the message to your professor. You should receive a copy of it as well.

ANALYSIS QUESTION: Why is it important to set up user roles and permissions?

Chapter 3

New Company Setup for a Merchandising Business

OBJECTIVES

1. Open company called Your Name Retailers Inc.
2. Set preferences.
3. Edit the chart of accounts.
4. Enter beginning balances.
5. Record check register entries.
6. Edit to correct an error.
7. Complete account reconciliation.
8. Display the trial balance.
9. Display the financial statements.
10. Make backup of work.[1]

In this text you are the sole stockholder and manager of a merchandising corporation that sells inventory. Merchandising businesses are retail stores that resell goods and services.

In Chapter 3, you open the merchandising business called Your Name Retailers Inc. that you set up in Chapter 1. Then, you complete the accounting tasks for the month of October using your check register and bank statement as source documents.

Source documents are used to show written evidence of a business transaction. In this chapter the source documents used are the check register and bank statement.

---

[1]The chart in the Preface, pages x–xi, shows the file name and size of each backup file. Refer to this chart for backing up data. Remember, you can back up to a hard drive location or external media.

GETTING STARTED

1. Start QuickBooks 2018.

Read me: What should I do if a QuickBooks Update Service window appears?

Product updates, also called maintenance releases, prompt you to install the update when you first start QuickBooks. The updates are identified using release numbers.

To install the QuickBooks update, follow steps a. though e.

Update QuickBooks

a. If a QuickBooks Update Service window appears, read the information. The authors suggest installing updates. To update, follow the screen prompts.

b. After selecting <Install Now>, the update starts to install. Wait for the Update complete window to appear.

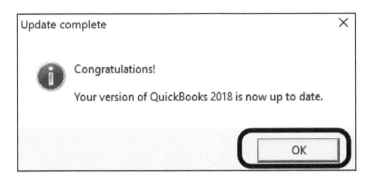

c. After clicking <OK>, the Update Company window appears saying "QuickBooks needs to update your company file."

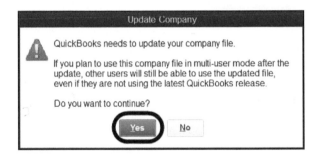

d. After clicking <Yes>, the title bar shows Your Name Retailers Inc. - QuickBooks Accountant Desktop 2018.

e. When you update QB, the release number changes. To check that the release number changed, press the function key <F2>.

The Product Information on the author's screen shows ACTIVATED R1_38. Your release number may differ. (*Hint:* Refer to pages 7 and 8 for activation information and, if needed, the Validation code.)

2. If you do **not** see **Your Name Retailers Inc.** on the title bar, select File > Close Company. If an Automatic Backup window appears, that says "Intuit highly recommends backing up your data. . . .", click <No>.

3. From the No Company Open window, select Open or restore an existing company.

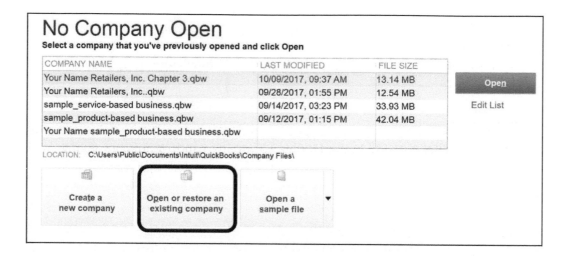

4. On the Open or Restore Company window, select Restore a backup copy. Click <Next>. The Is the backup copy stored locally or online? window appears. If necessary, select Local backup. Click <Next>. Go to the location of the Your Name Retailers Inc. backup file that you made in Chapter 1, pages 16-19, steps 1-7.

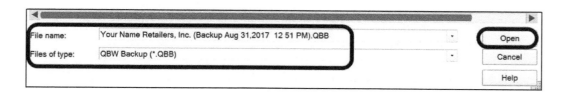

5. After selecting <Open>, the Where do you want to restore the file? window appears, click <Next>.

6. Rename Your Name Retailers Inc. to **Your Name Retailers Inc. Chapter 3** on the Save Company File as window. (*Hint:* Company files have a .qbw extension. QuickBooks Files (*.QBW) is shown in the Save as type field.)

File name:	Your Name Retailers, Inc. Chapter 3	˅	Save
Save as type:	QuickBooks Files (*.QBW)	˅	Cancel
			Help

7. After clicking <Save>, the screen prompts Your data has been restored successfully. Click <OK>. The title bar shows Your Name Retailers Inc. - QuickBooks Accountant Desktop 2018.

Your Name Retailers Inc. - QuickBooks Accountant Desktop 2018

COMPANY PREFERENCES

Set *preferences* to customize QuickBooks to suit the needs of your business and personal style of working. Preferences allow you to configure the way in which some functions and keys work in QuickBooks. In the example that follows you set preferences for account numbers.

Use the steps that follow to set the company preferences for Your Name Retailers Inc.

1. From the menu bar, select Edit > Preferences > Company Preferences tab > Accounting.

2. Check the box next to Use account numbers. Uncheck the boxes next to Date Warnings. Click <OK>.

   The Preferences window is shown on the next page.

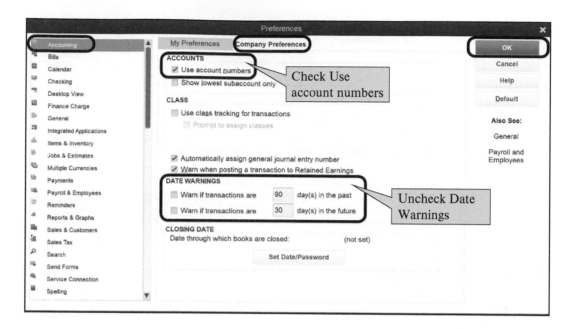

3. From the menu bar, select Edit > Preferences. Click on My Preferences tab > Desktop View. In the Company File Color Scheme field, select a Color Scheme of your choice. Click <OK>.

4. Select Edit > Preferences > My Preferences > Checking. Put a check mark next to Open the Write Checks form with . . . account, the Open the Pay Bills form with . . . account, and Open the Make Deposits form with . . . account. Make sure you have the three checkmarks shown below.

   a. For Open the Write Checks, click on the down-arrow to select the **Home State Bank** account.

   b. Select **Home State Bank** for Open the Pay Bills.

   c. Select **Home State Bank** for Open the Make Deposits.

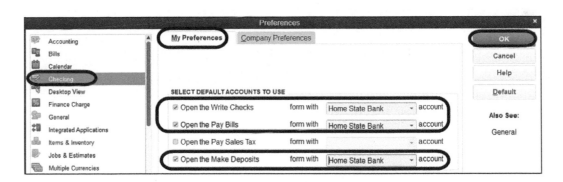

d. Make sure Home State Bank appears in the form with fields for Write Checks, Pay Bills, and Make Deposits. Click <OK>.

5. Select Edit > Preferences > My Preferences > Send Forms. Uncheck box next to Auto-check the "Email Later" checkbox if customer's Preferred Delivery Method is e-mail. In the Send E-Mail Using section, select Web Mail. (Since the author has Outlook, that e-mail selection is also shown.)

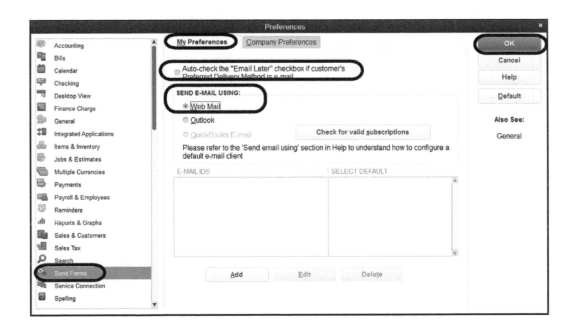

6. Click <OK>. If the Warning window appears, read it, then click <OK>. If necessary, click [🏠 Home] to go to the Home Page.

CHART OF ACCOUNTS

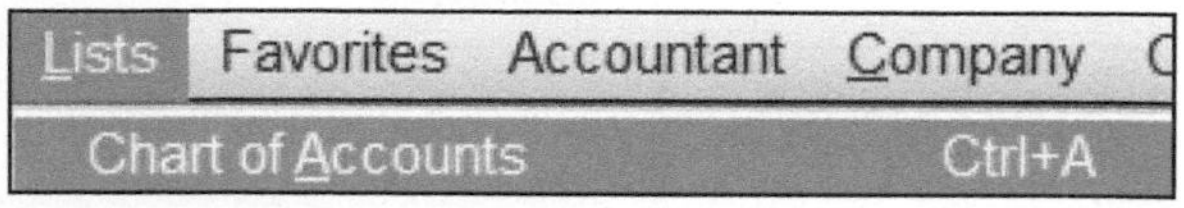
Lists
Favorites
Accountant
Company
Chart of Accounts
Ctrl+A

Examine the Home Page to learn there are many ways to access a company's chart of accounts. The ***chart of accounts*** is a list of all accounts in the company's general ledger. Notice you can click on the Home Page's Chart of Accounts icon; press <Ctrl>+<A>; or from the menu bar, select Lists > Chart of Accounts; or Company, Chart of Accounts.

1. From Home Page, click 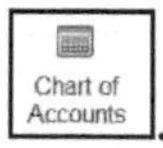Chart of
Accounts.

2. The Chart of Accounts appears. If necessary, resize it so you can view all accounts. Notice all have 0.00 balance totals.

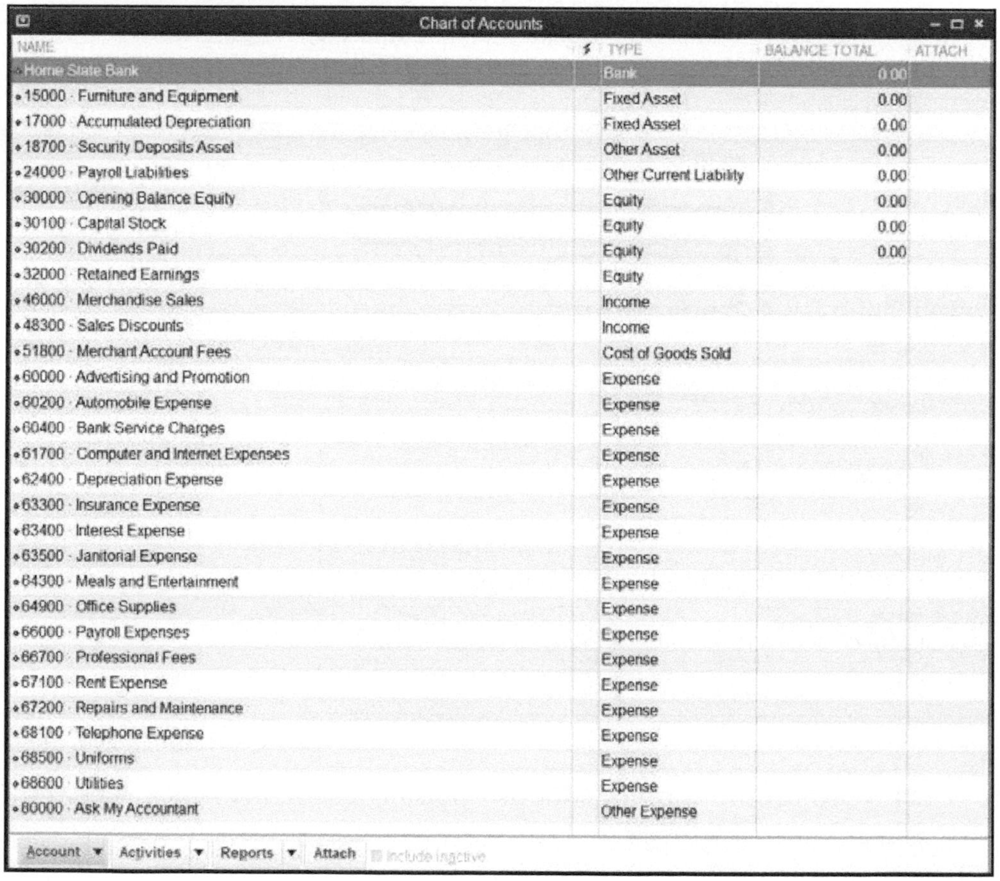
Chart of Accounts
Account
Activities
Reports
Attach
Include inactive

NAME	TYPE	BALANCE TOTAL	ATTACH
Home State Bank	Bank	0.00	
15000 · Furniture and Equipment	Fixed Asset	0.00	
17000 · Accumulated Depreciation	Fixed Asset	0.00	
18700 · Security Deposits Asset	Other Asset	0.00	
24000 · Payroll Liabilities	Other Current Liability	0.00	
30000 · Opening Balance Equity	Equity	0.00	
30100 · Capital Stock	Equity	0.00	
30200 · Dividends Paid	Equity	0.00	
32000 · Retained Earnings	Equity		
46000 · Merchandise Sales	Income		
48300 · Sales Discounts	Income		
51800 · Merchant Account Fees	Cost of Goods Sold		
60000 · Advertising and Promotion	Expense		
60200 · Automobile Expense	Expense		
60400 · Bank Service Charges	Expense		
61700 · Computer and Internet Expenses	Expense		
62400 · Depreciation Expense	Expense		
63300 · Insurance Expense	Expense		
63400 · Interest Expense	Expense		
63500 · Janitorial Expense	Expense		
64300 · Meals and Entertainment	Expense		
64900 · Office Supplies	Expense		
66000 · Payroll Expenses	Expense		
66700 · Professional Fees	Expense		
67100 · Rent Expense	Expense		
67200 · Repairs and Maintenance	Expense		
68100 · Telephone Expense	Expense		
68500 · Uniforms	Expense		
68600 · Utilities	Expense		
80000 · Ask My Accountant	Other Expense		

Follow these steps to add, edit, and change accounts.

Delete Accounts

Follow these steps to delete accounts.

1. Highlight Account No. 48300, Sales Discounts. Right-click on the highlighted account, left-click Delete.

2. When the window prompts "Are you sure you want to delete this account?," click <OK>. Account No. 48300, Sales Discounts, is removed.

3. Delete these accounts

No.	Name
18700	Security Deposits Asset
63500	Janitorial Expense
64300	Meals and Entertainment
66700	Professional Fees
68500	Uniforms
80000	Ask My Accountant

Make Accounts Inactive

Follow these steps to make Account No. 24000, Payroll Liabilities, inactive.

1. Highlight Account No. 24000, Payroll Liabilities and right-click. Left-click Make Account Inactive.

2. Repeat step 1 to make Account 66000, Payroll Expenses inactive.

3. Check Include inactive box at bottom of the Chart of Accounts to reveal all inactive accounts. Notice inactive accounts have an X beside them.

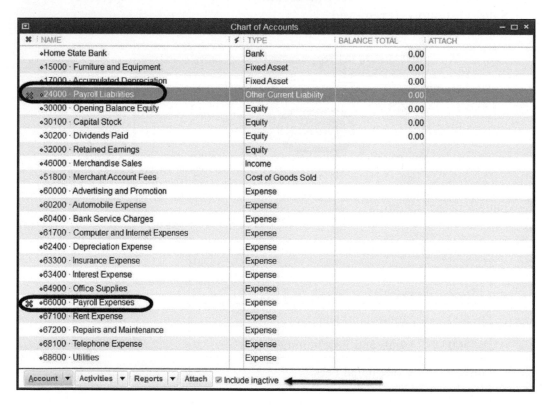

Change/Edit Accounts

Follow these steps to change or edit an account.

1. Right-click on Account No. 30000, Opening Balance Equity.

2. Left-click Edit Account.

3. Change the Account name field to **Common Stock.** Change Description field to **Common Stock par value.**

4. For Tax-Line Mapping select: B/S-Liabs/Eq.: Capital Stock-Common Stk.

5. After clicking <Save & Close>, observe that Account No. 30000 name is Common Stock.

6. Change the following accounts.

No.	New Name	Change
30100	Paid in Capital	Description: Paid in Capital Tax-Line Mapping: B/S-Liabs/Eq.: Paid in or capital surplus
30200	Dividends	
46000	Sales	
51800	Freight In	Description: FOB shipping
60000	Advertising and Promotion Exp.	
60400	Bank Service Charges Expense	
64900	Supplies Expense	Description: Supplies expense
67200	Repairs and Maintenance Expense	
68600	Utilities Expense	
10000	Home State Bank (*Hint:* In the Number field, type **10000**)	Description: Cash in bank Tax-Line Mapping: B/S-Assets: Cash
17000	Accumulated Depreciation-F&E	Tax-Line Mapping: B/S-Assets: Accumulated depreciation

Add Accounts

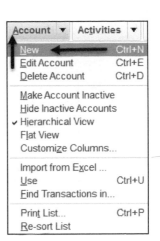

1. To add Account No. 14000, Computer Equipment, click on the down-arrow next to Account, select New.

2. On the Add New Account: Choose Account Type window, select Fixed Asset (major purchases).

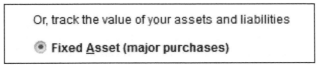

3. Click <Continue>. The Add New Account window appears. In Number field, type **14000,** in Account Name field type **Computer Equipment.** For Description, type **Computer equipment.** The Tax-Line Mapping field is automatically completed.

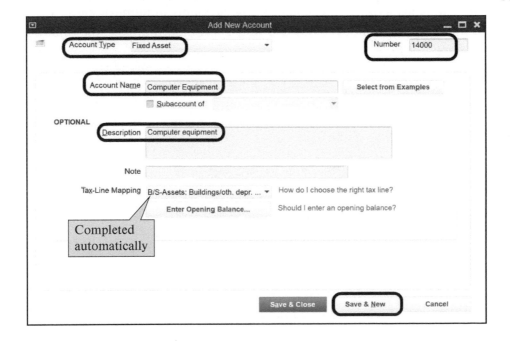

4. After clicking <Save & New>, add these accounts.

No.	Name	Account Type	Tax-Line Mapping
13000	Supplies	Other Current Asset	B/S-Assets: Other current assets
16000	Accumulated Depreciation-CEqmt.	Fixed Asset	B/S-Assets: Accumulated depreciation
18000	Prepaid Insurance	Other Current Asset	B/S-Assets: Other current assets
22000	Accounts Payable	Accounts Payable	B/S-Liabs/Eq.: Accounts payable
26000	Your Name Notes Payable	Long Term Liability	B/S-Liabs/Eq.: Loans from stockholders

5. When done adding each account, click <Save & Close>. View your chart of accounts list. (*Hint:* If needed, sort the accounts in numeric order by clicking on the Name column.) Compare your chart of accounts to the one shown on the next page.

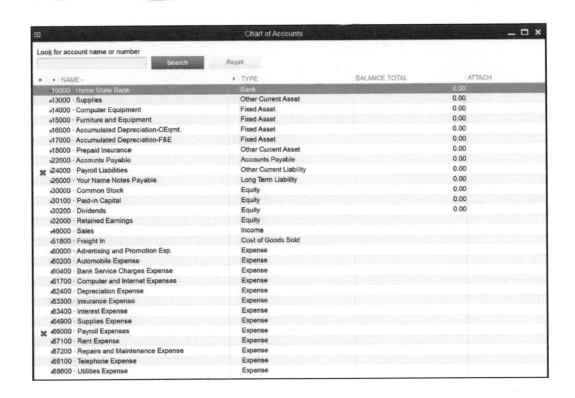

BEGINNING BALANCES

The *Balance Sheet* establishes the beginning balances as of October 1, 20XX (current year). The Balance Sheet lists the types and amounts of assets, liabilities, and equity as of a specific date. A balance sheet is also called a *statement of financial position.* Since QuickBooks asks you to enter the account balances on the day prior to your start date, the September 30 balance sheet is shown here.

Your Name Retailers Inc. Balance Sheet, September 30, 20XX (current year)		
ASSETS		
Current Assets:		
10000 - Home State Bank	$54,000.00	
Other Current Assets:		
13000 - Supplies	2,500.00	
18000 -Prepaid Insurance	2,500.00	
Total Current Assets		$59,000.00
Fixed Assets:		
14000 - Computer Equipment	1,000.00	
15000 - Furniture and Equipment	4,000.00	
Total Fixed Assets		5,000.00
Total Assets		$64,000.00
LIABILITIES AND STOCKHOLDERS' EQUITIES		
Long-Term Liabilities:		
26000 – Your Name Notes Payable	20,000.00	
Total Long-Term Liabilities		$20,000.00
Stockholders' Equities:		
30000 - Common Stock		44,000.00
Total Liabilities & Equities		$64,000.00

Use the steps shown to enter opening balances for Your Name Retailers Inc. on September 30, 20XX, the day before your QuickBooks start date. If needed, click on the Chart of Accounts icon. Notice all accounts have 0.00 balance totals.

1. Right-click on Account No. 10000 Home State Bank.

2. Select Edit Account > Enter Opening Balance. The Enter Opening Balance: Bank Account window appears.

3. In Statement Ending Balance field, type **54000.00,** press <Tab>. In the Statement Ending Date field, type **9/30/20XX (Use your current year).** Press <Tab>.

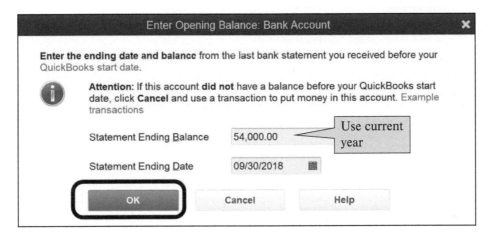

4. After clicking <OK>, you are returned to the Edit Account screen. Make sure 54,000.00 as of 09/30/20XX (current year) is shown. Click <Save & Close>. Observe that the Chart of Accounts shows that Account 10000 Home State Bank has a balance total of 54,000.

5. Edit the following accounts to add their beginning balances. To complete the Opening Balance and as of date fields, type **09/30/20XX** (current year).

No.	Name	Opening Balance as of 09/30/20XX
13000	Supplies	2,500.00
14000	Computer Equipment	1,000.00
15000	Furniture and Equipment	4,000.00
18000	Prepaid Insurance	2,500.00
26000	Your Name Notes Payable	20,000.00

6. Compare your chart of accounts to the one shown. Edit yours until it agrees. Uncheck Include inactive.

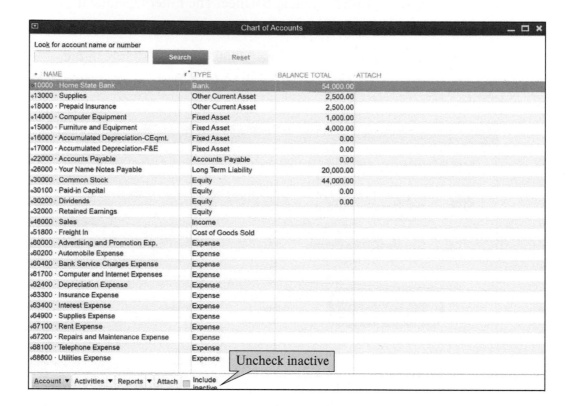

7. Close the Chart of Accounts.

October 1 Balance Sheet

To make sure that you have entered the October 1 balances correctly, display a balance sheet and compare it to the balance sheet on page 98. Follow these steps to do that.

1. From the Icon Bar, click [📊 Reports]. Company & Financial is the default.

   Scroll down the Report Center to the Balance Sheet & Net Worth area. Select Balance Sheet Standard. In the Dates and Custom fields, type or select **10/1/20XX** (current year). The date appears in both fields.

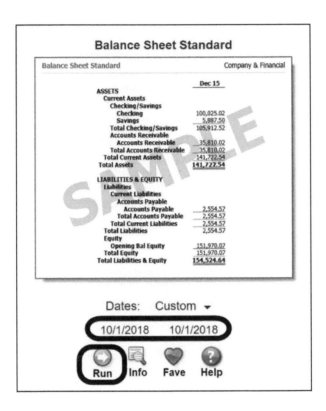

2. After clicking [🔵 Run], the October 1, 20XX Balance Sheet displays. Compare it to the one shown on page 98. (The PDF file is used to display the October 1 Balance Sheet.)

Your Name Retailers, Inc.
Balance Sheet
As of October 1, 2018

Accrual Basis

	Oct 1, 18
ASSETS	
Current Assets	
Checking/Savings	
10000 · Home State Bank	54,000.00
Total Checking/Savings	54,000.00
Other Current Assets	
13000 · Supplies	2,500.00
18000 · Prepaid Insurance	2,500.00
Total Other Current Assets	5,000.00
Total Current Assets	59,000.00
Fixed Assets	
14000 · Computer Equipment	1,000.00
15000 · Furniture and Equipment	4,000.00
Total Fixed Assets	5,000.00
TOTAL ASSETS	**64,000.00**
LIABILITIES & EQUITY	
Liabilities	
Long Term Liabilities	
26000 · Your Name Notes Payable	20,000.00
Total Long Term Liabilities	20,000.00
Total Liabilities	20,000.00
Equity	
30000 · Common Stock	44,000.00
Total Equity	44,000.00
TOTAL LIABILITIES & EQUITY	**64,000.00**

3. Click on the down-arrow next to <Print>, then select either Report or Save as PDF. If you Save as PDF, browse to your USB drive and name file: **Your Name October 1 BS.pdf.**

4. From the menu bar, select Window, Close All. Click **Home** to return to the Home Page.

BACKUP BEGINNING COMPANY DATA

Follow these steps to backup Your Name Retailers Inc. October 1 data.

1. Insert your USB flash drive. From menu bar, select File > Back Up Company > Create Local Backup. The Create Backup window appears

2. After selecting <Next>, the Backup Options window appears. If necessary, click <Browse>. Go to the location of the Your Name QB Backups

    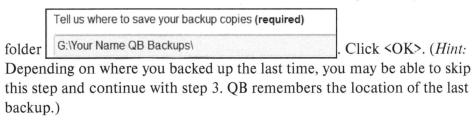

    folder   G:\Your Name QB Backups\   . Click <OK>. (*Hint:* Depending on where you backed up the last time, you may be able to skip this step and continue with step 3. QB remembers the location of the last backup.)

3. Accept the default for Save it now by clicking <Next>. Type the File name, **Your Name Chapter 3 October 1.**

    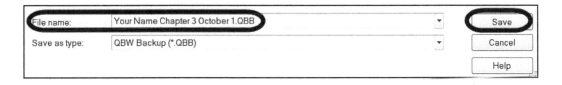

4. After clicking <Save>, your file backs up. When the window prompts "QuickBooks has saved a backup of the company file . . . .", click <OK>. You are returned to the Your Name Retailers Inc. Home Page.

ACCOUNT REGISTER

An account register for cash transactions is a listing of all deposits and checks. It is similar to your checkbook's transaction register. Your Name Retailers Inc. transaction register is shown here. Your Name Retailers Inc. writes checks and deposits manually in their checkbook and then records them in QuickBooks 2018.

Check Number	Date	Description of Transaction	Payment	Deposit	Balance
					54,000.00
	10/2	Deposit (Acct. No. 30000, Common Stock)		1,500.00	55,500.00
4002	10/4	The Business Store (Acct.14000, Computer Equipment) for computer storage	1,000.00		54,500.00
4003	10/25	The Office Supply Store (Acct. No. 13000, Supplies)	200.00		54,300.00

Source documents are used to show written evidence of a business transaction. Examples of source documents are sales invoices, purchase invoices, and in this case, the checkbook's transaction register for the Home State Bank account.

Make Deposits

Follow these steps to use your checkbook's transaction register to record the October entries related to cash.

1. On the Home Page in the Banking section, notice there are icons to Record Deposits, Write Checks, Print Checks, Reconcile, and Check Register.

2. Since the first transaction is a deposit, click on the Record Deposits icon 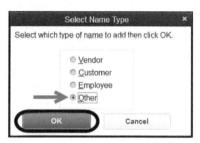.

3. The Make Deposits window appears. For Deposit To, make sure Account No. 10000 Home State Bank is selected. Type **10/2/20XX** (current year) as the Date. The Memo field shows Deposit. In the From Account field (second column), select **30000 Common Stock.** For Pmt Meth., select Cash. For Amount, type **1500.00.**

4. For Received From, select <Add New>. The Select Name Type window appears. On the Select Name Type window, pick **Other.**

5. After clicking <OK>, the New Name window appears. Type **Your Name, address,** and **phone number.**

6. After clicking <OK>, the Received From field shows Your Name, From Account shows 30000 – Common Stock; Pmt Meth., Cash; and Amount, $1,500.00.

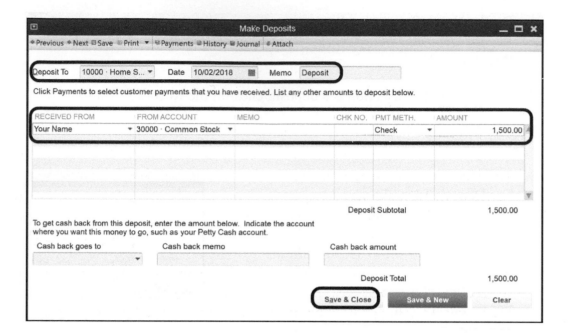

7. After clicking <Save & Close>, you are returned to the Home Page. Click on the icon for Check Register [Check Register].

8. Compare your Check Register to the one shown. Notice both the opening cash balance and the 10/2 deposit are shown. The updated cash balance in account 10000 is $55,500.00 which agrees with the checkbook's transaction register on page 104.

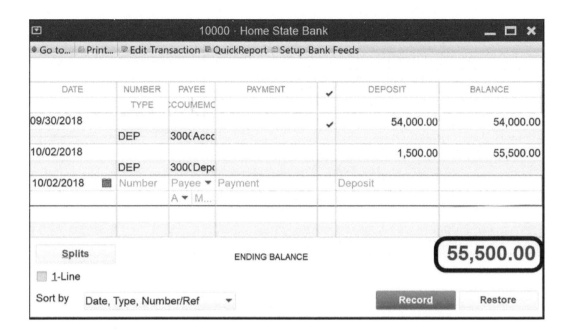

9. Close the Check Register by clicking on the title bar's <X>.

Write Checks for Assets

Follow these steps to record a purchase of computer storage.

1. From the Home Page, click on the Write Checks icon.

2. The Write Checks – Home State Bank window appears. The Bank Account field shows Account No. 10000 - Home State Bank. Observe that the Ending Balance field shows $55,500. This is the same balance as the checkbook's transaction register.

3. Click on the Print Later box to uncheck it - .

4. The No. field shows 1. Delete it, then type **4002** in the No. field.

5. Type **10/4/20XX (use your current year)** in the Date field.

6. Type **1000** in the $ field.

7. In the Pay To The Order Of field, select
   <Add New>. The Select Name Type window appears. If necessary, pick Vendor
   and click <OK>.

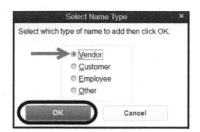

8. The New Vendor window appears. Type **The
   Business Store** for Vendor Name, **0.00** for the
   Opening Balance as of **10/04/20XX (current year).**

9. Click <OK>. You are returned to the Write Checks window.

10. In the Expenses and Items fields, Expenses should be selected. In the
    Account field, select Account No. 14000, Computer Equipment. In
    Memo field type **Computer storage.**

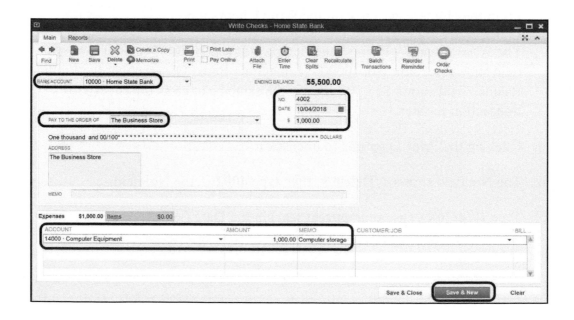

11. After clicking <Save & New>, the Write Checks – Home State Bank window is ready for the next transaction. In the Bank Account field Account No. 10000, Home State Bank is shown. If not, select it. Observe that the Ending Balance field shows $54,500.00. This is the same balance shown earlier on your checkbook's transaction register.

12. The Print Later box should be unchecked. The No. field displays 4003. Type **10/25/20XX (current year)** in the Date field.

13. Type **300** in the $ field.

14. In the Pay To The Order Of field, type **The Office Supply Store.** Press <Tab>. When the Name Not Found window appears. Click <Quick Add>; Vendor is the default. Click <OK>. You are returned to the Write Checks window.

15. The Expenses tab should be selected. In the Account field, select Account No. 13000, Supplies. The Amount field shows 300.00. Type **Store supplies** in the memo field.

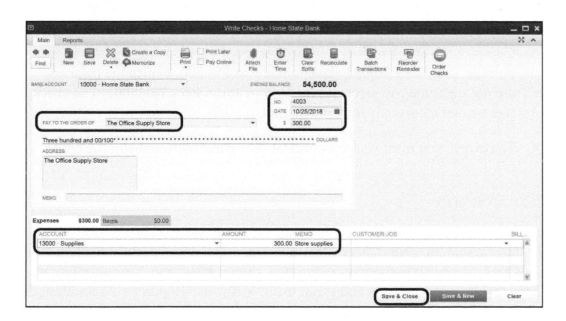

16. After clicking <Save & Close>, the Home Page appears.

Home State Bank Check Register

Periodically view the check register to confirm the account balance equals what is shown on the checkbook's transaction register and that there are no errors.

1. From the Banking section of the Home Page, click .

2. The 10000 Home State Bank window appears.

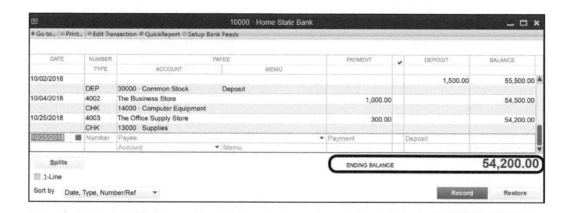

3. Compare the check register to your checkbook's transaction register shown on page 104. The Ending Balance should be $54,300. Notice the balances are <u>not</u> the same. An error was made in writing Check No. 4003. The check was written incorrectly for $300 instead of $200.

4. To correct, you must void the check in your checkbook and edit the entry.

EDIT AN ENTRY

When you notice a mistake, you can void the check in your checkbook and edit the transaction in your Check Register. Since QuickBooks 2018 includes an audit trail, it tracks every transaction and shows when and how an entry was changed. You can view this audit trail using Menu Bar Reports > Accountant &

Taxes > Audit Trail. When you void a check and edit a transaction, the audit trail shows the original entry (Prior) and the edited entry (Latest). Follow these steps to correct the error.

1. You should be viewing the Check Register. If not, from the Banking section of the Home Page, click [Check Register].

2. Using the mouse, click on the 10/25 transaction. Click [Edit Transaction]. This takes you to the original 10/25 entry. To edit the entry, type the correct check No. **4004** and amount **200.00** over the incorrect entries (*HINT*: Press <Tab> to move between fields.)

4003 4004	10/25	The Office Supply Store (Acct. No. 13000, Store Supplies)	200.00		52,300.00

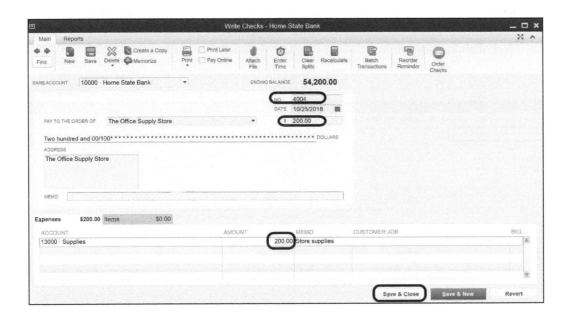

3. Make sure the 10/25 check has been edited. Click <u>Save & Close</u>. The Recording Transaction window appears. Read the information.

4. After clicking <Yes>, you are returned to the Check Register. Notice Home State Bank ending balance is $54,300.00. This agrees with the checkbook's transaction register on page 104. Close the Check Register.

5. To view the audit trail of this edit, go to the Report Center or the Reports menu; select Accountant & Taxes > Audit Trail (Dates: All) > Run. Notice edited check 4003 is not in bold and its State is labeled Prior, meaning it has been replaced. Boldface and italics indicate that Check No. 4004 is added.

6. Close the Audit Trail. Do not memorize the report.

Write Check for Dividends

Follow these steps to record the payment of a cash dividend to the sole stock-holder, Your Name. The checkbook's transaction register is:

4005	10/30	Your Name (Acct. No. 30200 Dividends)	200.00		54,100.00

1. Go to the Write Checks – Home State Bank window

2. The Bank Account field shows Account No. 10000, Home State Bank. Observe that the Ending Balance field shows $54,300, the same as the checkbook's transaction register. The Print Later box should be unchecked.

3. Type **4005** in the No. field.

4. Type **10/30/20XX (use your current year)** in the Date field.

5. Type **200** in the Amount field.

6. In the Pay To The Order Of field, type **Your Name.** Press <Tab>.

7. The Expenses tab should be selected. For the Account, select Account No. 30200, Dividends.

8. In Memo field type **Cash dividend to stockholder.**

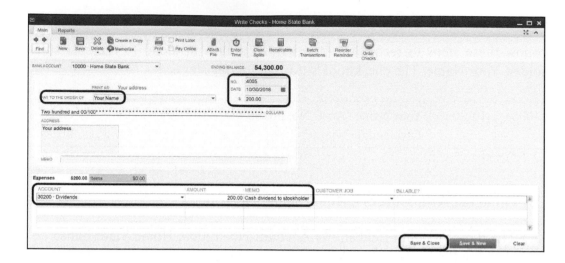

9. After clicking <Save & Close>, you are returned to the Home Page. To make sure your ending balance is $54,100, display the Check Register for Home State Bank.

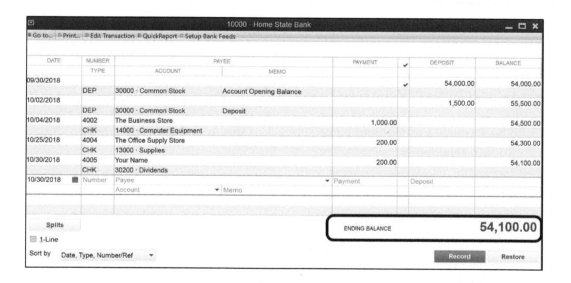

10. Close all windows except the Home Page.

BACKUP THE OCTOBER CHECK REGISTER

Before you complete *account reconciliation,* back up your data.

1. From menu bar, select File > Backup Up Company > Create Local Backup.

2. Create a local backup and click <Next>.

3. If necessary, select Save it now, click <Next>.

4. Browse to your USB drive. Use this file name, **Your Name Chapter 3 October Check Register.** Click <Save>.

5. When the window prompts, QuickBooks has saved a backup of the company file. . . . , click <OK>.

6. Exit QuickBooks 2018 or continue to the next section.

ACCOUNT RECONCILIATION

You receive a bank statement every month for the Home State Bank account, Account No. 10000, which shows the checks and deposits that have cleared the bank. Your bank statement for Home State Bank Account is shown here.

Statement of Account			Your Name Retailers Inc.	
Home State Bank			Your Address	
October 1 to October 31	Account 930-631891		Reno, NV 89557	
REGULAR HOME STATE BANK				
Previous Balance		$54,000.00		
1 Deposits (+)		1,500.00		
2 Checks (−)		1,200.00		
Service Charges (−)	10/31	10.00		
Ending Balance	10/31	**$54,290.00**		

Contiuned

DEPOSITS				
		10/4	1,500.00	
CHECKS (Asterisk * indicates break in check number sequence)				
	10/5	4002	1,000.00	
	10/30	4005*	200.00	

These steps reconcile your bank statement balance to Account 10000, Home State Bank.

1. Select [Reconcile].

2. The Begin Reconciliation window appears. If necessary, in the Account field, select **10000 - Home State Bank.**

3. Type **10/31/20XX (use your current year)** in the Statement Date field.

4. Confirm 54,000.00 appears as the Beginning Balance.

5. Type **54290.00** in the Ending Balance field.

6. In Service Charge field, type **10.00** for the amount and **10/31/20XX** for the Date. Select account **60400 Bank Service Charges Expense.**

7. Compare your Begin Reconciliation window to the one shown on the next page. (*Hint:* Your year may differ, as well as the date in the Interest Earned field.)

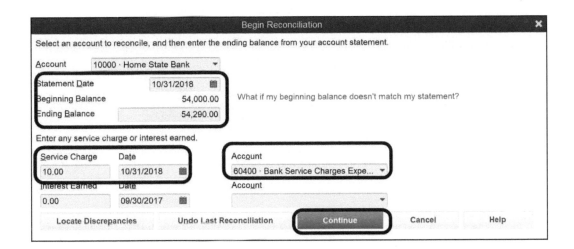

8. After clicking <Continue>, the Reconcile – Home State Bank window appears.

9. Click on the rows next to the checks and deposits that have cleared the bank. Make sure the checks that have *not* cleared the bank remain unchecked; for example, Check No. 4004 should *not* be checked.

10. Compare your Reconcile Account – Home State Bank window to the one shown below. Notice the Difference is 0.00. (*Hint:* Only Reconcile if Difference is 0.00!)

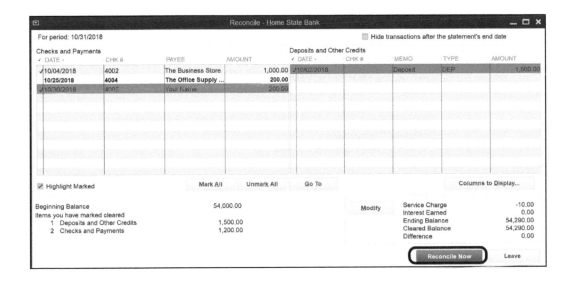

11. After clicking <Reconcile Now>, the Information window appears. Read it, then click <OK>. The Select Reconciliation Report window appears. Display both the summary and detail reports.

12. After clicking <Display>, a Reconcilation Report window appears. Read it, then click <OK>. The Reconciliation Summary report appears. Both the Reconciliation Detail and the Reconciliation Summary report display. If necessary, move them around your screen. Compare your Reconciliation Summary report to the one shown.

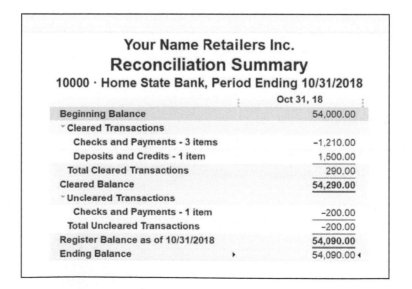

13. Compare your Reconciliation Detail to the one shown. You may need to enlarge it.

Your Name Retailers Inc.
Reconciliation Detail
10000 · Home State Bank, Period Ending 10/31/2018

Type	Date	Num	Name	Clr	Amount	Balance
Beginning Balance						54,000.00
Cleared Transactions						
Checks and Payments - 3 items						
▸ Check	10/04/2018	4002	The Business Store	✓	−1,000.00	−1,000.00 ◂
Check	10/30/2018	4005	Your Name	✓	−200.00	−1,200.00
Check	10/31/2018			✓	−10.00	−1,210.00
Total Checks and Payments					−1,210.00	−1,210.00
Deposits and Credits - 1 item						
Deposit	10/02/2018			✓	1,500.00	1,500.00
Total Deposits and Credits					1,500.00	1,500.00
Total Cleared Transactions					290.00	290.00
Cleared Balance					290.00	54,290.00
Uncleared Transactions						
Checks and Payments - 1 item						
Check	10/25/2018	4004	The Office Supply Store		−200.00	−200.00
Total Checks and Payments					−200.00	−200.00
Total Uncleared Transactions					−200.00	−200.00
Register Balance as of 10/31/2018					90.00	54,090.00
Ending Balance					90.00	54,090.00

14. Close the reports. If a Memorize Report pop-up appears, click <No>.

You have successfully completed your transactions for October. Now let's look at how these transactions were debited and credited.

DISPLAY THE JOURNAL

To see the journal, follow these steps.

1. From the Report Center or Reports menu, select Accountant & Taxes, Journal. If the Collapsing and Expanding window appears, click <OK>.

2. For the Date, type **9/30/20XX** to **10/31/20XX.** If you select Reports from the Icon Bar to go to the Report Center, after typing or selecting

dates, click <Run>. If you go to Reports from the menu bar, after typing the date range, select <Refresh>. (*Hint:* If a Collapsing and Expanding Transactions window appears, read the information. Put a checkmark in the Do not display this message in the future box. Click <OK>.)

Your Name Retailers Inc.
Journal
September 30 through October 31, 2018

Trans #	Type	Date	Num	Adj	Name	Memo	Account	Debit	Credit
1	Deposit	09/30/2018				Account Opening Balance	10000 · Home State Bank	54,000.00	
						Account Opening Balance	30000 · Common Stock		54,000.00
								54,000.00	54,000.00
2	Deposit	09/30/2018				Account Opening Balance	13000 · Supplies	2,500.00	
						Account Opening Balance	30000 · Common Stock		2,500.00
								2,500.00	2,500.00
3	General Journal	09/30/2018	1			Account Opening Balance	14000 · Computer Equipment	1,000.00	
						Account Opening Balance	30000 · Common Stock		1,000.00
								1,000.00	1,000.00
4	General Journal	09/30/2018	2			Account Opening Balance	15000 · Furniture and Equipment	4,000.00	
						Account Opening Balance	30000 · Common Stock		4,000.00
								4,000.00	4,000.00
5	Deposit	09/30/2018				Account Opening Balance	18000 · Prepaid Insurance	2,500.00	
						Account Opening Balance	30000 · Common Stock		2,500.00
								2,500.00	2,500.00
6	General Journal	09/30/2018	3			Account Opening Balance	26000 · Your Name Notes Payable		20,000.00
						Account Opening Balance	30000 · Common Stock	20,000.00	
								20,000.00	20,000.00
7	Deposit	10/02/2018				Deposit	10000 · Home State Bank	1,500.00	
					Your Name	Deposit	30000 · Common Stock		1,500.00
								1,500.00	1,500.00
8	Check	10/04/2018	4002		The Business Store		10000 · Home State Bank		1,000.00
					The Business Store	Computer storage	14000 · Computer Equipment	1,000.00	
								1,000.00	1,000.00
9	Check	10/25/2018	4004		The Office Supply Store		10000 · Home State Bank		200.00
					The Office Supply Store	Store supplies	13000 · Supplies	200.00	
								200.00	200.00
10	Check	10/30/2018	4005		Your Name		10000 · Home State Bank		200.00
					Your Name	Cash dividend to stockholder	30200 · Dividends	200.00	
								200.00	200.00
11	Check	10/31/2018				Service Charge	10000 · Home State Bank		10.00
						Service Charge	60400 · Bank Service Charges Expense	10.00	
								10.00	10.00
TOTAL								86,910.00	86,910.00

In the Trans # column, the first six transactions are the beginning balances that you entered from the October 1 balance sheet earlier in the chapter. Notice the edited transaction, check 4003, does not appear.

3. Close the Journal report. Do not memorize the report.

TRANSACTION DETAIL BY ACCOUNT

Transaction Detail by Account report is similar to a general ledger (GL). For purposes of seeing each account balance, use the steps below to display the Transaction Detail by Account report.

1. From the Report Center or Reports menu, select Accountant & Taxes, Transaction Detail by Account.

2. The date range is 9/30/20XX to 10/31/20XX > Refresh. Scroll down the report to see all the accounts. (*Hint:* Use current year.)

Your Name Retailers Inc.
Transaction Detail by Account
September 30 through October 31, 2018

Type	Date	Num	Adj	Name	Memo	Clr	Split	Debit	Credit	Balance
10000 · Home State Bank										
Deposit	09/30/2018				Account Opening Balance	✓	30000 · Common Stock	54,000.00		54,000.00
Deposit	10/02/2018				Deposit	✓	30000 · Common Stock	1,500.00		55,500.00
Check	10/04/2018	4002		The Business Store		✓	14000 · Computer Equipment		1,000.00	54,500.00
Check	10/25/2018	4004		The Office Supply Store			13000 · Supplies		200.00	54,300.00
Check	10/30/2018	4005		Your Name			30200 · Dividends		200.00	54,100.00
Check	10/31/2018				Service Charge	✓	60400 · Bank Service Charge...		10.00	54,090.00
Total 10000 · Home State Bank								55,500.00	1,410.00	54,090.00
13000 · Supplies										
Deposit	09/30/2018				Account Opening Balance	✓	30000 · Common Stock	2,500.00		2,500.00
Check	10/25/2018	4004		The Office Supply Store	Store supplies		10000 · Home State Bank	200.00		2,700.00
Total 13000 · Supplies								2,700.00	0.00	2,700.00
18000 · Prepaid Insurance										
Deposit	09/30/2018				Account Opening Balance	✓	30000 · Common Stock	2,500.00		2,500.00
Total 18000 · Prepaid Insurance								2,500.00	0.00	2,500.00
14000 · Computer Equipment										
General Journal	09/30/2018	1			Account Opening Balance	✓	30000 · Common Stock	1,000.00		1,000.00
Check	10/04/2018	4002		The Business Store	Computer storage		10000 · Home State Bank	1,000.00		2,000.00
Total 14000 · Computer Equipment								2,000.00	0.00	2,000.00
15000 · Furniture and Equipment										
General Journal	09/30/2018	2			Account Opening Balance	✓	30000 · Common Stock	4,000.00		4,000.00
Total 15000 · Furniture and Equipment								4,000.00	0.00	4,000.00
26000 · Your Name Notes Payable										
General Journal	09/30/2018	3			Account Opening Balance	✓	30000 · Common Stock		20,000.00	-20,000.00
Total 26000 · Your Name Notes Payable								0.00	20,000.00	-20,000.00
30000 · Common Stock										
Deposit	09/30/2018				Account Opening Balance		10000 · Home State Bank		54,000.00	-54,000.00
Deposit	09/30/2018				Account Opening Balance		13000 · Supplies		2,500.00	-56,500.00
General Journal	09/30/2018	1			Account Opening Balance		14000 · Computer Equipment		1,000.00	-57,500.00
General Journal	09/30/2018	2			Account Opening Balance		15000 · Furniture and Equipm...		4,000.00	-61,500.00
Deposit	09/30/2018				Account Opening Balance		18000 · Prepaid Insurance		2,500.00	-64,000.00
General Journal	09/30/2018	3			Account Opening Balance		26000 · Your Name Notes Pa...	20,000.00		-44,000.00
Deposit	10/02/2018			Your Name	Deposit		10000 · Home State Bank		1,500.00	-45,500.00
Total 30000 · Common Stock								20,000.00	65,500.00	-45,500.00
30200 · Dividends										
Check	10/30/2018	4005		Your Name	Cash dividend to stockholder		10000 · Home State Bank	200.00		200.00
Total 30200 · Dividends								200.00	0.00	200.00
60400 · Bank Service Charges Expense										
Check	10/31/2018				Service Charge		10000 · Home State Bank	10.00		10.00
Total 60400 · Bank Service Charges Expense								10.00	0.00	10.00
TOTAL								86,910.00	86,910.00	0.00

3. Close the report. Do not memorize it.

TRIAL BALANCE

A *trial balance* lists the ending debit and credit balances at the end of a reporting period. The trial balance shows that debits and credits are equal. To display Your Name Retailers' trial balance, follow these steps.

1. From the Report Center or Reports menu, select Accountant & Taxes > Trial Balance.

2. The date range is 9/30/20XX (current year) to 10/31/20XX. Compare your Trial Balance with the one shown. (*Hint:* Remember to use current year.)

Your Name Retailers Inc.
Trial Balance
As of October 31, 2018

	Oct 31, 18	
	Debit	Credit
10000 · Home State Bank	54,090.00	
13000 · Supplies	2,700.00	
18000 · Prepaid Insurance	2,500.00	
14000 · Computer Equipment	2,000.00	
15000 · Furniture and Equipment	4,000.00	
26000 · Your Name Notes Payable		20,000.00
30000 · Common Stock		45,500.00
30200 · Dividends	200.00	
60400 · Bank Service Charges Expense	10.00	
TOTAL	**65,500.00**	**65,500.00**

---

3. Close the Trial Balance without saving or memorizing.

FINANCIAL STATEMENTS

To display Your Name Retailers' Profit & Loss follow these steps.

1. From the Report Center or Reports menu, select Company & Financial, Profit & Loss Standard.

2. The date range is 10/1/20XX (use current year) to 10/31/20XX.

	Oct 18
Your Name Retailers Inc.	
Profit & Loss	
October 2018	

Your Name Retailers Inc.
Profit & Loss
October 2018

	Oct 18
Expense	
60400 · Bank Service Charges Expense	10.00
Total Expense	10.00
Net Income	–10.00

3. Close the profit and loss without saving or memorizing.

4. From the Report Center or Reports menu, select Company & Financial > Balance Sheet Standard. The report date is **10/31/20XX.** Compare yours with the one shown on the next page.

Your Name Retailers Inc.
Balance Sheet
As of October 31, 2018

	Oct 31, 18
ASSETS	
Current Assets	
Checking/Savings	
10000 · Home State Bank	54,090.00
Total Checking/Savings	54,090.00
Other Current Assets	
13000 · Supplies	2,700.00
18000 · Prepaid Insurance	2,500.00
Total Other Current Assets	5,200.00
Total Current Assets	59,290.00
Fixed Assets	
14000 · Computer Equipment	2,000.00
15000 · Furniture and Equipment	4,000.00
Total Fixed Assets	6,000.00
TOTAL ASSETS	**65,290.00**
LIABILITIES & EQUITY	
Liabilities	
Long Term Liabilities	
26000 · Your Name Notes Payable	20,000.00
Total Long Term Liabilities	20,000.00
Total Liabilities	20,000.00
Equity	
30000 · Common Stock	45,500.00
30200 · Dividends	-200.00
Net Income	-10.00
Total Equity	45,290.00
TOTAL LIABILITIES & EQUITY	**65,290.00**

5. Close the balance sheet without saving or memorizing.

6. From the Company & Financial menu, select Statement of Cash Flows. The date range is 10/01/20XX to 10/31/20XX **(use your current year).**

Your Name Retailers Inc.
Statement of Cash Flows
October 2018

	Oct 18
OPERATING ACTIVITIES	
Net Income	–10.00
Adjustments to reconcile Net Income	
to net cash provided by operations:	
13000 · **Supplies**	–200.00
Net cash provided by Operating Activities	–210.00
INVESTING ACTIVITIES	
14000 · **Computer Equipment**	–1,000.00
Net cash provided by Investing Activities	–1,000.00
FINANCING ACTIVITIES	
30000 · **Common Stock**	1,500.00
30200 · **Dividends**	–200.00
Net cash provided by Financing Activities	1,300.00
Net cash increase for period	90.00
Cash at beginning of period	54,000.00
Cash at end of period	**54,090.00**

7. Close reports without saving or memorizing.

BACKUP CHAPTER 3 DATA

Before completing the end-of-chapter exercises, follow these steps to backup Chapter 3 data.

1. From menu bar, select File > Backup Company > Create Local Backup.

2. Accept the default for Local Backup by clicking <Next>.

3. Accept the default for Save it now by clicking <Next>.

4. Browse to your USB drive or other location for your backup files. Use the file name **Your Name Chapter 3 October End.** Click <Save>.

5. To increase the number of backups, do this.

   a. Click File > Back up Company > Create Local Backup > Options button. If necessary go to the Your Name QB Backups folder. In the Limit the number of backup copies in this folder, type **20.**

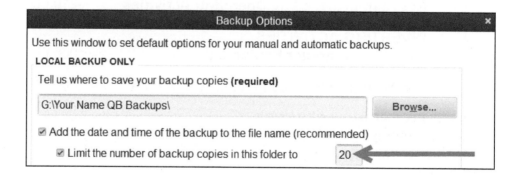

   b. When through, click OK > Finish. A Your Name Retailers Inc. Chapter 3 (Backup [today's date and time]).QBB file is backed up.

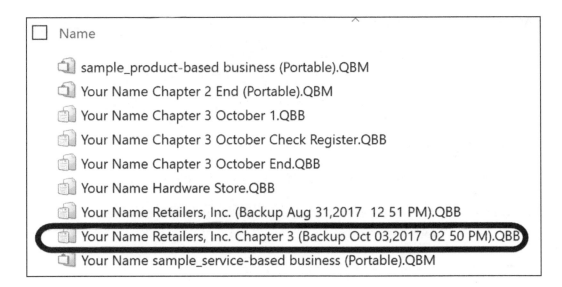

c. When the window prompts that QuickBooks has saved a backup of the company file. . . . , click <OK>.

6. Exit QuickBooks 2018 or continue to the next section.

SUMMARY AND REVIEW

Additional resources are on the textbook's Online Learning Center (OLC) at www.mhhe.com/qbd2018. The OLC includes Student Edition links and Information Center links. When you link to the Student Edition, choose a chapter to populate more resources.

RESOURCEFUL QUICKBOOKS

Go to Help > New Features > New Feature Tour > select Search in Chart of Accounts.

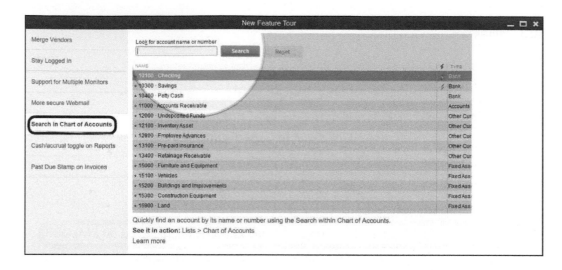

1. How do you find an account in the Chart of Accounts?
2. List the features included within the Chart of Accounts search feature.

Multiple Choice Questions: The Online Learning Center includes the multiple-choice questions at www.mhhe.com/qbd2018 > Student Edition > Chapter 3 > Multiple Choice.

_____ 1. How many backups were made of company data in Chapter 3?

     a. One.

     b. Two.

     c. Three.

     d. Four.

_____ 2. The Business Store is a:

     a. Vendor.

     b. Customer.

     c. Employee.

     d. Other.

_____ 3. The Home Page area that includes write checks is:

    a. Employees.

    b. Vendors.

    c. Banking.

    d. Company.

_____ 4. An Audit Trail report shows:

    a. All transactions.

    b. Only edited transactions.

    c. Only voided transactions.

    d. Only duplicate transactions.

_____ 5. How often should an account be reconciled?

    a. Daily.

    b. Weekly.

    c. Monthly.

    d. Quarterly.

_____ 6. Reconciliation reports generated when an account is reconciled include:

    a. Summary.

    b. Detail.

    c. Both.

    d. No report is generated.

_____ 7. In Report Center under Accountant & Taxes, all of the following reports can be generated except:

    a. Transaction Detail by Account.

    b. Transaction List by Date.

    c. Audit Trail.

    d. Unclassified.

_____ 8. In the Report Center under Company & Financial all of the following reports can be found for Profit & Loss except:

    a.   Prev Year Comparison.

    b.   By Job.

    c.   By Class.

    d.   By Date.

_____ 9. In the Report Center under Company & Financial all of the following reports can be found for Balance Sheet & Net Worth except:

    a.   Summary.

    b.   YTD Comparison.

    c.   Prev Year Comparison.

    d.   Net Worth Graph.

_____ 10. In the Report Center under Company & Financial all of the following sections are included *except:*

    a.   Profit & Loss (income statement).

    b.   Income & Expenses.

    c.   Balance Sheet & Net Worth.

    d.   A/R Aging.

True/Make True: To answer these questions, go online to www.mhhe.com/qbd2018 > Student Edition > Chapter 3 > QA Templates. The analysis question is also included.

1. In Chapter 3, the checkbook's transaction register and September 30, 20XX balance sheet are used as source documents.

2. Written evidence of a business transaction is called an account register.

3. Two actions are necessary when a company writes a check in error, the check must be voided and the entry must be edited in QuickBooks.

4. Two backups were made in Chapter 3 of Your Name Retailers Inc. company data.

5. The first date for recording transactions is 10/01/20XX.

6. The company preference for write checks and record deposits is Account No. 10000, Home State Bank.

7. The total cash balance on 10/31/20XX is $50,000.00.

8. The 10/31/20XX Profit & Loss report for Your Name Retailers Inc. had a net income.

9. The total assets on the 10/31/20XX Balance Sheet for Your Name Retailers Inc. were $100,000.00.

10. Your Name Retailers Inc. had a positive cash flow for the month of October.

Exercise 3-1: Follow the instructions to complete Exercise 3-1. You must complete Chapter 3 activities *before* you can do Exercise 3-1.

1. Print the Chart of Accounts: [Reports] > Accountant & Taxes > Account Listing > Dates 9/30/20XX to 10/31/20XX > Run. (*Hint:* Refer to the Read me box on the next page for saving reports as PDF files.)

2. Print the 9/30/20XX to 10/31/20XX journal.

3. Print the 9/30/20XX to 10/31/20XX transaction detail by account.

Exercise 3-2: Follow the instructions below to complete Exercise 3-2.

1. Print the 9/30/20XX to 10/31/20XX trial balance.

2. Print the 10/01/20XX to 10/31/20XX profit and loss report.

3. Print the 10/31/20XX balance sheet.

4. Print the 09/30/20XX to 10/31/20XX statement of cash flows.

Read Me: Save QB reports as PDF Files

Your instructor may want you to email the QB reports as PDF attachments. To do that, follow these steps:

1. Display the report.

2. Click the Print button > Save as PDF. If report is emailed to your instructor, select E-mail > Send report as PDF.

3. The suggested file name is **Exercise 3-1 Chart of Accounts.pdf,** etc. (*Hint:* The current date is shown on the Account Listing *or* Chart of Accounts.)

You need Adobe Reader to save as PDF files. If needed, download the free Adobe Reader, https://get.adobe.com/reader/.

If your instructor prefers receiving reports as an Excel file, refer to pages 307-308, Use Excel with QuickBooks, Appendix B, Troubleshooting.

Analysis Question: Why are the trial balance totals different from the balance sheet totals?

Chapter 4 | Working with Inventory, Vendors, and Customers

OBJECTIVES:

1. Open the company, Your Name Retailers Inc.
2. Enter items and inventory preferences.
3. Enter vendor records.
4. Enter inventory items.
5. Print the vendor list and item list.
6. Enter bills and record purchase returns.
7. Pay bills.
8. Enter customer records and defaults.
9. Record customer sales on account and sales returns.
10. Receive customer payments.
11. Make backups.[1]

GETTING STARTED

Your Name Retailers Inc. started operations on October 1, 20XX (use current year) in Reno, NV and is organized as a corporation. Customers purchase three products from Your Name Retailers Inc.

The three products sold by Your Name Retailers are:

▶ Podcasts (audio files).

---

[1]The chart in the Preface, pages x-xi, shows the file name and size of each backup file. Refer to this chart for backing up data. Remember, you can back up to a hard drive location or external media.

► ebooks (PDF files). PDF is an abbreviation of portable document format.

► TV programs (video files).

Follow these steps to open Your Name Retailers Inc.

1. Start QuickBooks.[2] You should see Your Name Retailers Inc. - QuickBooks Accountant Desktop 2018 on the title bar.

> Your Name Retailers Inc. - QuickBooks Accountant Desktop 2018

2. If you do <u>not</u> see Your Name Retailers Inc. on the title bar, follow these steps.

    a. Select File > Close Company. If an Automatic Backup window appears, click <No> to backing up. From the No Company Open window, select Open or restore an existing company.

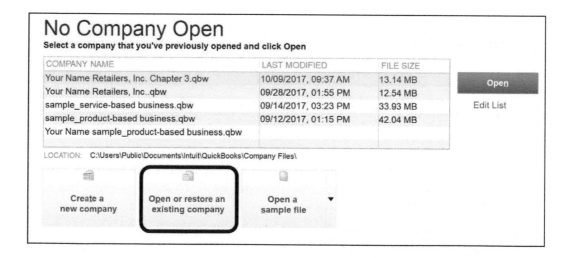

---

[2] If an Update Company window appears, refer to pages 84-85. The authors recommend installing the update.

b. On the Open or Restore Company window, select Restore a backup copy > click <Next> two times. Go to the location of the Your Name Chapter 3 October End.QBB backup file that you made in Chapter 3. This backup was made on pages 126-127 > click <Open> > then <Next>.

c. In the Where do you want to restore the file? window, click <Next>.

d. Rename the Your Name Retailers Inc.Chapter 3.qbw file to **Your Name Chapter 4 October Begin** in the Save Company File as

window–

File name:	Your Name Chapter 4 October Begin.qbw

.

e. Click <Save>. When the screen prompts Your data has been restored successfully, click <OK>. The title bar shows Your Name Retailers Inc. - QuickBooks Accountant Desktop 2018.

3. To confirm that you are starting in the correct place, display the 10/31 trial balance. (Your year may differ.) Compare your trial balance account balances with the ones shown at the end of Chapter 3 on page 122.

Your Name Retailers Inc.
Trial Balance
As of October 31, 2018

	Oct 31, 18	
	Debit	Credit
10000 · Home State Bank	54,090.00	
13000 · Supplies	2,700.00	
18000 · Prepaid Insurance	2,500.00	
14000 · Computer Equipment	2,000.00	
15000 · Furniture and Equipment	4,000.00	
26000 · Your Name Notes Payable		20,000.00
30000 · Common Stock		45,500.00
30200 · Dividends	200.00	
60400 · Bank Service Charges Expense	10.00	
TOTAL	65,500.00	65,500.00

---

4. Close the trial balance without saving.

ITEMS & INVENTORY PREFERENCES

Follow these steps to set preferences for items and inventory.

1. From the menu bar, select Edit > Preferences.
2. Select Items & Inventory > Company Preferences tab.
3. Click on the box next to Inventory and purchase orders are active to place a checkmark in the box. Compare your Items & Inventory Preferences to the screen image below.

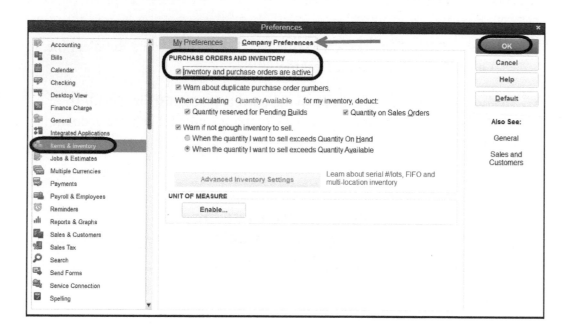

4. After clicking <OK>, if a Warning window prompts, QuickBooks must close all its open windows to change this preference, click <OK>. Click [🏠 Home].

MERCHANDISING BUSINESSES

Merchandising businesses purchase the merchandise they sell from suppliers known as *vendors.* A vendor is a person or company from whom Your Name Retailers buys products or services. When Your Name Retailers makes a purchase on account from vendors, the transaction is known as an *accounts payable transaction.* Purchases made on account involve payment terms; for example, Your Name Retailers purchases inventory on account from a vendor. The vendor offers the Your Name Retailers 30 days to pay for the purchase. This is shown as Net 30 in the Payment terms field of the vendor record.

QuickBooks organizes and monitors Your Name Retailers' *accounts payable.* Accounts Payable is a group of accounts that show the amounts owed to vendors or creditors for goods, supplies, or services purchased on account.

When entering a purchase, you select the vendor's name and item. The vendor's address information, payment terms, and appropriate accounts are automatically debited and credited. This works similarly for accounts receivable.

The Vendors section of the Home Page illustrates the work flow of entering and paying a vendor bill as well as the tracking of any inventory items purchased on account.

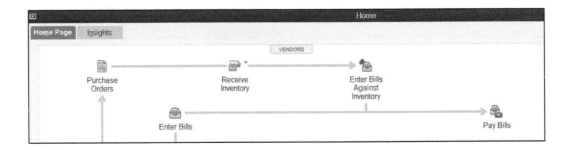

VENDORS

The Vendor Center gives you quick access to your vendors, their contact and billing information, and vendor transactions. In the Vendor Center, you perform all the tasks related to vendors and payables. The Vendor Center is the starting point for managing vendor purchases and the tracking of inventory items purchased.

To see the Vendor Center, select [Vendors]. You can also select Vendors > Vendor Center from the menu bar.

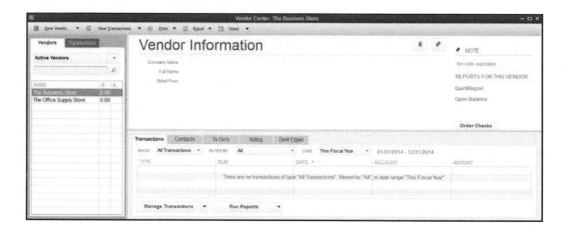

The steps that follow show how to set up vendors.

1. If necessary, on the Icon Bar, select [Vendors].

2. Select the down-arrow next to New Vendor > New Vendor

. The New Vendor window appears.

Complete the following fields:

Vendor Name:	**Podcast Ltd.**
Opening Balance:	**0** as of **10/01/20XX (use current year)**
Company Name:	**Podcast Ltd.**
Full Name	**Howie Henson**
Work Phone:	**669-555-0100**
Fax:	**669-555-0300**
Main Email:	**howie@podcast.net**
Website:	**www.podcast.net**

In the Address Details, Billed From field, type the following:

5113 Barrington Road

Los Gatos, CA 95008 USA

3. Click Payment Settings. Complete the following fields:

Account No.:	**22000**
Payment Terms:	**Net 30**
Credit limit:	**10,000.00**
Print Name on Check as:	Podcast Ltd.

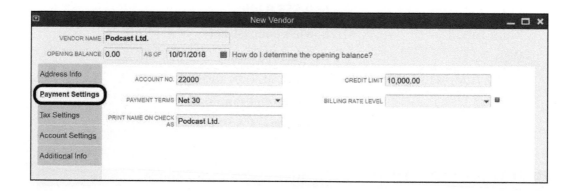

4. Click Additional Info. In the Vendor Type field, select **Suppliers.**

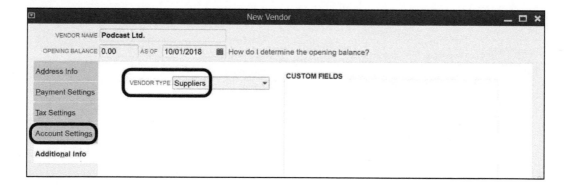

5. Review data under Address Info, Payment Settings, and Additional Info. When satisfied, click <OK>. Podcast Ltd. is added to the Name list along with The Business Store and The Office Supply Store.

6. Set up the next vendor record:

Vendor Name:	**eBooks Express**
Opening Balance:	**0** as of **10/01/20XX (use current year)**
Company Name:	**eBooks Express**
Full Name:	**Nan Norton**
Work Phone:	**253-555-4320**
Fax:	**253-555-8808**
Main Email:	**nan@ebooks.com**
Website:	**www.ebooks.com**
Address:	**175 NW First Street**
	Gig Harbor, WA 98332 USA

Payment Settings:

Account No.:	**22000**
Payment Terms:	**Net 30**
Credit limit:	**10,000.00**
Print Name on Check as:	eBooks Express

Additional Info:

Vendor Type:	**Suppliers**

7. Review data under Address Info, Payment Settings, and Additional Info. When satisfied, click <OK>.

8. Set up the next vendor record.

Vendor Name:	**TV Flix**
Opening Balance:	**0** as of **10/01/20XX (use current year)**
Company Name:	**TV Flix**
Full Name:	**Hugh Singer**
Work Phone:	**818-555-1690**
Fax:	**818-555-6320**
Main Email:	**hugh@tvflix.com**
Website:	**www.tvflix.com**
Address:	**673 Sunset Lane Burbank, CA 91501 USA**

Payment Settings:

Account No.:	**22000**
Payment Terms:	**Net 30**
Credit limit:	**10,000.00**
Print Name on Check as:	TV Flix

Additional Info:

Vendor Type:	**Suppliers**

9. Click <OK> to return to the Vendor Center.

    Notice all of your vendors, the three you added this chapter plus the two you added previously when you purchased supplies and furniture (Chapter 3) are listed in the left pane of the Vendor Center window with account balances of zero.

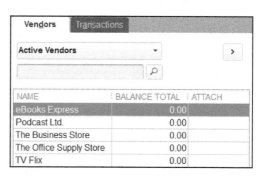

10. Close the Vendor Center.

INVENTORY ITEMS

An *inventory item* is a product that is purchased for sale and is tracked in Account No. 12100, Inventory Asset, on the balance sheet. Because the Inventory account is increased or decreased for every purchase, sale or return, its balance in the general ledger is current. In QuickBooks when you purchase and receive inventory items, they are added to inventory. When you sell these items and they are added to an invoice, the items are subtracted from inventory.

Complete the following steps to add a new item to inventory.

1. From the Home Page's Company area, click on the down-arrow next to Inventory Activities > Inventory Center.

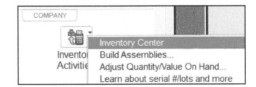

2. From the Inventory Center, select New Inventory Item > New Inventory Item .

3. If necessary, in the Type field, select Inventory Part. Complete the fields shown on the next page. Some accounts are automatically completed. Double-check that that COGS Account, Income Account, and Asset Account agree with the New Item window below.

Type: Inventory Part
Item Name/Number: **Podcast**

Description on Purchase Transactions and Sales Transactions:

audio files (Sales automatically fills)

Cost:	**15.00**
COGS Account:	50000 - Cost of Goods Sold
Preferred Vendor:	**Podcast Ltd.**
Sales Price:	30.00
Income Account:	46000 - Sales
Asset Account:	12100 - Inventory Asset
On Hand:	0.00
Total Value:	0.00
As of:	**10/01/20XX** (use current year)

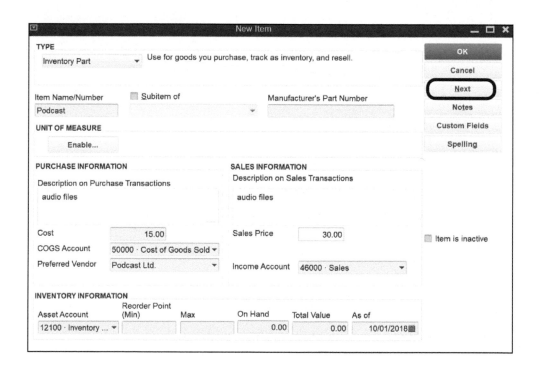

4. Make sure your New Item window agrees. (*Hint:* Your As of year may differ).
    Click <Next>. When the New Item window appears, make sure Inventory
    Part is selected.

5. The New Item window is ready for the next inventory item. Complete these fields.

Type:	Inventory Part
Item Name/Number:	**eBook**
Description on Purchase Transactions and Sales Transactions:	
	PDF files
Cost:	**25.00**
COGS Account:	Account No. 50000, Cost of Goods Sold
Preferred Vendor:	**eBooks Express**
Sales Price:	**50.00**
Income Account:	46000 - Sales
Asset Account:	12100 - Inventory Asset
On Hand:	0.00
Total Value:	0.00
As of:	**10/01/20XX** (use current year)

6. Check each field. Click <Next>. If Check Spelling on Form window appears to check the spelling of PDF, select <Ignore All>.

7. The New Item window is ready for the next inventory part. Complete these fields.

Type:	Inventory Part
Item Name/Number:	**TV Programs**
Description on Purchase Transactions and Sales Transactions:	
	video files
Cost:	**30.00**
COGS Account:	50000 - Cost of Goods Sold

Preferred Vendor:	TV Flix
Sales Price:	**60.00**
Income Account:	46000 - Sales
Asset Account:	12100 - Inventory Asset
On Hand:	0.00
Total Value:	0.00
As of:	**10/01/20XX** (use current year)

8. Check each field. Click <OK> to return to the Inventory Center.

NAME	PRICE
◆ eBook	50.00
◆ Podcast	30.00
◆ TV Programs	60.00

Close the Inventory Center. To accommodate inventory tracking, two accounts are automatically added to the Chart of Accounts — Account 12100 Inventory Asset and Account 50000 Cost of Goods Sold. Display the chart of accounts to see these accounts.

The Chart of Accounts is shown on the next page. Inactive accounts are not shown. (*Hint:* If needed, uncheck Include inactive.)

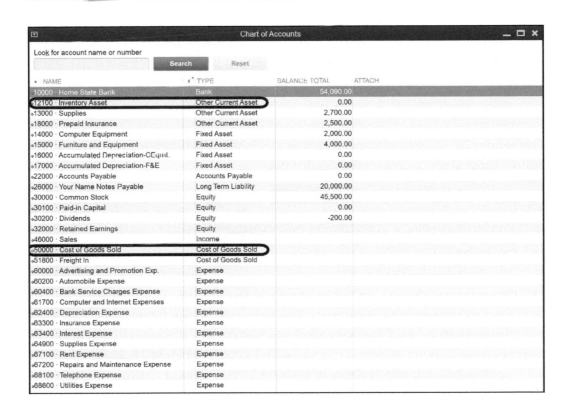

Account 12100 Inventory Asset tracks the current value of inventory. QuickBooks automatically adds the Inventory Asset account to the Chart of Accounts the first time you create an inventory item.

Account 50000 Cost of Goods Sold is also added to your Chart of Accounts the first time you add an inventory item. QuickBooks uses this account to track how much you paid for goods and materials that were held in inventory and then sold.

The New Item window on page 144 includes two fields for these accounts, COGS Account and Asset Account. After checking the Chart of accounts for Account 12100 Inventory Asset and Account 50000 Cost of Goods sold, close the Chart of Accounts window.

LISTS

You just added three vendors and three inventory items. QuickBooks' list feature shows the details of each record.

Vendor List

The vendor list shows information about the vendors with whom you do business. Follow these steps to display the vendor list.

1. From the Icon Bar, select **Vendors** > click on the Vendors tab. The Vendor List appears. Observe you can view list by All Vendors, Active Vendors, Vendors with Open Balances, or Custom Filter.
2. To see The Business Store vendor record, drill down. (*Hint:* Double-click on The Business Store.)
3. Since this vendor was added on the fly in the previous chapter, you need to add vendor information. The Company Name field shows The Business Store. The Business Store is located at 2001 Range Road, Reno, NV 89555; Work Phone, 775-555-3400; Fax is 775-555-3404; Main Email, james@tbs.com; and Website is www.tbs.com. Payment Settings include Account No. 22000; Payment Terms, Net 30; Print name on check as The Business Store; and Credit Limit, 5,000.00. Additional Info includes Suppliers as the Vendor Type.
4. To see The Office Supply Store vendor record, drill down. Add the following vendor information. The Company Name fields shows The Office Supply Store: The Office Supply Store is located at 8915 Hogback Lane, Reno, NV 89555; Work Phone 775-555-8874; Fax, 775-555-7992; Main Email: sally@oss.com; Website, www.oss.com. Payment Settings include Account No. 22000, Payment Terms Net 30, Print Name on Check as The Office Supply Store, Credit Limit 5,000.00. Additional Info includes Suppliers as the Vendor Type. Click <OK> to return to the Vendors List.

5. If you need to edit Vendor Information, click on the pencil icon.

6. Click on the arrow button at the top of the Vendor list to show the full list.

7. Click to return to the Vendor Center.

Item List

The Item List shows information about inventory items including name, description, type, account, on hand, and price. When you open the list, you view the active items.

Follow the steps below to display the item list.

1. From the Menu Bar, select Vendors > Items List. The Item List appears. If necessary, click on the Name column to list the items in alphabetic order.

2. Notice there are several items listed that you did not add, Total Sales - Non-taxable and Total Sales - Taxable. Since Your Name Retailers Inc. is located in Nevada, there is no sales tax.
3. To delete Total Sales - Non-Taxable, highlight it. Right-click then select Delete Item. When asked "Are you sure you want to delete this item?" Select <OK>.
4. Delete Total Sales - Taxable, too.
5. Now the three items you added appear in the list.

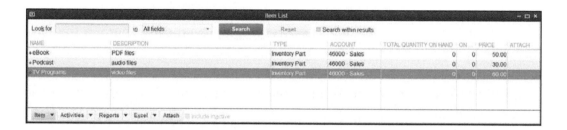

6. To see an item record, drill-down by double-clicking on it.
7. Close all Windows. (*HINT:* Select Window > Close all. Then, click

    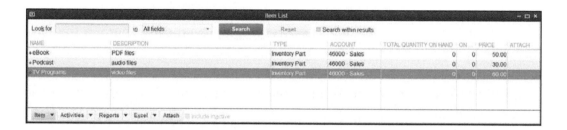.)
8. Backup if you are working in a computer lab to your USB drive or continue to the next section. The suggested file name is **Your Name Chapter 4 Vendors and Inventory.QBB.** (*Hint:* From the menu bar, select File > Backup Company > Create Local Backup.)

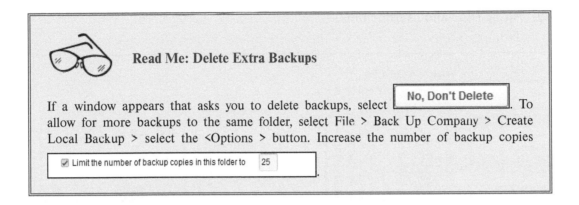

Read Me: Delete Extra Backups

If a window appears that asks you to delete backups, select [No, Don't Delete]. To allow for more backups to the same folder, select File > Back Up Company > Create Local Backup > select the <Options > button. Increase the number of backup copies

☑ Limit the number of backup copies in this folder to   25

VENDOR TRANSACTIONS

In the Vendors section of the Home Page, you perform all the tasks related to vendors and payables. It is the starting point for managing vendor purchases and inventory. In this section, you work with some of these features.

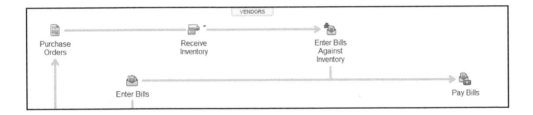

On the Vendors icons, notice you can enter purchase orders placed with vendors, receive inventory, enter bills against inventory, enter bills, and pay bills.

Vendor and Payable Reports

In the Report Center, there are many Vendors & Payables reports, including those that focus on A/P Aging, Vendor Balances, Lists, and related reports. In this chapter you will use them to gain quick access to vendor or payable information.

A/P Aging (due and overdue bills)

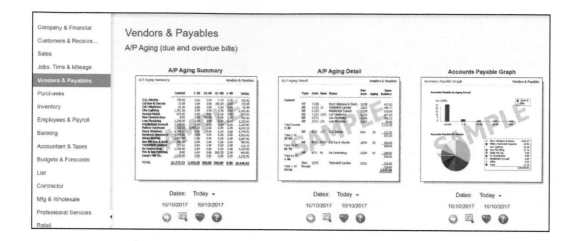

Vendor Balances

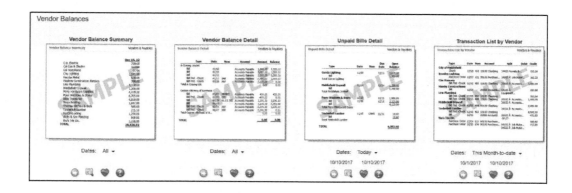

Accounts Payable Tasks

In QuickBooks, all information about a purchase is recorded in the Vendors area of the Home Page. Then, QuickBooks takes the necessary information from the Vendors pane and automatically does the accounting debits and credits.

There are two ways to record a purchase on account in QuickBooks. You can use a purchase order tracking system where a purchase is followed from its initial request until payment. In the accounting work flow diagram, Purchase Order to Receive Inventory to Enter Bills Against Inventory to Pay Bills is shown. (To illustrate, the work flow was altered slightly.)

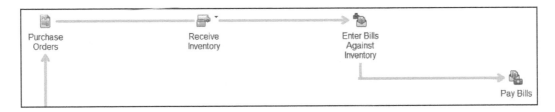

Or, a purchase on account can be tracked from when the bill is received until it is paid. In the accounting work flow diagram, Enter Bill to Pay Bill is shown.

In the following section, you use the Enter Bill and Pay Bill icons to purchase inventory on account from vendors. Transaction processing is dependent on which defaults are set for vendors and inventory items. Since vendor defaults were set up earlier in this chapter, this means that vendor information is completed automatically in the Enter Bills window.

Purchases from vendors are posted to both the General Ledger and to detailed vendors and payables accounts. In accounting, vendors and payables details are shown in the *accounts payable ledger*

When Your Name Retailers pays vendors, QuickBooks' Pay Bills feature is used. Purchases work hand in hand with payments. Once you have entered a bill, it is available when you pay bills. Then, QuickBooks distributes the appropriate amounts.

The next section explains how to enter bills. The term bill and invoice are used interchangeably. A **bill** or *invoice* is a request for payment for products or services.

Enter Bills

The transaction you are going to record is:

Date	Description of Transaction
11/2	Invoice No. 5 received from Podcast Ltd. for the purchase of 20 audio files, $15 each, for a total of $300.

Follow these steps to record this transaction.

1. From the Vendors area on the Home Page, select the Enter Bills icon.

2. On the Enter Bills window, complete the following fields:

Date:	**11/2/20XX (use current year)**
	(Press <Tab> between fields)
Vendor:	Podcast Ltd.
Ref. No.	Invoice No. 5

   Click on Items tab, complete the following fields:

Item:	Podcast
Description:	audio files is completed automatically
Qty:	**20**
Cost:	15.00 is completed automatically

Amount: 300.00 is completed automatically

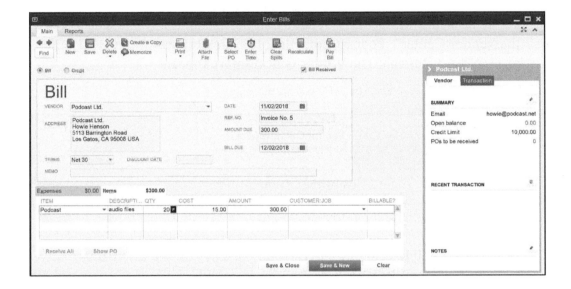

3. Click <Save & Close>. Before completing the next transaction, let's see how QuickBooks debited and credited this information.

4. Select the Report Center (from either the Icon Bar or menu bar) > Accountant & Taxes > Journal. Type **11/1/20XX** (your current year) in the From field and **11/2/20XX** (your current year) in the To field. Click Run (or Refresh) to display the report.

5. The transaction was debited and credited as follows:

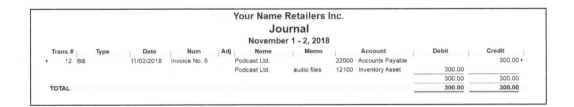

When the 12100 Inventory Asset account is debited, it is increased. When the 22000 Accounts Payable account is credited it is also increased. Your Name

Retailers owes Podcast Ltd. $300 for this purchase. Close the Journal without saving.

6. To see how this transaction is recorded in the accounts payable ledger, go to the Vendor Center > Podcast Ltd. > link to QuickReport > From 11/1/XX to 11/2/XX > Refresh. The Vendor QuickReport appears.

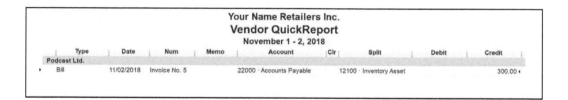

	Type	Date	Num	Memo	Account	Clr	Split	Debit	Credit
Podcast Ltd.									
▸	Bill	11/02/2018	Invoice No. 5		22000 · Accounts Payable		12100 · Inventory Asset		300.00 ◂

7. Double-click Bill to drill down to the original entry on the Enter Bills window. Close windows.

8. Enter the following bills. (*Hint:* Select the Enter Bills icon. Type the Invoice No. in the Ref. No. field.) Remember to click <Save & New> after each transaction. Saving posts the transaction to the appropriate accounts in the general ledger and accounts payable ledger.

Date   ***Description of Transaction***

11/3   Invoice No. 90eB received from eBooks Express for the purchase of 15 PDF files, $25 each, for a total of $375. (Hint: In the Item field, select eBook for PDF files.)

11/3   Invoice No. 210TV received from TV Flix for the purchase of 25 video files, $30 each, for a total of $750. (Hint: In the Item field, select TV Programs.)

11/5   Invoice No. 78 received from Podcast Ltd. for the purchase of 18 audio files, $15 each, for a total of $270. (Hint: After entering this transaction, click <Save & Close.>

Purchase Returns

Sometimes it is necessary to return merchandise that has been purchased from a vendor. When entering a purchase return, you need to record it as a Credit instead of a Bill in the Enter Bills window.

The following transaction is for merchandise returned to a vendor.

Date	Description of Transaction
11/10	Returned two video files to TV Flix from Invoice No. 210TV, Credit Memo No. CM1, for a total of $60.

Follow these steps to record a credit memo.

1. If Enter Bills window is not displayed, click on the Home Page's Enter Bills icon.

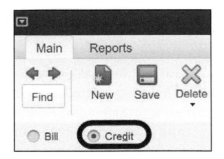

2. When the Enter Bills window appears, select the Credit radio button and complete the following fields:

Date:	**11/10/20XX (use current year)**
Vendor:	TV Flix
Ref. No.	**CM1**
Memo:	**Invoice No. 210TV**
Item:	TV Programs
Qty:	**2**

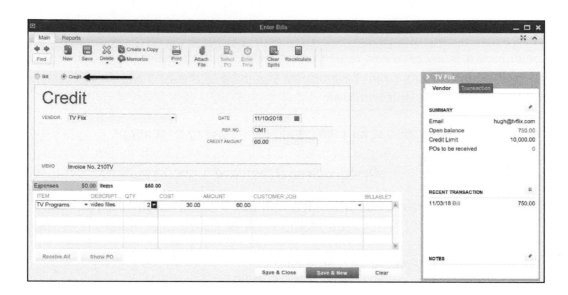

3. After comparing your Enter Bills, Credit window click <Save & Close>.

4. Let's see how this entry is journalized. Go to Report Center > Accountant & Taxes > Journal > date is 11/10/20XX. Observe that 22000 Accounts Payable TV Flix is debited for $60. This reduces the accounts payable account balance by $60. Also, 12100 Inventory Asset is credited for $60. This reduces the inventory account balance by the amount of the return. After viewing, close Journal without saving it.

Your Name Retailers Inc.
Journal
November 10, 2018

Trans #	Type	Date	Num	Adj	Name	Memo	Account	Debit	Credit
16	Credit	11/10/2018	CM1		TV Flix	Invoice No. 210TV	22000 · Accounts Payable	60.00	
					TV Flix	video files	12100 · Inventory Asset		60.00
								60.00	60.00
TOTAL								60.00	60.00

5. To see the return on a QB report, display the Vendor Center. In Vendors tab, highlight TV Flix > link to QuickReport. Type **11/1/20XX** to **11/10/20XX**, [Refresh]. Observe that Account 22000 Accounts Payable is debited for 60.00 on 11/10/20XX.

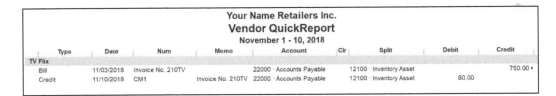

	Type	Date	Num	Memo	Account	Clr	Split	Debit	Credit
TV Flix									
	Bill	11/03/2018	Invoice No. 210TV		22000 · Accounts Payable		12100 · Inventory Asset		750.00 ‹
	Credit	11/10/2018	CM1	Invoice No. 210TV	22000 · Accounts Payable		12100 · Inventory Asset	60.00	

6. To determine the balance in the Accounts Payable account on 11/10/20XX, go to Report Center > Vendors & Payables > Vendor Balance Summary. Select All Dates. Observe that the Total of all Vendor Balances is $1,635.

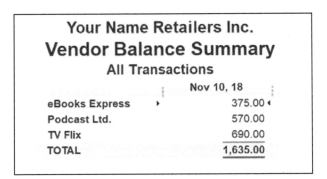

Your Name Retailers Inc.
Vendor Balance Summary
All Transactions

	Nov 10, 18
eBooks Express ▸	375.00 ‹
Podcast Ltd.	570.00
TV Flix	690.00
TOTAL	**1,635.00**

7. This should agree with the 11/10/20XX Balance Sheet for Accounts Payable. (Report Center > Company & Financial > Balance Sheet & Net Worth > Balance Sheet Summary. Custom Dates as of 11/10/20XX.) The general ledger balance for accounts payable is 1,635.00. This is the *same* amount that is shown on the Vendor Balance Summary report.

LIABILITIES & EQUITY	
Liabilities	
Current Liabilities	
Accounts Payable	
22000 · Accounts Payable	1,635.00
Total Accounts Payable	1,635.00
Total Current Liabilities	1,635.00

8. Close all windows. Do not save reports. Click 🏠 Home .

Vendor Payments

Use the Pay Bills icon on the Home Page to pay vendor bills. The Pay Bills form will display a list of the company's unpaid bills. You can choose to pay individual bills or pay all of them.

In the transaction that follows, all vendor bills are paid.

Date	*Description of Transaction*
11/20	Your Name Retailers pays all outstanding vendor bills for a total of $1,635.

1. Click .
2. When the Pay Bills window appears, if necessary select the Show all bills radio button .

3. Confirm Method field shows Check .
4. Confirm the Account field shows 10000 - Home State Bank

5. Type Payment Date, **11/20/20XX** (use current year)

6. Since Your Name Retailers returned merchandise to TV Flix, highlight TV Flix and place a checkmark in the box. The Discount & Credit Information for Highlighted Bill field appears. Observe that the Total Credits Available field shows $60.00.

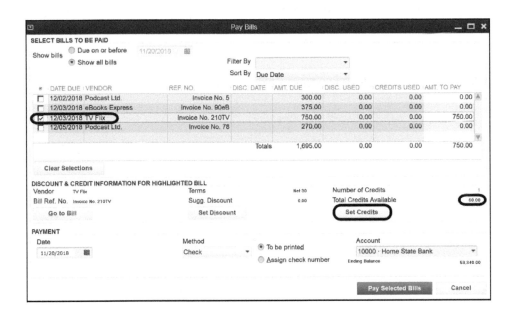

7. After clicking <Set Credits>, the Discount and Credits window appears.

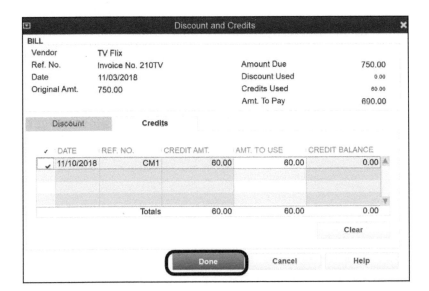

8. After clicking <Done>, observe that the Credits used for TV Flix shows $60.00 and the Amt. To Pay shows 690 (750 − 60 = 690).

9. To place a checkmark next to each vendor, click on the box next to the Date Due column. Compare your Pay Bills window to the one below. Observe that the Totals row shows $1,635. This agrees with the accounts payable balance shown on page 159.

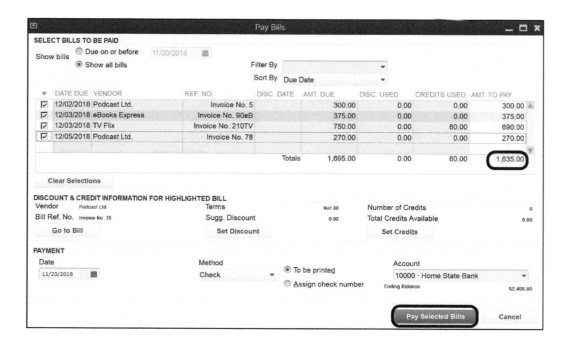

10. After clicking <Pay Selected Bills> the Payment Summary window appears. Observe that the Total shows 1,635.00 which is in agreement with the Accounts Payable balance. (*Hint:* Use the vertical scroll bar to see each payment: 375 + 300 + 270 + 690 = 1,635.)

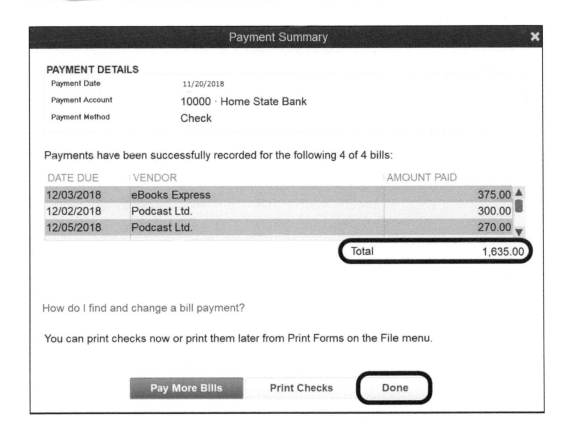

11. After clicking <Done>, you are returned to the Home Page. (*NOTE*: If this were a real business you would have printed and mailed the checks.)
12. Display the detailed account balance for Account No. 22000, Accounts Payable. (Report Center > Company & Financial > Balance Sheet & Net Worth > Balance Sheet Detail. Custom Dates From 10/01/20XX To 11/20/20XX.) Observe that the Balance Sheet Detail shows that the balance in Accounts Payable is 0.00 as of 11/20/20XX. Close report without saving it.

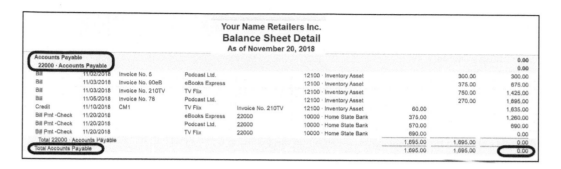

Your Name Retailers Inc.
Balance Sheet Detail
As of November 20, 2018

								Debit	Credit	Balance
Accounts Payable										0.00
22000 · Accounts Payable										0.00
Bill	11/02/2018	Invoice No. 5	Podcast Ltd.		12100 · Inventory Asset				300.00	300.00
Bill	11/03/2018	Invoice No. 90eB	eBooks Express		12100 · Inventory Asset				375.00	675.00
Bill	11/03/2018	Invoice No. 210TV	TV Flix		12100 · Inventory Asset				750.00	1,425.00
Bill	11/05/2018	Invoice No. 78	Podcast Ltd.		12100 · Inventory Asset				270.00	1,695.00
Credit	11/10/2018	CM1	TV Flix	Invoice No. 210TV	12100 · Inventory Asset		60.00			1,635.00
Bill Pmt -Check	11/20/2018		eBooks Express	22000	10000 · Home State Bank		375.00			1,260.00
Bill Pmt -Check	11/20/2018		Podcast Ltd.	22000	10000 · Home State Bank		570.00			690.00
Bill Pmt -Check	11/20/2018		TV Flix	22000	10000 · Home State Bank		690.00			0.00
Total 22000 · Accounts Payable								1,695.00	1,695.00	0.00
Total Accounts Payable								1,695.00	1,695.00	0.00

13. Display the Vendor Center. Observe that each vendor shows a zero balance.

14. To see how the vendor payments are journalized, display the 11/20/20XX Journal. (Report Center > Accountant & Taxes > Journal > date is 11/20/20XX) Observe that each vendor payment is journalized separately; for example, the November 20 vendor payment to eBooks Express shows a debit to Account No. 22000 for $375; and a credit to Account No. 10000, Home State Bank for $375. If you add the three payments together they equal, $1,635, which is the total of the three payments—375 + 570 + 690 = 1,635.

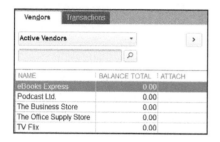

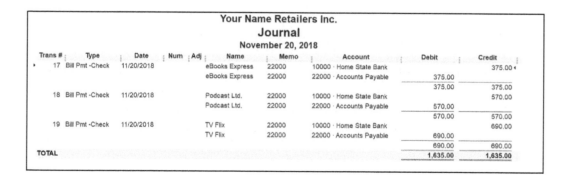

Your Name Retailers Inc.
Journal
November 20, 2018

Trans #	Type	Date	Num	Adj	Name	Memo	Account	Debit	Credit
17	Bill Pmt -Check	11/20/2018			eBooks Express	22000	10000 · Home State Bank		375.00
					eBooks Express	22000	22000 · Accounts Payable	375.00	
								375.00	375.00
18	Bill Pmt -Check	11/20/2018			Podcast Ltd.	22000	10000 · Home State Bank		570.00
					Podcast Ltd.	22000	22000 · Accounts Payable	570.00	
								570.00	570.00
19	Bill Pmt -Check	11/20/2018			TV Flix	22000	10000 · Home State Bank		690.00
					TV Flix	22000	22000 · Accounts Payable	690.00	
								690.00	690.00
TOTAL								**1,635.00**	**1,635.00**

Purchasing Assets from Vendors

In the previous chapter you purchased assets for cash and used the check register as your source document. Now, along with credit purchases for inventory, assets can also be purchased on account from vendors. To see how to purchase assets on account, complete the following steps.

Date	*Description of Transaction*
11/21	Purchased notebook computer equipment on account from The Business Store, Invoice BOS44, for a total of $400, terms Net 30 days.

1. Record the 11/21/20XX credit purchase using Enter Bills. In the Vendor name field, select The Business Store; Ref No., Invoice No. BOS44.

2. If necessary, click on Expenses tab and complete the following fields:

Account:	14000, Computer Equipment
Amount:	400.00
Memo:	Notebook computer

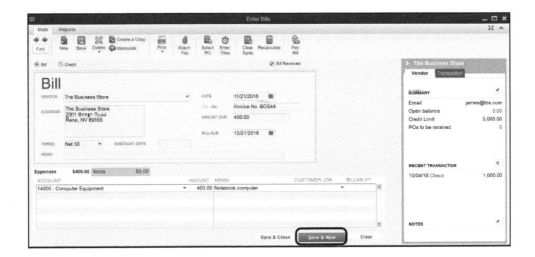

3. Verify that your Enter Bills window is correct. When satisfied, click <Save & Close>.

4. Backup your work. (*Hint:* File > Back Up Company > Create Local Backup.) Name backup file **Your Name Chapter 4 Vendors.QBB.**

CUSTOMERS

Now that you have purchased items from vendors, you are ready to sell that inventory. To do that, you need to learn how to use QuickBooks' customers and receivables tasks. This section shows you how to establish customer records and defaults and explains how QuickBooks' customer work flows are organized. *Accounts receivable* is a group of accounts that show the amounts customers owe for services or products sold on credit. Credit transactions from customers are called *accounts receivable transactions.*

Customer receipts work similarly to paying vendor invoices. A *customer invoice* is defined as a request for payment to a customer for products or services sold.

The Home Page's Customers area is where you perform all the tasks related to customers and receivables. The Customers area shows the work flow of customer tasks. You will work with some of these Customers work flow icons.

Once a new invoice is recorded using the Create Invoices icon, the Receive Payments icon is used to record customer payments or collections. The Create Sales Receipts icon is used for cash sales. The Refunds & Credits icon is used when dissatisfied customers receive a refund or some kind of consideration resulting from a previous sale.

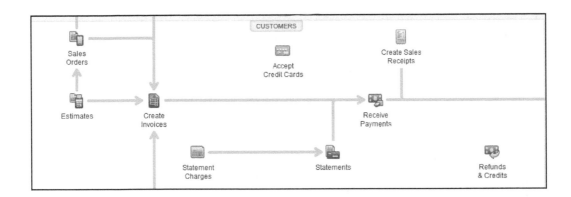

QuickBooks has a Customer Center (Icon Bar, 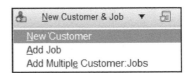; or menu bar, Customers) to track tasks related to customers and receivables. The center provides easy access to customer records, contact information, transaction details, and history. The Customer Center is the starting point for managing customers and the tracking of items sold.

CUSTOMER RECORDS

On the Customer Center, you set up customers and receivables. Follow the steps shown to set up customer records and defaults.

1. From the Icon Bar, select [Customers] > New Customer & Job > New Customer. The New Customer window appears.

2. Complete the Address Info fields shown here.

Customer Name:	**Audio Answers**
Opening Balance:	**0.00** as of **10/01/20XX (current year)**
Company Name:	**Audio Answers**
Full Name:	**Kate Mason**

Work Phone:	**970-555-3912**
Fax:	**970-555-4381**
Main Email:	**kate@audio.biz**
Address:	**1200 Clark Street**
	Telluride, CO 81410

Click Copy >> . The Add Shipping Address Information window appears. Check the information, then click <OK>.

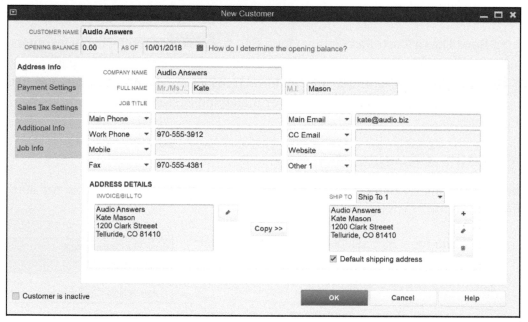

Payment Settings:

Account No.:	**AA1**
Credit Limit:	**7,500.00**
Payment Terms:	Net 30
Preferred Delivery Method:	Mail
Preferred Payment Method:	Check

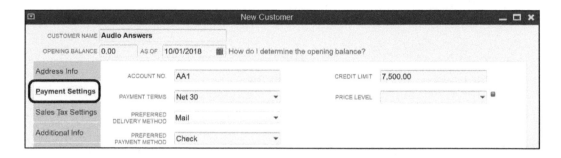

Additional Info:

Customer Type: Retail

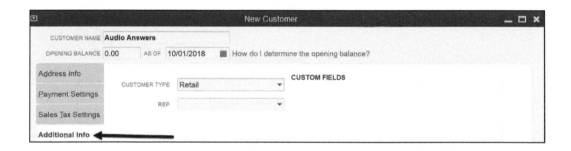

3. Check the information entered. Click <OK>.

4. Enter the following customers:

Customer Name:	**iPrint Design**
Opening Balance:	**0.00** as of **10/01/20XX (current year)**
Company Name:	**iPrint Design**
Full Name:	**Randy Carter**
Work Phone:	**310-555-3277**
Fax:	**310-555-8823**
Main Email:	**randy@iprint.com**
Address:	**810 Springfield Blvd.**
	Palos Verdes, CA 90275
	<Copy> to Ship To

Payment Settings:

Account No.:	**IP2**
Credit Limit:	**7,500.00**
Payment Terms:	Net 30
Preferred Delivery Method:	Mail
Preferred Payment Method:	Check

Additional Info:

Type:	Retail

Customer Name:	**Video Solutions**
Opening Balance:	**0.00** as of **10/01/20XX (current year)**
Company Name:	**Video Solutions**
Full Name:	**Les Haney**
Work Phone:	**352-555-0613**
Fax:	**352-555-0417**
Main Email:	**lh@video.com**
Address:	**1706 NE Highway 16**
	Fanning Springs, FL 32693
	<Copy> to Ship To

Payment Settings:

Account No.:	**VS3**
Credit Limit:	**7,500.00**
Payment Terms:	Net 30
Preferred Delivery Method:	Mail
Preferred Payment Method:	Check

Additional Info:

Type: Retail

5. Click <OK> to return to Customer Center.

Customer List

The customer list shows information about the customers with whom you do business. Follow these steps to display the customer list.

1. If necessary, go to the Customer Center> click on the Customers & Jobs tab. The Customer List appears. Observe you can view list by All Customers, Active Customers (the default), Customers with Open Balances, Customers with Overdue Invoices, Customers with Almost Due Invoices, or Custom Filter.

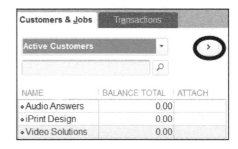

2. Click on the [<] button show the full list.

3. Click on the [>] button to return to the Customer Center.
4. To see the detailed record and transaction history of a specific customer, click on the customer name in the customer list. Information about the customer will appear in the right pane of the Customer Center.

Customers & Receivables and Sales Reports

QuickBooks' Report Center provides many customer, receivable, and sales reports that are used in this chapter. Customers & Receivables reports provide information about A/R Aging, Customer Balance, Lists, and other related reports. To see the Customers & Accounts Receivables reports, from the Icon Bar, select Reports > Customers & Receivables.

Customers & Receivables: A/R Aging (what my customers owe me and what is overdue). A partial window is shown. Scroll down the Customers & Receivables report center to see more.

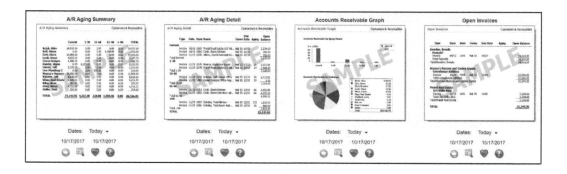

Lists (scroll down to see Lists):

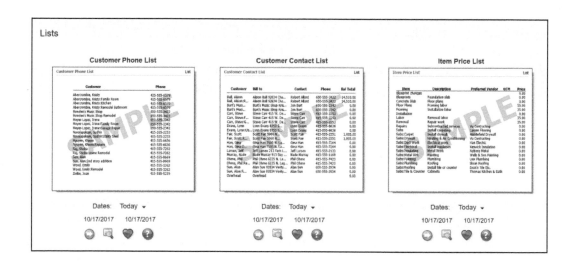

Sales: Sales reports include various reports within these sections – Sales by Customer, Sales by Item, Sales by Rep, and Open Sales Order. In the Report

Center, select Sales. Sales by Customer reports are shown below. Scroll down the Sales Report Center to see more.

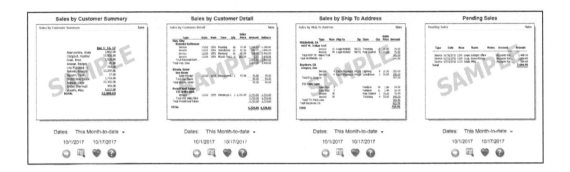

CUSTOMER TRANSACTIONS

In the Customers section of the Home Page, you perform the tasks related to customers and accounts receivables. In this section, you work with some of these features.

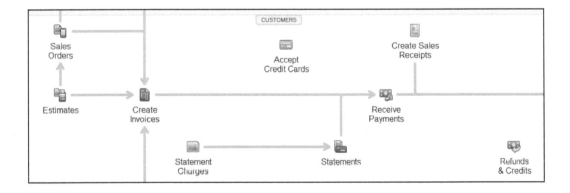

In QuickBooks, all information about a sale on account is recorded on the Create Invoice form. Then, QuickBooks takes the necessary information from the Invoice window and automatically creates the transaction's debits and credits. Credit sales from customers are posted to both the General Ledger and to the customers and receivables accounts. In accounting, customers and receivables accounts grouped together are called the *accounts receivable ledger.*

Use the QuickBooks Create Invoices icon to record credit sales to customers. *Credit sales* or sales on account refer to sales made to customers that will be paid for later. Your Name Retailers offers customers payment terms of Net 30 days.

Sales Invoices

The transaction you are going to record is:

Date	Description of Transaction

11/15/20XX   Sold 5 eBooks (PDF files) on account to iPrint Design for a total credit sale of $250, Invoice # 1.

Follow these steps to enter the transaction.

1. Click [Create Invoices]. The Create Invoices window appears.

2. Complete these fields.

> Customer:Job: iPrint Design
> Date: **11/15/20XX**
> Invoice #:   1 is completed automatically
> Qty.:   **5**
> Item Code: eBook
> Description: PDF files is completed automatically
> Unit Price: 50.00 is completed automatically
> Amount: 250.00 is completed automatically

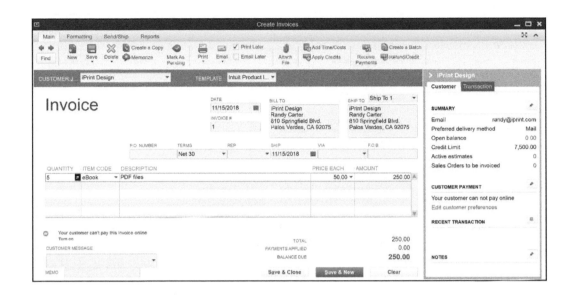

3. Check the Create Invoices window. When satisfied, click <Save & New>.

4. If Check Spelling on Form window appears, select <Ignore All>. The Create Invoices window is ready for the next two transactions.

Date	Description of Transaction
11/15/20XX	Sold 15 Podcasts (audio files) on account to Audio Answers for a total credit sale of $450, Invoice # 2.
11/15/20XX	Sold 8 TV Programs (video files) on account to Video Solutions for a total credit sale of $480, Invoice # 3.

5. Click <Save & Close>.

6. Look at how QuickBooks journalizes these sales by displaying the 11/15/20XX Journal. (Report Center > Accountant & Taxes > Journal > date is 11/15/20XX)

Your Name Retailers Inc.
Journal
November 15, 2018

Trans #	Type	Date	Num	Adj	Name	Memo	Account	Debit	Credit
21	Invoice	11/15/2018	1		iPrint Design		11000 · Accounts Receivable	250.00	
					iPrint Design	PDF files	46000 · Sales		250.00
					iPrint Design	PDF files	12100 · Inventory Asset		125.00
					iPrint Design	PDF files	50000 · Cost of Goods Sold	125.00	
								375.00	375.00
22	Invoice	11/15/2018	2		Audio Answers		11000 · Accounts Receivable	450.00	
					Audio Answers	audio files	46000 · Sales		450.00
					Audio Answers	audio files	12100 · Inventory Asset		225.00
					Audio Answers	audio files	50000 · Cost of Goods Sold	225.00	
								675.00	675.00
23	Invoice	11/15/2018	3		Video Solutions		11000 · Accounts Receivable	480.00	
					Video Solutions	video files	46000 · Sales		480.00
					Video Solutions	video files	12100 · Inventory Asset		240.00
					Video Solutions	video files	50000 · Cost of Goods Sold	240.00	
								720.00	720.00
TOTAL								1,770.00	1,770.00

7. Look closely at the accounts debited and credited for the sale made to iPrint Design.

   Observe that *both* the sales price, $250, and the cost of the inventory item are debited and credited. When Your Name Retailers sells PDF files the customer pays $50 each (5 PDF files were sold for a total of $250). When Your Name Retailers buys PDF files from the vendor, it pays $25 × 5 = $125. QuickBooks tracks both the sales price *and* the purchase price when items are sold. The sales price is debited and credited to AR/Customer and Sales; the cost of the item is debited and credited to Cost of Goods Sold and Inventory, respectively. This entry keeps the Inventory account perpetually up to date.

8. Close the Journal without saving.

Inventory

Before recording more sales, let's look at the status of inventory as of November 15, 20XX (use current year). Follow these steps to do that.

1. From the menu bar or Icon Bar, select Reports > Inventory > Inventory Valuation Detail. The dates are 10/1/20XX to 11/15/20XX > click <Refresh>. Observe that the following quantities are on hand.

eBook	PDF files	10
Podcast	audio files	23
TV Programs	video files	15

Your Name Retailers Inc.
Inventory Valuation Detail
October 1 through November 15, 2018

Type	Date	Name	Num	Qty	Cost	On Hand	Avg Cost	Asset Value
Inventory								
eBook (PDF files)								
Bill	11/03/2018	eBooks Express	Invoice No. 90eB	15	375.00	15	25.00	375.00
Invoice	11/15/2018	iPrint Design	1	-5		10	25.00	250.00
Total eBook (PDF files)						10		250.00
Podcast (audio files)								
Bill	11/02/2018	Podcast Ltd.	Invoice No. 5	20	300.00	20	15.00	300.00
Bill	11/05/2018	Podcast Ltd.	Invoice No. 78	18	270.00	38	15.00	570.00
Invoice	11/15/2018	Audio Answers	2	-15		23	15.00	345.00
Total Podcast (audio files)						23		345.00
TV Programs (video files)								
Bill	11/03/2018	TV Flix	Invoice No. 210TV	25	750.00	25	30.00	750.00
Credit	11/10/2018	TV Flix	CM1	-2	-60.00	23	30.00	690.00
Invoice	11/15/2018	Video Solutions	3	-8		15	30.00	450.00
Total TV Programs (video files)						15		450.00
Total Inventory						48		1,045.00
TOTAL						48		1,045.00

2. Close windows without saving.

Sales Returns

When a customer returns a product or requires a refund, you can create a customer credit memo with the Credit Memo/Refunds form.

The following transaction is for a sales return.

Date	*Description of Transaction*
11/17/20XX	Audio Answers returned 2 Podcasts (audio files).

Follow these steps to enter the sales return.

1. Click [Refunds & Credits]. The Create Credit Memos/Refunds window appears.
2. Select Audio Answers as the Customer.
3. Type **11/17/20XX** in the date field. The Credit No. field shows 4 which is automatically completed.
4. In the Item field, select Podcast.
5. Type **2** in the Qty field.

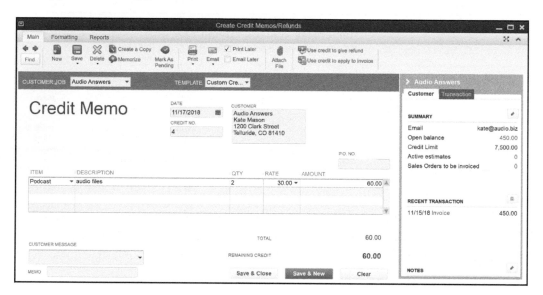

6. Check the Create Credit Memos/ Refunds window. When satisfied, click <Save & Close>.

7. When the Available Credit window appears, select Apply to an invoice, then <OK>.

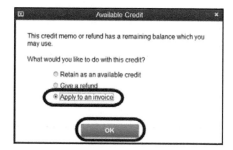

8. When the Apply Credit to Invoices window appears, confirm the Audio Answers 11/15/20XX Invoice is checked.

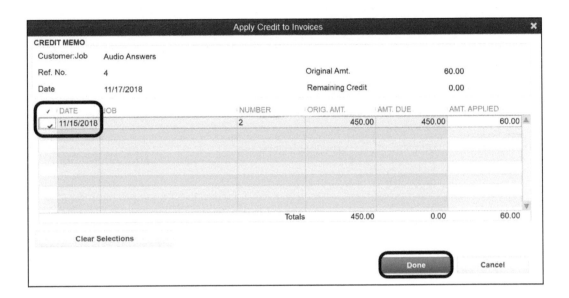

9. Click <Done> to apply the credit to the invoice. The Home Page appears.
10. To see how this entry is journalized. Display the 11/17/20XX Journal. (Report Center > Accountant & Taxes > Journal > 11/17/20XX > click <Refresh>.) Close Journal without saving it.

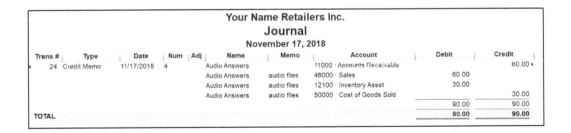

11. Display the Customer Balance Detail Report to see how the accounts receivable account records customer transactions. (*Hint:* Report Center > Customers & Receivables > Customer Balance Detail > All Dates) Observe that the balance in the Audio Answers account is reduced by the amount of the 11/17/20XX return. Also, notice that the Total on

the report is $1,120. This total should agree with the 11/17 balance for Account No. 11000, Accounts Receivable.

Type	Date	Num	Account	Amount	Balance
Your Name Retailers Inc. **Customer Balance Detail** All Transactions					
Audio Answers					
Invoice	11/15/2018	2	11000 · Accounts Receivable	450.00	450.00
Credit Memo	11/17/2018	4	11000 · Accounts Receivable	-60.00	390.00
Total Audio Answers				390.00	390.00
iPrint Design					
Invoice	11/15/2018	1	11000 · Accounts Receivable	250.00	250.00
Total iPrint Design				250.00	250.00
Video Solutions					
Invoice	11/15/2018	3	11000 · Accounts Receivable	480.00	480.00
Total Video Solutions				480.00	480.00
TOTAL				1,120.00	1,120.00

12. Close the Customer Balance Detail report without saving.
13. Display the Balance Sheet Detail Report From 10/01/20XX To 11/20/20XX. (*Hint:* Report Center > Company & Financial > Balance Sheet Detail.) Notice the Account No. 11000, Accounts Receivable, shows the same balance as the Customer Balance Detail, $1,120.00.

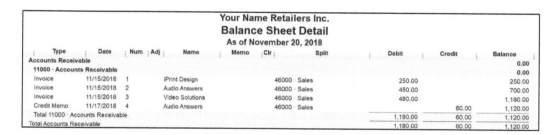

Type	Date	Num	Adj	Name	Memo	Clr	Split	Debit	Credit	Balance
Your Name Retailers Inc. **Balance Sheet Detail** As of November 20, 2018										
Accounts Receivable										0.00
11000 · Accounts Receivable										0.00
Invoice	11/15/2018	1		iPrint Design			46000 · Sales	250.00		250.00
Invoice	11/15/2018	2		Audio Answers			46000 · Sales	450.00		700.00
Invoice	11/15/2018	3		Video Solutions			46000 · Sales	480.00		1,180.00
Credit Memo	11/17/2018	4		Audio Answers			46000 · Sales		60.00	1,120.00
Total 11000 · Accounts Receivable								1,180.00	60.00	1,120.00
Total Accounts Receivable								1,180.00	60.00	1,120.00

14. Close the report without saving.

Credit Card Sales

Your Name Retailers accepts credit cards for customer sales but does not use QuickBooks' credit card processing service. (QuickBooks charges a fee for processing credit card sales.) Observe that on the Icon Bar, there is a Credit Cards selection **Credit Cards**. (*Hint:* You may need to scroll through the Icon Bar.) Also, within the Home Page's Customers area, there is an Accept Credit Cards. Since there is a charge for using the Credit Cards selections, do *not* make these selections.

Your Name Retailers Inc. is set up to accept credit cards for customer payments and processes credit card sales at their bank, Home State Bank. For our purposes, you will see how a company can process credit cards but you will *not* set up the online credit card processing.

The transaction you are going to record is:

Date	Description of Transaction
11/18	Sold 5 eBooks for $250; 8 Podcasts for $240; and 6 TV Programs for $360; for total credit card sales of $850, Sale No. 1.

Follow these steps to enter a new customer on the fly and record credit card sales.

1. Click **Create Sales Receipts**. The Enter Sales Receipts window appears.

2. Type **11/18/20XX** in the Date field.

3. Accept the default Sale No. 1.

4. In the Customer:Job field, select <Add New>. On the New Customer form, complete these fields.

Customer Name: **Credit Card Sales**
Opening Balance   **0.00** as of **10/1/20XX**
Company Name: **Credit Card Sales**

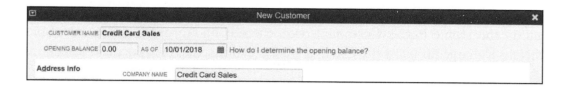

Payment Settings:

Account No.: **CCS**

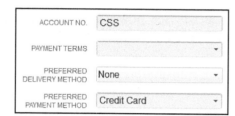

Preferred Delivery Method: None

Preferred Payment Method: Select
<Add New>. In the Payment Method field, type **Credit Card.**

Payment Type: Cash. Click <OK>. The New Customer, Payment Settings window looks like this.

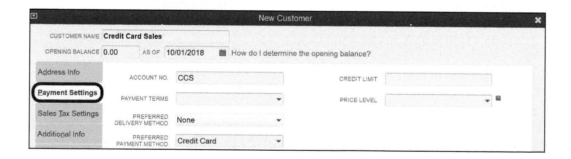

5. After clicking <OK>, the Enter Sales Receipts window appears. Credit Cards Sales is shown in the Customer:Job field. Observe that the Sale No. field is completed automatically with the number 1.

6. In the Item field, select eBook.

7. Type **5** in the Qty field.

8. Go to the Item field, select Podcast.

9. Type **8** in the Qty field.

10. Go to the Item field, select TV Programs.

11. Type **6** in the Qty. field.

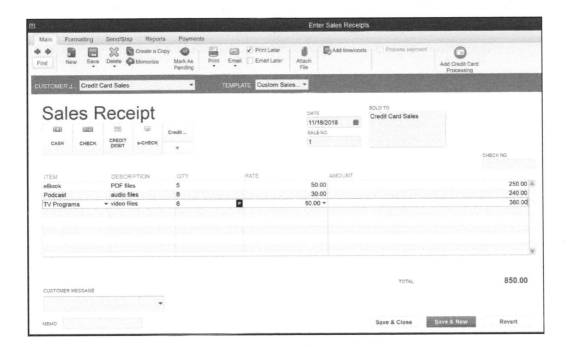

12. Check the Enter Sales Receipts window. Click <Save & Close>. Ignore the spelling window about PDF.

13. To see how this transaction is journalized, display the Journal for 11/18/20XX. Observe that each item amount is individually debited and credited to Undeposited Funds, Sales, Inventory Asset, and Cost of Goods Sold.

Your Name Retailers Inc.
Journal
November 18, 2018

Trans #	Type	Date	Num	Adj	Name	Memo	Account	Debit	Credit
25	Sales Receipt	11/18/2018	1		Credit Card Sales		12000 · Undeposited Funds	850.00	
					Credit Card Sales	-MULTIPLE-	46000 · Sales		850.00
					Credit Card Sales	-MULTIPLE-	12100 · Inventory Asset		425.00
					Credit Card Sales	-MULTIPLE-	50000 · Cost of Goods Sold	425.00	
								1,275.00	1,275.00
TOTAL								1,275.00	1,275.00

The Memo column shows MULTIPLE. This indicates more than one inventory item. Drill down (double-click) MULTIPLE to see the Enter Sales Receipts window which indicates the three items sold: eBooks (5 PDF files), Podcast (8 audio files), and TV Programs (6 video files). Close the Enter Sales Receipts window and the Journal without saving.

Customer Payments

When a customer sends a payment, enter the customer payment on the Receive Payment window. You can then apply the payment to the invoices that are due. A payment might cover one or more invoice, or it may be for part of the invoice. You can select which invoice to settle against a payment as well as the amount to apply to each invoice. *Or,* you can have QuickBooks automatically apply the payment to invoices in chronological order from the oldest outstanding invoice.

In the following transactions, customers pay their outstanding invoices.

Date	Description of Transaction
11/23	Received a check in full payment of Audio Answers' account, $390.

Using the payment from Audio Answers as an example, follow these steps to record a customer payment.

1. Click [Receive Payments]. On the Receive Payments window, complete these fields.

Received From:	Audio Answers
Payment Amount:	**390.00**
Date:	**11/23/20XX**

2. A check mark is placed next to the 11/15 invoice automatically. Notice the original amount $450.00 was reduced to $390.00 by the previously applied credit memo for $60.00 since Audio Answers returned merchandise.

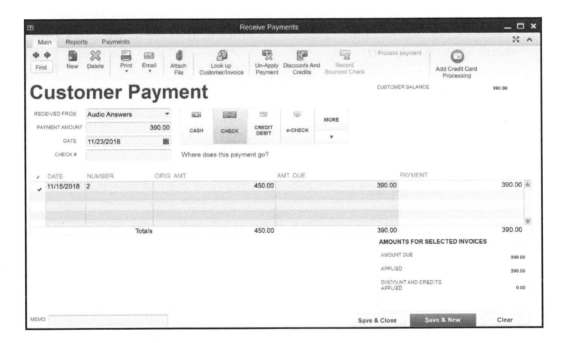

3. Click <Save & Close>. Display the 11/23/20XX Journal. When a customer payment is received, Undeposited Funds and Accounts Receivable are debited and credited respectively. (The example shows the customer payment received from Audio Answers.)

Your Name Retailers Inc.									
Journal									
November 23, 2018									
Trans #	Type	Date	Num	Adj	Name	Memo	Account	Debit	Credit
26	Payment	11/23/2018			Audio Answers		12000 · Undeposited Funds	390.00	
					Audio Answers		11000 · Accounts Receivable		390.00
								390.00	390.00
TOTAL								390.00	390.00

What are undeposited funds? Account No. 12000, Undeposited Funds, is a cash account for amounts received from customers but not yet deposited to the bank account. When bank deposits are made, Undeposited Funds will be credited and Home State Bank will be debited. Think of undeposited funds as a clearing account. The undeposited funds account holds the cash until it is deposited and cleared by the bank. The November bank statement will show which customer payments cleared Account No. 10000, Home State Bank, which is Your Name Retailers' bank account.

4. Record the two November 24, 20XX payments received from customers.

    Date   *Description of Transaction*

    11/24   Received a check in full payment of iPrint Design's
              account, $250.

    11/24   Received a check in full payment of Video Solutions'
              account, $480.

5. Click <Save & Close> to return to Home Page. After you record the customer payments received on 11/23 and 11/24, you deposit the payments received.

6. Click ![Record Deposits]. The Payments to Deposit window appears.

Place a check mark next to the 11/23 and 11/24 checks included in the deposit. (Customer checks for $390.00 + $250.00 + $480.00.) Place a check mark next to Credit Card Sales of $850.00, too. The Payments Subtotal is $1,970.00 (4 of 4 payments selected for deposit.)

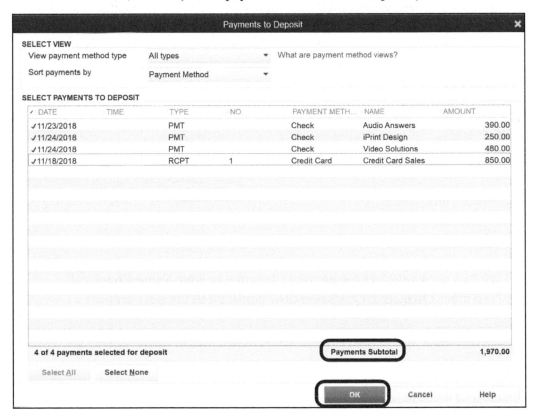

7. *Before* clicking <OK>, check the Payments to Deposit window. Verify that the Payments Subtotal is 1,970.00. The Make Deposits window appears. Observe that the Deposit To field shows Home State Bank.

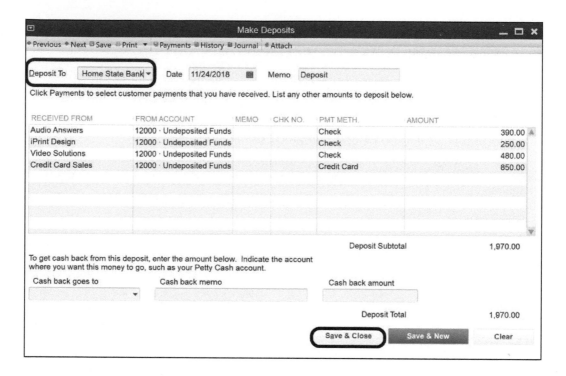

8. After clicking <Save & Close>, the Home Page appears.

9. Backup your work. The suggested file name is **Your Name Chapter 4 November.QBB.** Exit QuickBooks or continue to the next section.

> **Comment:**
>
> ***Separation of duties*** means work is divided between different employees to ensure data integrity and minimize the opportunity for wrongdoing. This is a basic internal control. For example, to keep employees from stealing customer payments, the tasks of opening the mail, recording customer payments, and making deposits at the bank are assigned to three different employees.

ACCOUNT RECONCILIATION

To reconcile Account 10000 for November, use the bank statement. (*Hint:* See previous chapter for October's Account Reconciliation steps.) Check numbers are shown on the following bank statement. Depending on whether you recorded a check number for each vendor payment, check numbers may or may not be included on the Reconcile window shown on the next page.

Statement of Account			Your Name Retailers Inc.	
Home State Bank			Your address	
November 1 to November 30		Account # 930-631891	Reno, NV 89557	
REGULAR CHECKING				
Previous Balance	10/31	$54,290.00		
Deposits(+)		1,970.00		
Checks (−)		1,835.00		
Service Charges (−)	11/30	10.00		
Ending Balance	11/30	**54,415.00**		
DEPOSITS				
	11/24	1,120.00	Customers	
	11/24	850.00	Credit Card	
CHECKS (Asterisk * indicates break in check number sequence)				
	11/3	200.00	4004	
	11/25	375.00	4006*	
	11/25	570.00	4007	
	11/25	690.00	4008	

1. After placing check marks beside the cleared deposits and checks per the bank statement, compare your window to the following. (*Hint:* On the Reconcile – Home State Bank window, check numbers 4006, 4007, and 4008 are <u>not</u> shown. Refer to the amounts.)

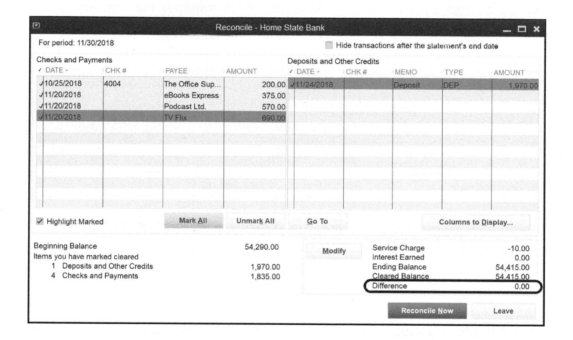

2. The Reconcile - Home State Bank window shows a Difference of 0.00.
3. Click <Reconcile Now>. If necessary, on the Select Reconcilatiation Report window, select Both > Display > OK.

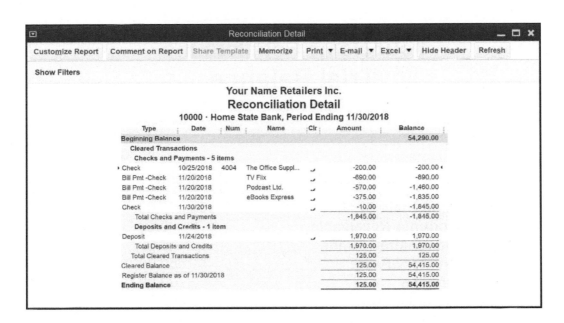

4. Close the Reconciliation Detail and Reconciliation Summary windows. (*Hint:* The Reconciliation Summary report is not shown.)

REPORTS

Print the following reports. If you have made errors in your entries, void and edit your original entries to correct your reports. (*Hint:* See pages 110-112.)

1. Trial Balance from 10/01/20XX to 11/30/20XX.

Your Name Retailers Inc.
Trial Balance
As of November 30, 2018

	Nov 30, 18	
	Debit	Credit
10000 · Home State Bank	54,415.00	
11000 · Accounts Receivable	0.00	
12000 · Undeposited Funds	0.00	
12100 · Inventory Asset	650.00	
13000 · Supplies	2,700.00	
18000 · Prepaid Insurance	2,500.00	
14000 · Computer Equipment	2,400.00	
15000 · Furniture and Equipment	4,000.00	
22000 · Accounts Payable		400.00
26000 · Your Name Notes Payable		20,000.00
30000 · Common Stock		45,500.00
30200 · Dividends	200.00	
46000 · Sales		1,970.00
50000 · Cost of Goods Sold	985.00	
60400 · Bank Service Charges Expense	20.00	
TOTAL	67,870.00	67,870.00

2. Journal 11/01/20XX to 11/30/20XX.

Your Name Retailers Inc.
Journal
November 2018

Trans #	Type	Date	Num	Adj	Name	Memo	Account	Debit	Credit
12	Bill	11/02/2016	Invoice No. 5		Podcast Ltd.		22000 · Accounts Payable		300.00
					Podcast Ltd.	audio files	12100 · Inventory Asset	300.00	
								300.00	300.00
13	Bill	11/03/2016	Invoice No. 90eB		eBooks Express		22000 · Accounts Payable		375.00
					eBooks Express	PDF files	12100 · Inventory Asset	375.00	
								375.00	375.00
14	Bill	11/03/2016	Invoice No. 210TV		TV Flix		22000 · Accounts Payable		750.00
					TV Flix	video files	12100 · Inventory Asset	750.00	
								750.00	750.00
15	Bill	11/05/2018	Invoice No. 78		Podcast Ltd.		22000 · Accounts Payable		270.00
					Podcast Ltd.	audio files	12100 · Inventory Asset	270.00	
								270.00	270.00
16	Credit	11/10/2016	CM1		TV Flix	Invoice No. 210TV	22000 · Accounts Payable	60.00	
					TV Flix	video files	12100 · Inventory Asset		60.00
								60.00	60.00
17	Bill Pmt -Check	11/20/2016			eBooks Express	22000	10000 · Home State Bank		375.00
					eBooks Express	22000	22000 · Accounts Payable	375.00	
								375.00	375.00
18	Bill Pmt -Check	11/20/2016			Podcast Ltd.	22000	10000 · Home State Bank		570.00
					Podcast Ltd.	22000	22000 · Accounts Payable	570.00	
								570.00	570.00
19	Bill Pmt -Check	11/20/2018			TV Flix	22000	10000 · Home State Bank		690.00
					TV Flix	22000	22000 · Accounts Payable	690.00	
								690.00	690.00
20	Bill	11/21/2018	Invoice No. BOS44		The Business Store		22000 · Accounts Payable		400.00
					The Business Store	Notebook computer	14000 · Computer Equipment	400.00	
								400.00	400.00
21	Invoice	11/15/2018	1		iPrint Design		11000 · Accounts Receivable	250.00	
					iPrint Design	PDF files	46000 · Sales		250.00
					iPrint Design	PDF files	12100 · Inventory Asset		125.00
					iPrint Design	PDF files	50000 · Cost of Goods Sold	125.00	
								375.00	375.00

Trans #	Type	Date	Num	Adj	Name	Memo	Account	Debit	Credit
21	Invoice	11/15/2018	1		iPrint Design		11000 · Accounts Receivable	250.00	
					iPrint Design	PDF files	46000 · Sales		250.00
					iPrint Design	PDF files	12100 · Inventory Asset		125.00
					iPrint Design	PDF files	50000 · Cost of Goods Sold	125.00	
								375.00	375.00
22	Invoice	11/15/2018	2		Audio Answers		11000 · Accounts Receivable	450.00	
					Audio Answers	audio files	46000 · Sales		450.00
					Audio Answers	audio files	12100 · Inventory Asset		225.00
					Audio Answers	audio files	50000 · Cost of Goods Sold	225.00	
								675.00	675.00
23	Invoice	11/15/2018	3		Video Solutions		11000 · Accounts Receivable	480.00	
					Video Solutions	video files	46000 · Sales		480.00
					Video Solutions	video files	12100 · Inventory Asset		240.00
					Video Solutions	video files	50000 · Cost of Goods Sold	240.00	
								720.00	720.00
24	Credit Memo	11/17/2018	4		Audio Answers		11000 · Accounts Receivable		60.00
					Audio Answers	audio files	46000 · Sales	60.00	
					Audio Answers	audio files	12100 · Inventory Asset	30.00	
					Audio Answers	audio files	50000 · Cost of Goods Sold		30.00
								90.00	90.00
25	Sales Receipt	11/18/2018	1		Credit Card Sales		12000 · Undeposited Funds	850.00	
					Credit Card Sales	-MULTIPLE-	46000 · Sales		850.00
					Credit Card Sales	-MULTIPLE-	12100 · Inventory Asset		425.00
					Credit Card Sales	-MULTIPLE-	50000 · Cost of Goods Sold	425.00	
								1,275.00	1,275.00
26	Payment	11/23/2018			Audio Answers		12000 · Undeposited Funds	390.00	
					Audio Answers		11000 · Accounts Receivable		390.00
								390.00	390.00
27	Payment	11/24/2018			iPrint Design		12000 · Undeposited Funds	250.00	
					iPrint Design		11000 · Accounts Receivable		250.00
								250.00	250.00
28	Payment	11/24/2018			Video Solutions		12000 · Undeposited Funds	480.00	
					Video Solutions		11000 · Accounts Receivable		480.00
								480.00	480.00
29	Deposit	11/24/2018			-MULTIPLE-	Deposit	10000 · Home State Bank	1,970.00	
						Deposit	12000 · Undeposited Funds		1,970.00
								1,970.00	1,970.00
30	Check	11/30/2018				Service Charge	10000 · Home State Bank		10.00
						Service Charge	60400 · Bank Service Charges Expense	10.00	
								10.00	10.00
TOTAL								**10,025.00**	**10,025.00**

3. Inventory Valuation Detail 10/01/20XX to 11/30/20XX.

Your Name Retailers Inc.
Inventory Valuation Detail
October through November 2018

Type	Date	Name	Num	Qty	Cost	On Hand	Avg Cost	Asset Value
Inventory								
eBook (PDF files)								
Bill	11/03/2018	eBooks Express	Invoice No. 90eB	15	375.00	15	25.00	375.00
Invoice	11/15/2018	iPrint Design	1	-5		10	25.00	250.00
Sales Receipt	11/18/2018	Credit Card Sales	1	-5		5	25.00	125.00
Total eBook (PDF files)						5.00		125.00
Podcast (audio files)								
Bill	11/02/2018	Podcast Ltd.	Invoice No. 5	20	300.00	20	15.00	300.00
Bill	11/05/2018	Podcast Ltd.	Invoice No. 78	18	270.00	38	15.00	570.00
Invoice	11/15/2018	Audio Answers	2	-15		23	15.00	345.00
Credit Memo	11/17/2018	Audio Answers	4	2		25	15.00	375.00
Sales Receipt	11/18/2018	Credit Card Sales	1	-8		17	15.00	255.00
Total Podcast (audio files)						17.00		255.00
TV Programs (video files)								
Bill	11/03/2018	TV Flix	Invoice No. 210TV	25	750.00	25	30.00	750.00
Credit	11/10/2018	TV Flix	CM1	-2	-60.00	23	30.00	690.00
Invoice	11/15/2018	Video Solutions	3	-8		15	30.00	450.00
Sales Receipt	11/18/2018	Credit Card Sales	1	-6		9	30.00	270.00
Total TV Programs (video files)						9.00		270.00
Total Inventory						31.00		650.00
TOTAL						**31.00**		**650.00**

4. Transaction List by Vendor 11/01/20XX to 11/30/20XX.

Your Name Retailers Inc.
Transaction List by Vendor
November 2018

Type	Date	Num	Memo	Account	Clr	Split	Debit	Credit
eBooks Express								
Bill	11/03/2018	Invoice No. 90eB		22000 · Accounts Payable		12100 · Inventory Asset		375.00
Bill Pmt -Check	11/20/2018		22000	10000 · Home State Bank	X	22000 · Accounts Payable		375.00
Podcast Ltd.								
Bill	11/02/2018	Invoice No. 5		22000 · Accounts Payable		12100 · Inventory Asset		300.00
Bill	11/05/2018	Invoice No. 78		22000 · Accounts Payable		12100 · Inventory Asset		270.00
Bill Pmt -Check	11/20/2018		22000	10000 · Home State Bank	X	22000 · Accounts Payable		570.00
The Business Store								
Bill	11/21/2018	Invoice No. BOS44		22000 · Accounts Payable		14000 · Computer Equipm...		400.00
TV Flix								
Bill	11/03/2018	Invoice No. 210TV		22000 · Accounts Payable		12100 · Inventory Asset		750.00
Credit	11/10/2018	CM1	Invoice No. 210TV	22000 · Accounts Payable		12100 · Inventory Asset	60.00	
Bill Pmt -Check	11/20/2018		22000	10000 · Home State Bank	X	22000 · Accounts Payable		690.00

5. Purchases by Item Summary 11/01/20XX to 11/30/20XX. (*Hint:* This is a Purchases report.)

Your Name Retailers Inc.
Purchases by Item Summary
November 2018

	Nov 18	
	Qty	Amount
Inventory		
eBook (PDF files)	15	375.00
Podcast (audio files)	38	570.00
TV Programs (video files)	23	690.00
Total Inventory	76	1,635.00
TOTAL	**76.00**	**1,635.00**

6. Purchases by Vendor Detail 11/01/20XX to 11/30/20XX.

Your Name Retailers Inc.
Purchases by Vendor Detail

Accrual Basis

November 2018

Type	Date	Num	Memo	Name	Item	Qty	Cost Price	Amount	Balance
eBooks Express									
Bill	11/03/2018	Invoice No. 90eB	PDF files	eBooks Express	eBook (PDF files)	15	25.00	375.00	375.00
Total eBooks Express						15		375.00	375.00
Podcast Ltd.									
Bill	11/02/2018	Invoice No. 5	audio files	Podcast Ltd.	Podcast (audio files)	20	15.00	300.00	300.00
Bill	11/05/2018	Invoice No. 78	audio files	Podcast Ltd.	Podcast (audio files)	18	15.00	270.00	570.00
Total Podcast Ltd.						38		570.00	570.00
TV Flix									
Bill	11/03/2018	Invoice No. 210TV	video files	TV Flix	TV Programs (video files)	25	30.00	750.00	750.00
Credit	11/10/2018	CM1	video files	TV Flix	TV Programs (video files)	-2	30.00	-60.00	690.00
Total TV Flix						23		690.00	690.00
TOTAL						76		1,635.00	1,635.00

7. Transaction List by Customer 11/01/20XX to 11/30/20XX.

Your Name Retailers Inc.
Transaction List by Customer

November 2018

Type	Date	Num	Memo	Account	Clr	Split	Debit	Credit
Audio Answers								
Invoice	11/15/2018	2		11000 · Accounts Receivable		46000 · Sales	450.00	
Credit Memo	11/17/2018	4		11000 · Accounts Receivable		46000 · Sales		60.00
Payment	11/23/2018			12000 · Undeposited Funds	X	11000 · Accounts Receivable	390.00	
Credit Card Sales								
Sales Receipt	11/18/2018	1		12000 · Undeposited Funds	X	-SPLIT-	850.00	
iPrint Design								
Invoice	11/15/2018	1		11000 · Accounts Receivable		46000 · Sales	250.00	
Payment	11/24/2018			12000 · Undeposited Funds	X	11000 · Accounts Receivable	250.00	
Video Solutions								
Invoice	11/15/2018	3		11000 · Accounts Receivable		46000 · Sales	480.00	
Payment	11/24/2018			12000 · Undeposited Funds	X	11000 · Accounts Receivable	480.00	

8. Income by Customer Summary 11/01/20XX to 11/30/20XX. (*Hint:* Company & Financial reports.)

Your Name Retailers Inc. Income by Customer Summary November 2018	
	Nov 18
Audio Answers	195.00
Credit Card Sales	425.00
iPrint Design	125.00
Video Solutions	240.00
TOTAL	985.00

9. Income and Expense Graph: *Hint:* Company & Financial > Income & Expense Graph > Dates > 11/01/20XX to 11/30/20XX.

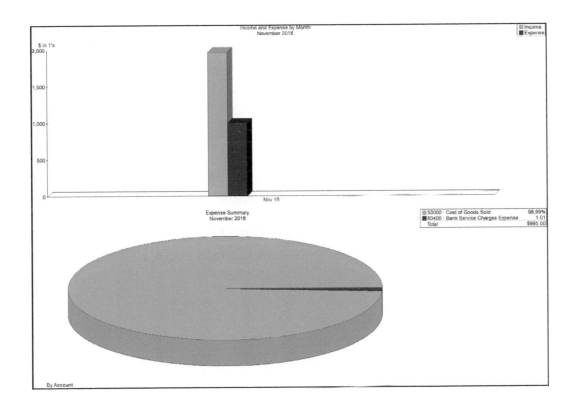

10. Sales by Item Summary 11/01/20XX to 11/30/20XX. (*Hint:* Sales report.)

Your Name Retailers Inc.
Sales by Item Summary
November 2018

Accrual Basis

	Qty	Amount	% of Sales	Avg Price	COGS	Avg COGS	Gross Margin	Gross Margin %
Inventory								
eBook (PDF files)	10	500.00	25.4%	50.00	250.00	25.00	250.00	50.0%
Podcast (audio files)	21	630.00	32.0%	30.00	315.00	15.00	315.00	50.0%
TV Programs (video files)	14	840.00	42.6%	60.00	420.00	30.00	420.00	50.0%
Total Inventory	45	1,970.00	100.0%	43.78	985.00	21.89	985.00	50.0%
TOTAL	45	1,970.00	100.0%	43.78		21.89		

BACKUP CHAPTER 4 DATA

1. Backup your work to your USB drive. (*Hint:* File > Back Up Company > Create Local Backup). Name your file **Your Name Chapter 4 End.QBB.**
2. Exit QuickBooks or continue with the next section.

SUMMARY AND REVIEW

Additional resources are on the textbook's Online Learning Center (OLC) at www.mhhe.com/qbd2018. The OLC includes Information Center links and Student Edition links. When you link to the Student Edition, choose a chapter to populate more resources.

RESOURCEFUL QUICKBOOKS

The Online Learning Center at www.mhhe.com/qbd2018 > Student Edition > Chapter 4 > Narrated PowerPoints includes a link to the article and video.

1. Read the article "Consider Your Costs When Pricing Your Product," and watch the video at https://quickbooks.intuit.com/r/pricing-strategy/video-consider-your-costs-when-pricing-your-product/.

2. Answer these questions.

    a.   Why do Dennis Kahn's prices fluctuate?

    b.   When compared to other surfboards, why are his retail prices higher?

Multiple Choice Questions: The Online Learning Center includes the multiple-choice questions at www.mhhe.com/qbd2018 > Student Edition > Chapter 4 > Multiple Choice.

_____ 1. A group of posting accounts that shows the amounts owed to vendors or suppliers is called:

    a.   Accounts receivable.

    b.   Inventory.

    c.   Accounts payable.

    d.   Entering bills.

    e.   All of the above.

_____ 2. Your Name Retailers describes eBooks as:

    a.   Video files.

    b.   PDF files.

    c.   Audio files.

    d.   None of the above.

    e.   All of the above.

_____ 3. QuickBooks Lists include all of the following except:

    a.   Items.

    b.   Customers.

    c.   Vendors.

    d.   Accounts.

    e.   All are QuickBooks Lists.

_____ 4. Products that are purchased for sale are tracked in the following account:

    a.   Account No. 46000, Sales.

    b.   Account No. 11000, Accounts Receivable.

    c.   Account No. 12100, Inventory Asset.

    d.   Account No. 13000, Supplies.

    e.   None of the above.

_____ 5. Which of the following shows information about inventory items?

    a.   Vendor list.

    b.   Trial Balance.

    c.   Item list.

    d.   Vendor record.

    e.   None of the above.

_____ 6. An in-depth view of the amounts the company owes its vendors as of a selected date.

    a.   Transaction list by vendor.

    b.   Invoice.

    c.   Purchases by item detail.

    d.   A/P aging summary.

    e.   All of the above.

_____ 7. When merchandise is returned to the vendor, the following accounts are debited and credited:

    a.   Debit Account No. 12100, Inventory Asset; Credit Account No. 50000, Cost of Goods Sold.

    b.   Debit Account No. 50000, Cost of Goods Sold and Account No. 12100, Inventory Asset; Credit Account No. 50000, Cost of Goods Sold and Account No. 22000, Accounts Payable.

    c.   Debit Account No. 50000, Cost of Goods Sold and Account No. 22000, Accounts Payable; Credit Account No. 50000, Cost of Goods Sold and Account No. 12100, Inventory Asset.

    d.   Debit Account No. 22000 Accounts Payable; credit Account No. 12100, Inventory Asset.

    e.   None of the above.

_____ 8. When a vendor payment is made, the following accounts are debited and credited:

    a.   Debit Account No. 22000, Accounts Payable/vendor; Credit Account No. 10000, Home State Bank.

    b.   Credit Account No. 10000, Home State Bank; Debit Account No. 12100, Inventory Asset

    c.   Debit Account No. 50000, Cost of Goods Sold and Credit Account No. 10000, Home State Bank.

    d.   Debit Account No. 22000 Accounts Payable; credit Account No. 50000, Cost of Goods Sold.

    e.   None of the above.

_____ 9. In the Report Center under Customers & Receivables all of the following sections are included *except:*

    a.   A/R Aging.

    b.   Customer Balance.

    c.   Lists.

    d.   Sales by Item.

    e.   None of the above.

_____ 10. The A/P aging report shows:

    a.   Purchases by vendor detail.

    b.   An Item list.

    c.   Vendor transaction history and trial balance.

    d.   Payments made by customers.

    e.   Due and overdue bills.

True/Make True: To answer these questions, go online to www.mhhe.com/qbd2018 > Student Edition > Chapter 4 > QA Templates. The analysis question at the end of the chapter is also included.

1. Another term for vendor is supplier.

2. A vendor of Your Name Retailers Inc. is TV Flix.

3. Credit card sales are recorded using the Pay Bills icon.

4. Purchases from vendors are recorded using the Enter Bills icon.

5. Sales to customers are recorded using the Create Invoice icon.

6. Purchases returned to vendors are recorded using the Enter Bills icon.

7. Returns from customers are recorded using the Refunds and Credits icon.

8. Customer payments on account are recorded using the Receive Payments icon.

9. Inventory purchased on account is recorded using the Enter Bills icon.

10. Vendor payments are recorded using the Create Cash Receipt icon.

Exercise 4-1: Follow the instructions below to complete Exercise 4-1.

1. Start QuickBooks and open Your Name Retailers. Restore the Your Name Chapter 4 End file. (*Hint:* If you are using your own PC, you may not need to restore. To check that you are starting in the right place, display the 11/30/20XX trial balance. Compare it to the one on page 192.)

   When you start QB, if a pop-up message appears, click on the box next to "Please do not show this message again" to place a checkmark in it > close the pop-up.

2. Record the following transactions during the month of December:

Date	Description of Transaction
12/21	Pay BOS44 to The Business Store for the $400 laptop computer purchase on 11/21.
12/21	Invoice No. 101eB received from eBooks Express for the purchase of 16 PDF files, $25 each, for a total of $400.
12/21	Invoice No. 352TV received from TV Flix for the purchase of 22 video files, $30 each, for a total of $660.
12/21	Invoice No. 95 received from Podcast Ltd. for the purchase of 12 audio files, $15 each, for a total of $180.
12/23	Returned two PDF files to eBooks Express, Credit Memo No. CM2 for a total of $50.
12/24	Sold 8 eBooks (PDF files) on account to iPrint Design for a total credit sale of $400, Invoice # 5.
12/24	Sold 10 Podcasts (audio files) on account to Audio Answers for a total credit sale of $300 Invoice # 6.
12/24	Sold 12 TV Programs (video files) on account to Video Solutions for a total credit sale of $720, Invoice # 7.
12/26	Sold 4 eBooks for $200; 8 Podcasts for $240; and 6 TV Programs for $360; for total credit card sales of $800, Sale No. 2.
12/27	Video Solutions returned 2 TV Programs (video files), $120. Apply to invoice.
12/30	Received a check in full payment of Audio Answers' account, $300.
12/30	Received a check in full payment of iPrint Design's account, $400.

12/30	Your Name Retailers pays all outstanding vendor bills for a total of $1,190. (Hint: Remember to Set Credit for the 12/23/20XX return to eBooks Express.)
12/30	Invoice No. 152 received from Podcast Ltd. for the purchase of 10 audio files, $15 each, for a total of $150.
12/30	Make bank deposit into the Home State Bank account. Include all undeposited funds, $1,500.

3. Continue with Exercise 4-2.

Exercise 4-2: Follow the instructions below to complete Exercise 4-2. Exercise 4-1 *must* be completed before starting Exercise 4-2.

1. Print the following reports. Your instructor may want these reports saved as PDF files and attached in an email. Refer to the Read Me box on page 132, for saving reports as PDFs.

    a. Trial Balance 12/31/20XX.

    b. Journal 12/01/20XX to 12/31/20XX.

    c. Inventory Valuation Detail 12/1/20XX to 12/31/20XX.

    d. Transaction List by Vendor 12/01/20XX to 12/31/20XX.

    e. Purchases by Vendor Detail 12/01/20XX to 12/31/20XX.

    f. Transaction List by Customer 12/01/20XX to 12/31/20XX.

    g. Income and Expense Graph: Dates, By Customer, Income 12/01/20XX to 12/31/20XX.

2. If necessary, close all windows. Backup to USB drive. The suggested file name is **Your Name Exercise 4-2 December.QBB.**

ANALYSIS QUESTION

Does Your Name Retailers use the periodic or perpetual system for tracking inventory and sales?

<table>
<tr><td>**Chapter**
5</td><td># Accounting Cycle and Year End</td></tr>
</table>

OBJECTIVES:

1. Restore data from the Exercise 4-2 backup.
2. Record a compound journal entry.
3. Write checks for expenses.
4. Make deposits.
5. Complete account reconciliation.
6. Print a trial balance (unadjusted).
7. Record and post quarterly adjusting entries in the General Journal.
8. Print adjusted trial balance and financial statements.
9. Close the fiscal year.
10. Print a Postclosing Trial Balance.
11. Make backups of Chapter 5 data.[1]

GETTING STARTED:

1. Start QuickBooks and open Your Name Retailers. If necessary, restore the Your Name Exercise 4-2 December backup file. This backup was made on page 204. (*Hint:* If you are using your own PC, you may not need to restore. To check that you are starting in the right place, display the 12/31/20XX trial balance. Compare it to the one on the next page).

   Troubleshooting: When I start, a QuickBooks Update Service window appears. What should I do? Accept the update. Refer to Appendix A, Troubleshooting, Update QuickBooks, pages 313-316.

---

[1]The chart in the Preface, pages x-xi, shows the file name and size of each backup file. Refer to this chart for backing up data. Remember, you can back up to a hard drive location or external media.

2. Display the 12/31/20XX (use your current year) trial balance. Compare your trial balance with the one shown below.

Your Name Retailers Inc.
Trial Balance
As of December 31, 2018

	Dec 31, 18	
	Debit	Credit
10000 · Home State Bank	54,325.00	
11000 · Accounts Receivable	600.00	
12000 · Undeposited Funds	0.00	
12100 · Inventory Asset	940.00	
13000 · Supplies	2,700.00	
18000 · Prepaid Insurance	2,500.00	
14000 · Computer Equipment	2,400.00	
15000 · Furniture and Equipment	4,000.00	
22000 · Accounts Payable		150.00
26000 · Your Name Notes Payable		20,000.00
30000 · Common Stock		45,500.00
30200 · Dividends	200.00	
46000 · Sales		4,070.00
50000 · Cost of Goods Sold	2,035.00	
60400 · Bank Service Charges Expense	20.00	
TOTAL	69,720.00	69,720.00

3. Close the trial balance without saving.

COMPOUND TRANSACTIONS

A *compound transaction* is an entry that affects three or more accounts. The principle and interest payment on the Your Name Note Payable is an example of a compound transaction. A compound transaction can be recorded in either the *General Journal, or* if a check is issued, Write Checks can be used. In this example, the General Journal is used.

Follow these steps to record a compound journal entry.

1. From the Icon bar, select Accountant; *or* from the menu bar, select Company. Select Make General Journal Entries.

2. When the Assigning Numbers to Journal Entries screen appears, read it and click <OK>.

3. The Make General Journal Entries window appears. Uncheck the

    Adjusting Entry box– ADJUSTING ENTRY .

4. Record the following 12/31/20XX note payable payment.

    Date   *Date of Transaction*

    12/31   Pay $800 to Your Name for note payable principle
                    repayment with interest. The account distribution is
                    shown below. (*Hint:* No check is issued. This payment
                    is completed online.)

Acct. No.	Account	Debit	Credit
26000	Your Name Notes Payable	542.00	
63400	Interest Expense	258.00	
10000	Home State Bank		800.00

5. Compare your Make General Journal Entries window to the one shown here. (*Hint:* Either the General Journal *or* Write Checks, which is shown in the next section, can be used for compound transactions. In QB, compound transactions are identified as a "split." If necessary, *uncheck* Adjusting Entry.)

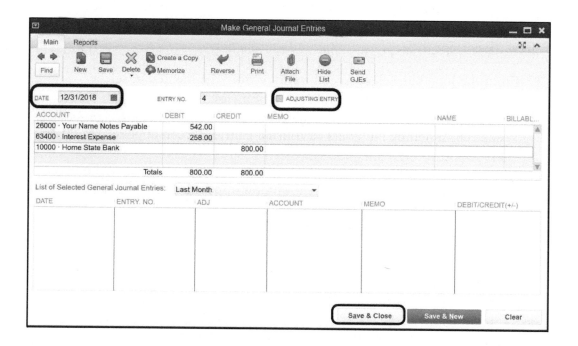

6. After clicking <Save & Close>, the Home page appears.

WRITE CHECKS

From the Home page, use the Banking section's Write Checks icon to issue the following checks.

12/31   Issue Check No. 4015 in the amount of $80 for cellular service. (*Hint:* Type the Check number in the No. field. Quick add the vendor, Mobile One. Debit Account No. 68100, Telephone Expense.)

12/31	Issue Check No. 4016 in the amount of $50 for Internet service. (*Hint:* The No. field automatically completes 4016. Quick add the vendor, ISP. Debit Account No. 61700, Computer and Internet Expenses.)
12/31	Issue Check No. 4017 in the amount of $68 for telephone service. (*Hint:* Quick add the vendor, Everywhere Telephone. Debit Account No. 68100, Telephone Expense.)
12/31	Issue Check No. 4018 in the amount of $111 for Electricity/Gas. (*Hint:* Quick add the vendor, Regional Utilities. Debit Account No. 68600 Utilities Expense.)
12/31	Issue Check No. 4019 in the amount of $74 for Water/Garbage service. (*Hint:* Quick add the vendor, Reno Water/Garbage. Debit Account No. 68600 Utilities Expense.)
12/31	Pay $200 Dividend to sole stockholder, Your Name. Check No. 4020 payable to you. Save & Close Write Checks window.

CHECK REGISTER

Click on the Check Register icon in the Banking section of the Home page to see Account No. 10000, Home State Bank activity. You can enlarge to 10000 Home State Bank window to see more transactions.

Check Register

The Account 10000 - Home State Bank check register is shown on the next page.

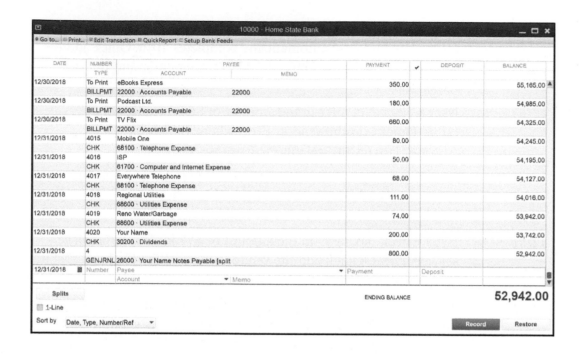

After comparing your Account No. 10000-Home State Bank account to the register, close. Observe that the 12/31 Your Name Notes Payable transaction is identified as a [split] which means that it is a compound entry with three or more accounts affected.

ACCOUNT RECONCILIATION

You may want to review detailed steps for account reconciliation, pages 115-119. Using the bank statement shown on the next page, reconcile the Home State Bank account. Remember the bank service charge of $10.00.

Follow these steps to complete account reconciliation.

1. From the Banking pane of the Home page, select the Reconcile icon. All checks have cleared the bank. To reconcile, use the bank statement on the next page.

Statement of Account			Your Name Retailers	
Home State Bank			Your Address	
December 1 to December 31, 20XX Account # 930-631891			Reno, NV 89557	
REGULAR CHECKING				
Previous Balance	11/30	54,415.00		
Deposits		1,500.00		
Checks (−)		2,973.00		
Service Charges (−)	12/31	10.00		
Ending Balance	12/31	**$52,932.00**		
DEPOSITS				
	12/31	300.00	Audio Answers	
	12/31	400.00	iPrint Design	
	12/31	800.00	Credit Card	
CHECKS				
	12/23	400.00		
	12/31	350.00		
	12/31	180.00		
	12/31	660.00		
	12/31	800.00		
	12/31	80.00	4015	
	12/31	50.00	4016	
	12/31	68.00	4017	
	12/31	111.00	4018	
	12/31	74.00	4019	
	12/31	200.00	4020	

2. Reconcile the account. Compare your Reconcile-Home State Bank screen to the one shown below.

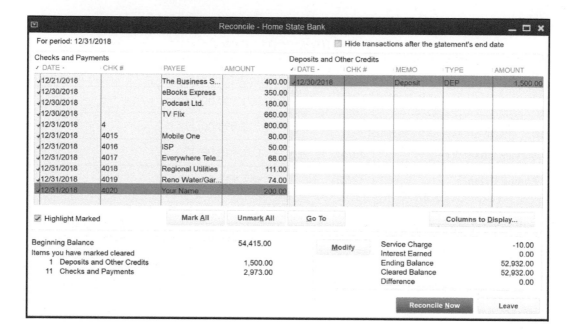

Observe that the Check Register on page 212 shows an ending balance of $52,942.00. The bank statement's ending balance shows $52,932.00. The difference is the bank service charge of $10.00. Once those fees are deducted from the check register balance, the bank statement and check register agree.

3. Make sure the Difference field shows 0.00. When satisfied, click <Reconcile Now>.

4. When the Select Reconciliation Report window displays, make sure Both is selected. Display the Reconciliation Summary report. (*Hint:* Two reports display, Reconciliation Detail and the Reconciliation Summary.) Compare your Reconciliation Summary report to the one shown on the next page.

Your Name Retailers Inc.
Reconciliation Summary
10000 · Home State Bank, Period Ending 12/31/2018

	Dec 31, 18
Beginning Balance	54,415.00
Cleared Transactions	
Checks and Payments - 12 items	-2,983.00
Deposits and Credits - 1 item	1,500.00
Total Cleared Transactions	-1,483.00
Cleared Balance	**52,932.00**
Register Balance as of 12/31/2018	52,932.00
Ending Balance	52,932.00

5. Close the reports.

ACCOUNTING CYCLE

Chapters 3-5 in this text work together to process the tasks in the accounting cycle for October through December. The steps of the Accounting Cycle that you do in this text are shown in the table below.

QuickBooks Accounting Cycle
1. Set up a company.
2. Record transactions.
3. Post entries automatically.
4. Account Reconciliation.
5. Print the Trial Balance (unadjusted).
6. Record and post adjusting entries.
7. Print the Trial Balance (adjusted).
8. Print the financial statements: balance sheet, profit and loss, cash flow statement.
9. Close the fiscal year.
10. Interpret accounting information.

At the end of December, which is also the end of the fiscal year, you complete the remaining tasks by printing an unadjusted trial balance, recording adjusting entries, printing financial statements, and closing the fiscal year.

UNADJUSTED TRIAL BALANCE

1. Print the 12/31/20XX Trial Balance (unadjusted). Compare your unadjusted trial balance to the one shown below.

Your Name Retailers Inc.
Trial Balance
As of December 31, 2018

	Dec 31, 18	
	Debit	Credit
10000 · Home State Bank	52,932.00	
11000 · Accounts Receivable	600.00	
12000 · Undeposited Funds	0.00	
12100 · Inventory Asset	940.00	
13000 · Supplies	2,700.00	
18000 · Prepaid Insurance	2,500.00	
14000 · Computer Equipment	2,400.00	
15000 · Furniture and Equipment	4,000.00	
22000 · Accounts Payable		150.00
26000 · Your Name Notes Payable		19,458.00
30000 · Common Stock		45,500.00
30200 · Dividends	400.00	
46000 · Sales		4,070.00
50000 · Cost of Goods Sold	2,035.00	
60400 · Bank Service Charges Expense	30.00	
61700 · Computer and Internet Expenses	50.00	
63400 · Interest Expense	258.00	
68100 · Telephone Expense	148.00	
68600 · Utilities Expense	185.00	
TOTAL	69,178.00	69,178.00

2. Backup the company data through the unadjusted trial balance to your USB drive. Name your backup **Your Name Chapter 5 December UTB** in the File name field. (*Hint:* UTB is an abbreviation of unadjusted trial balance.)
3. Exit QuickBooks or continue with the next section.

END-OF-QUARTER ADJUSTING ENTRIES

It is the policy of your company to record adjusting entries at the end of the quarter to properly reflect all the quarter's business activities.

Follow these steps to record and post the adjusting entries in the journal.

1. From the Icon Bar select Accountant; *or* from the menu bar, select Company > Make General Journal Entries.

2. When the Assigning Numbers to Journal Entries screen appears, read it and click <OK>.

3. Make sure the box next to Adjusting Entry is checked  .

   When you check the Adjusting Entry box, adjusting entries are identified on QB reports. Since QB includes an Adjusted Trial Balance, make sure you have selected Adjusting Entry on the Make General Journal Entries window.

4. If necessary, type **5** in the Entry No. field. That is the first adjusting entry number.

5. Type **12/31/20XX (use your current year)** in the Date field.

6. In the Account field, select the appropriate account to debit. (See transactions 1-4 below and on pages 219-221)

7. Type the appropriate amount in the Debit field.

8. Select the appropriate account to credit. Make sure the Credit field shows the appropriate amount.

9. Click <Save & New> to go to the next journal entry.

The adjusting entries that follow need to be recorded. Record and post these December 31, 20XX adjusting entries.

1. Supplies on hand are $2,400.00. (This is Entry No. 5.) The account distribution is shown below.

Acct. #	Account Name	Debit	Credit
64900	Supplies Expense	300.00	
13000	Supplies		300.00

Computation: Supplies $2,700.00

Office supplies on hand   −2,400.00

Adjustment $ 300.00

(*Hint:* To post your transaction, click <Save & New> after each journal entry.)

2. Adjust three months of prepaid insurance $150.00 ($50 per month × 3 months). (This is Entry No. 6.)

Acct. #	Account Name	Debit	Credit
63300	Insurance Expense	150.00	
18000	Prepaid Insurance		150.00

3. Use straight-line depreciation for computer equipment. Your computer equipment has a five-year service life and no salvage value. (Entry No. 7.)

To depreciate computer equipment for the fourth quarter, use this calculation:

$2,400 ÷ 5 years X 3/12 months = $120.00

Acct. #	Account Name	Debit	Credit
62400	Depreciation Expense	120.00	
16000	Accumulated Depreciation-CEqmt.		120.00

Read the Tracking Fixed Assets on Journal Entries window, then click <OK>.

4. Use straight-line depreciation to depreciate furniture. The furniture has a 5-year service life and no salvage value. (Entry No. 8.)

To depreciate furniture for the fourth quarter, use this calculation:

$4,000 ÷ 5 years X 3/12 months = $200.00

Acct. #	Account Name	Debit	Credit
62400	Depreciation Expense	200.00	
17000	Accumulated Depreciation-F&E		200.00

Read the Tracking Fixed Assets on Journal Entries box, then click <OK>.

5. After making the end-of-quarter adjusting entries, close the Make General Journal Entries window, then display the Adjusting Journal Entries for 12/31/20XX. (*Hint:* Report Center or Reports menu > Accountant & Taxes > Adjusting Journal Entries > 12/31/XX to 12/31/XX > Refresh.) If you placed a check mark next to adjusting entries (step 3, page 218) on the MakeGeneral Journal Entries window, only adjusting entries will display.

Your Name Retailers Inc.
Adjusting Journal Entries

Accrual Basis   December 31, 2018

Date	Num	Name	Memo	Account	Debit	Credit
12/31/2018	5			64900 · Supplies Expense	300.00	
				13000 · Supplies		300.00
					300.00	300.00
12/31/2018	6			63300 · Insurance Expense	150.00	
				18000 · Prepaid Insurance		150.00
					150.00	150.00
12/31/2018	7			62400 · Depreciation Expense	120.00	
				16000 · Accumulated Depreciation-CEqmt.		120.00
					120.00	120.00
12/31/2018	8			62400 · Depreciation Expense	200.00	
				17000 · Accumulated Depreciation-F&E		200.00
					200.00	200.00
TOTAL					770.00	770.00

If your adjusting journal entries in the Journal do *not* agree with the Adjusting Journal Entries window, edit them.

6. Close the Journal without saving.

7. Print the 12/31/20XX Adjusted Trial Balance. Compare your adjusted trial balance to the one shown. (*Hint:* On the Reports page, select Adjusted Trial Balance.)

Your Name Retailers Inc.
Adjusted Trial Balance
December 31, 2018

Accrual Basis

	Unadjusted Balance		Adjustments		Adjusted Balance	
	Debit	Credit	Debit	Credit	Debit	Credit
10000 · Home State Bank	52,932.00				52,932.00	
11000 · Accounts Receivable	600.00				600.00	
12000 · Undeposited Funds	0.00				0.00	
12100 · Inventory Asset	940.00				940.00	
13000 · Supplies	2,700.00			300.00	2,400.00	
18000 · Prepaid Insurance	2,500.00			150.00	2,350.00	
14000 · Computer Equipment	2,400.00				2,400.00	
15000 · Furniture and Equipment	4,000.00				4,000.00	
16000 · Accumulated Depreciation-CEqmt.				120.00		120.00
17000 · Accumulated Depreciation-F&E				200.00		200.00
22000 · Accounts Payable		150.00				150.00
26000 · Your Name Notes Payable		19,458.00				19,458.00
30000 · Common Stock		45,500.00				45,500.00
30200 · Dividends	400.00				400.00	
46000 · Sales		4,070.00				4,070.00
50000 · Cost of Goods Sold	2,035.00				2,035.00	
60400 · Bank Service Charges Expense	30.00				30.00	
61700 · Computer and Internet Expenses	50.00				50.00	
62400 · Depreciation Expense			320.00		320.00	
63300 · Insurance Expense			150.00		150.00	
63400 · Interest Expense	258.00				258.00	
64900 · Supplies Expense			300.00		300.00	
68100 · Telephone Expense	148.00				148.00	
68600 · Utilities Expense	185.00				185.00	
TOTAL	69,178.00	69,178.00	770.00	770.00	69,498.00	69,498.00

8. Print the 10/01/20XX to 12/31/20XX Profit & Loss-Standard (income statement). Compare yours to the one shown on the next page.

Your Name Retailers Inc.
Profit & Loss
October through December 2018

	Oct - Dec 18
Income	
46000 · Sales	4,070.00
Total Income	4,070.00
Cost of Goods Sold	
50000 · Cost of Goods Sold	2,035.00
Total COGS	2,035.00
Gross Profit	2,035.00
Expense	
60400 · Bank Service Charges Expense	30.00
61700 · Computer and Internet Expenses	50.00
62400 · Depreciation Expense	320.00
63300 · Insurance Expense	150.00
63400 · Interest Expense	258.00
64900 · Supplies Expense	300.00
68100 · Telephone Expense	148.00
68600 · Utilities Expense	185.00
Total Expense	1,441.00
Net Income	**594.00**

9. Print the 12/31/20XX Balance Sheet-Standard. Compare yours to the one shown on the next page.

Your Name Retailers Inc.
Balance Sheet
As of December 31, 2018

	Dec 31, 18
ASSETS	
Current Assets	
Checking/Savings	
10000 · Home State Bank	52,932.00
Total Checking/Savings	52,932.00
Accounts Receivable	
11000 · Accounts Receivable	600.00
Total Accounts Receivable	600.00
Other Current Assets	
12100 · Inventory Asset	940.00
13000 · Supplies	2,400.00
18000 · Prepaid Insurance	2,350.00
Total Other Current Assets	5,690.00
Total Current Assets	59,222.00
Fixed Assets	
14000 · Computer Equipment	2,400.00
15000 · Furniture and Equipment	4,000.00
16000 · Accumulated Depreciation-CEqmt.	-120.00
17000 · Accumulated Depreciation-F&E	-200.00
Total Fixed Assets	6,080.00
TOTAL ASSETS	**65,302.00**
LIABILITIES & EQUITY	
Liabilities	
Current Liabilities	
Accounts Payable	
22000 · Accounts Payable	150.00
Total Accounts Payable	150.00
Total Current Liabilities	150.00
Long Term Liabilities	
26000 · Your Name Notes Payable	19,458.00
Total Long Term Liabilities	19,458.00
Total Liabilities	19,608.00
Equity	
30000 · Common Stock	45,500.00
30200 · Dividends	-400.00
Net Income	594.00
Total Equity	45,694.00
TOTAL LIABILITIES & EQUITY	**65,302.00**

10. Print the 10/01/20XX to 12/31/20XX Statement of Cash Flows.

Your Name Retailers Inc.
Statement of Cash Flows
October through December 2018

	Oct - Dec 18
OPERATING ACTIVITIES	
Net Income	594.00
Adjustments to reconcile Net Income	
to net cash provided by operations:	
11000 · Accounts Receivable	-600.00
12100 · Inventory Asset	-940.00
13000 · Supplies	100.00
18000 · Prepaid Insurance	150.00
22000 · Accounts Payable	150.00
Net cash provided by Operating Activities	-546.00
INVESTING ACTIVITIES	
14000 · Computer Equipment	-1,400.00
16000 · Accumulated Depreciation-CEqmt.	120.00
17000 · Accumulated Depreciation-F&E	200.00
Net cash provided by Investing Activities	-1,080.00
FINANCING ACTIVITIES	
26000 · Your Name Notes Payable	-542.00
30000 · Common Stock	1,500.00
30200 · Dividends	-400.00
Net cash provided by Financing Activities	558.00
Net cash increase for period	-1,068.00
Cash at beginning of period	54,000.00
Cash at end of period	**52,932.00**

> **Comment**
>
> If your statement of cash flows or other financial statements *do not agree* with the textbook illustrations, drill-down to the appropriate entries. Edit the entries, then post and reprint your reports.

11. Back Up Company. The suggested file name is **Your Name Chapter 5 December Financial Statements.**

CLOSING THE FISCAL YEAR

When you close the fiscal year, all revenue and expense accounts are moved to Account No. 32000, Retained Earnings. Moving the expense and revenue accounts to retained earnings is called *closing the fiscal year.* The Dividends account must also be closed to Retained Earnings.

Follow these steps to close Dividends and close the fiscal year.

1. Journalize and post the following closing entries in the general journal (Journal Entry 9). When the Assigning Numbers to Journal Entries window appears, click <OK>. Make sure the Adjusting Entry box is unchecked—⬜ ADJUSTING ENTRY . Make the following December 31, 20XX closing entry for dividends.

Acct. #	Account Name	Debit	Credit
32000	Retained Earnings	400.00	
30200	Dividends		400.00

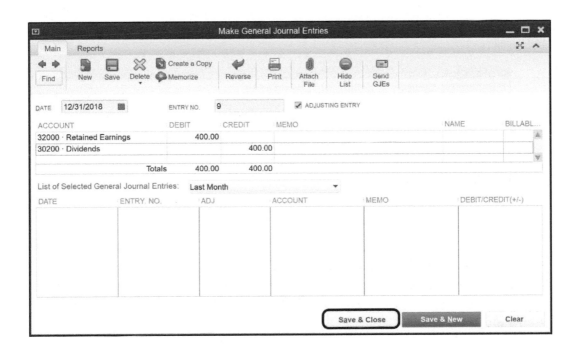

2.   After clicking <Save & Close>, the Retained Earnings warning screen appears. Read it and then click <OK>.

3.   From the menu bar, select Company > Set Closing Date.

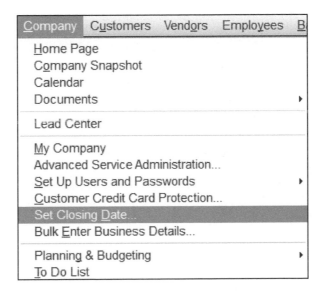

4. The Preferences window appears. Company Preferences is the default.

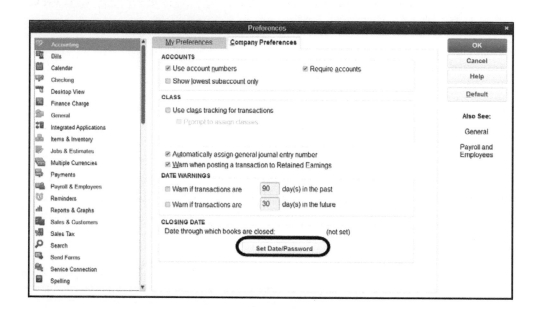

5. After clicking <Set Date/Password>, the Set Closing Date and Password window appears. For Closing Date, type **12/31/20XX** (use your current year). **Do not type a password!**

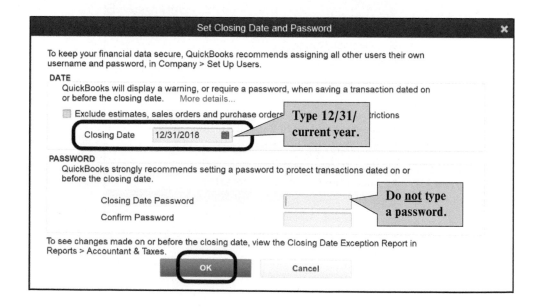

6. After clicking <OK>, the No Password Entered window appears. Read the information. Then, click <No>. To close the Preferences window, click <OK>.

PRINTING THE POSTCLOSING TRIAL BALANCE

After the fiscal year is closed, a postclosing trial balance is displayed and printed. Observe that the postclosing trial balance does *not* show dividends, revenue and expense accounts.

1. Display the 01/01/20XY (use the year after your current year) trial balance. (*Hint:* From the menu bar, select Reports > Accountant & Taxes > Trial Balance.) Compare yours to the one shown. When satisfied, print your postclosing trial balance.

Your Name Retailers Inc.
Trial Balance
As of January 1, 2019

	Jan 1, 19	
	Debit	Credit
10000 · Home State Bank	52,932.00	
11000 · Accounts Receivable	600.00	
12000 · Undeposited Funds	0.00	
12100 · Inventory Asset	940.00	
13000 · Supplies	2,400.00	
18000 · Prepaid Insurance	2,350.00	
14000 · Computer Equipment	2,400.00	
15000 · Furniture and Equipment	4,000.00	
16000 · Accumulated Depreciation-CEqmt.		120.00
17000 · Accumulated Depreciation-F&E		200.00
22000 · Accounts Payable		150.00
26000 · Your Name Notes Payable		19,458.00
30000 · Common Stock		45,500.00
30200 · Dividends	0.00	
32000 · Retained Earnings		194.00
TOTAL	65,622.00	65,622.00

Since the company's net income was greater than the dividends paid, Retained Earnings has a credit balance of $194.00.

2. Close the postclosing trial balance without saving.

BACKUP END-OF-YEAR DATA

1. Back up the data through year end to your USB drive. The suggested file name is **Your Name Chapter 5 EOY (Portable).QBM.** (*Hint:* EOY is an abbreviation of end of year.) Since you are going to email this file to your instructor, use the portable file format – File > Create Copy > Portable company file.

The Save Copy or Backup window is shown below. Portable company file is selected.

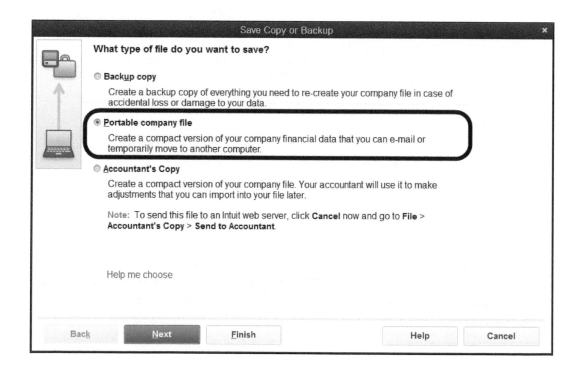

Portable company files create a compact version of your data. Files ending in a QBM extension are smaller than backups that have a .QBB file extension.

File name:	Your Name Chapter 5 EOY (Portable).QBM	▾	Save
Save as type:	QuickBooks Portable Company Files (*.QBM)	▾	Cancel
			Help

2. Exit QuickBooks or continue with the next section.

ACCOUNTANT TRANSFER

At year-end, external accountants or auditors review a company's accounting records. In this text, the external accountant is your professor. It is time to send your end-of-year portable company file via e-mail to you professor.

1. Start your e-mail program.
2. Create an e-mail message to your professor. Type **Your Name Retailers EOY** for the Subject. (Use your first and last name)
3. Attach the portable backup file **Your Name Chapter 5 EOY (Portable)** that you made on pages 230-231.
4. CC yourself on the message to be sure the message sends properly.
5. Send the message to your professor with attachment. You should receive a copy of it as well.

SUMMARY AND REVIEW

Additional resources are on the textbook's Online Learning Center (OLC) at www.mhhe.com/qbd2018. The OLC includes Student Edition links and Information Center links. When you link to the Student Edition, choose a chapter to populate more resources.

RESOURCEFUL QUICKBOOKS

The Online Learning Center at www.mhhe.com/qbd2018 > Student Edition > Chapter 5 > Narrated PowerPoints includes a link to the article.

Read the article "100 Best Business Blogs You Need to be Reading (and Taking Lessons From)" at https://quickbooks.intuit.com/r/starting-up/best-business-blogs/. List three business blogs and explain each blog.

Multiple Choice questions: The Online Learning Center includes the multiple-choice questions at www.mhhe.com/qbd2018 > Student Edition > Chapter 5 > Multiple Choice.

_____ 1. Compound entries affect at least how many accounts?

    a.   One.

    b.   Two.

    c.   Three.

    d.   None of the above.

_____ 2. Write checks icon is found in which pane on the Home page:

    a.   Banking.

    b.   Customers.

    c.   Company.

    d.   Vendors.

_____ 3. The Check Register displays information about:

    a.   Deposits.

    b.   Checks.

    c.   Cash balance.

    d.   All of the above.

_____ 4. An account reconciliation is completed:

    a.   When the bank statement is received.

    b.   Daily.

    c.   Weekly.

    d.   Annually.

_____ 5. The correct order of Accounting Cycle steps is:

    a.   Record transactions, Print the adjusted trial balance, Record and post adjusting entries, Close the fiscal year.

    b.   Record and post adjusting entries, Account reconciliation, Print the unadjusted trial balance, Close the fiscal year.

    c.   Record transactions, Print the unadjusted trial balance, Record and post adjusting entries, Close the fiscal year.

    d.   Record transactions, Print the adjusted trial balance, Account reconciliation, Close the fiscal year.

_____ 6. The adjusting entry for depreciation is:

    a.   Debit Accumulated Depreciation account and Credit Depreciation Expense account.

    b.   Debit Depreciation Expense account and Credit Accumulated Depreciation account.

    c.   Debit Computer Equipment account and Credit Accumulated Depreciation account.

    d.   Debit Depreciation Expense account and Credit Computer Equipment.

_____ 7. Make General Journal Entries window is used to record:

    a.   Compound entries.

    b.   Adjusting entries.

    c.   Closing entries.

    d.   All of the above.

_____ 8. Financial statements are prepared in the following order:

    a.   Balance Sheet, Income Statement, and Statement of Cash Flow.

    b.   Statement of Cash Flow, Income Statement, and Balance Sheet.

    c.   Income Statement, Balance Sheet, and Statement of Cash Flow.

    d.   Balance Sheet, Statement of Cash Flow, and Income Statement.

_____ 9. Closing entries move the following account balances to Retained Earnings at the end of the fiscal year:

    a.   Revenue and expense accounts.

    b.   Dividend and liability accounts.

    c.   Expense and asset accounts.

    d.   Asset and liability accounts.

_____ 10. Postclosing Trial Balance contains:

    a.   Only statement of cash flow accounts.

    b.   No revenue, expense, or dividend accounts.

    c.   Only profit and loss accounts.

    d.   Only stockholders' equity accounts.

Short-answer questions: To answer these questions, go online to www.mhhe.com/qbd2018 > Student Edition > Chapter 5 > QA Templates. The analysis question at the end of the chapter is also included.

1. Define a compound transaction.

2. What is the account distribution for the note payable payment?

3. What account is debited to pay dividends? What account is credited?

4. What account is debited to pay for cellular phone service? What account is credited?

5. What account is debited to pay for Internet service? What account is credited?

6. What account is debited to pay for water and garbage? What account is credited?

7. What is the check register and what does it show?

8. In Chapter 5 what steps of the accounting cycle did you complete?

9. Why does Your Name Retailers Inc. make adjusting journal entries?

10. What accounts never appear in a company's postclosing trial balance?

Exercise 5-1: Follow the instructions below to complete Exercise 5-1.

1. If necessary start QuickBooks and open Your Name Retailers.

2. Print the Audit Trail report for All dates. (*Hint:* Report Center > Accountant & Taxes > Audit Trail.)

 Read Me: Audit Trail

When changes are made to a transaction, the Num column is shown in italics; the State column shows Latest and Prior. If the amount was changed, it is shown in boldface.

3. Your instructor may want you to email the Audit Trial report as a **PDF** attachment. To do that, display the Audit Trail report (all dates), then select File > Save as PDF. (*Hint:* There is also an E-mail button on the Audit Trial's icon bar. Select E-mail, then send the report as a PDF–

.) The suggested file name is **Chapter 5 Audit Trail.pdf.**

Exercise 5-2: Answer the questions in the space provided. Use the following abbreviations to identify reports: IS (income statement); BS (balance sheet); CFS (cash flow statement).

1. What report(s) show the net income or net loss?

2. What report(s) show the cash balance?

3. What report(s) show total fixed assets?

4. What report(s) show common stock?

5. What reports(s) show cash at the beginning of the period?

6. What report(s) show note payable accounts?

7. What report(s) show total expenses?

8. What report(s) show the gross profit?

9. What report(s) show cost of goods sold?

10. What report(s) show dividends?

ANALYSIS QUESTION:

How is the December 31, 20XX retained earnings balance computed? Show the computation.

Chapter 6

First Month of the New Year

OBJECTIVES:

1. Restore data from Your Name Chapter 5 EOY file.

2. Record one month of transactions.

3. Make bank deposit.

4. Complete account reconciliation.

5. Print a trial balance (unadjusted).

6. Record adjusting entries and print an adjusted trial balance.

7. Print financial statements.

8. Make backups of Chapter 6 data.[1]

GETTING STARTED:

1. Start QuickBooks and open Your Name Retailers Inc.
2. If necessary, open or restore the Your Name Chapter 5 EOY. This backup was made in the previous chapter, pages 230–231. (*Hint:* If you are using your own PC, you may not need to restore.)
3. To make sure you are starting in the correct place, display the 01/01/20XY trial balance. 20XY is the year after your current year; for example, if your current year is 2018, use 2019 for year 20XY.

---

[1]The chart in the Preface, pages x-xi, shows the files names and size of each backup file. Refer to this chart for backing up data. Remember, you can back up to a hard drive location or external media.

The January 1, 20XY postclosing trial balance is shown below and on page 229.

Your Name Retailers Inc.
Trial Balance
As of January 1, 2019

	Jan 1, 19	
	Debit	Credit
10000 · Home State Bank	52,932.00	
11000 · Accounts Receivable	600.00	
12000 · Undeposited Funds	0.00	
12100 · Inventory Asset	940.00	
13000 · Supplies	2,400.00	
18000 · Prepaid Insurance	2,350.00	
14000 · Computer Equipment	2,400.00	
15000 · Furniture and Equipment	4,000.00	
16000 · Accumulated Depreciation-CEqmt.		120.00
17000 · Accumulated Depreciation-F&E		200.00
22000 · Accounts Payable		150.00
26000 · Your Name Notes Payable		19,458.00
30000 · Common Stock		45,500.00
30200 · Dividends	0.00	
32000 · Retained Earnings		194.00
TOTAL	65,622.00	65,622.00

4. Close the trial balance without saving.

In this chapter, you apply what you have learned so far to complete steps 2–8 in the accounting cycle for January.

The steps in the accounting cycle are shown on the next page.

	Accounting Cycle
1.	Set up company.
2.	Record transactions.
3.	Post entries.
4.	Account Reconciliation.
5.	Print the Trial Balance (unadjusted).
6.	Record and post adjusting entries.
7.	Print the Trial Balance (adjusted).
8.	Print the financial statements: Profit & Loss, Balance Sheet, and Statement of Cash Flow.
9.	Close the fiscal year.
10.	Interpret account information.

RECORD FIRST MONTH OF NEW FISCAL YEAR TRANSACTIONS

Record the following transactions from your Check Register for the month of January 20XY. (Hint: 20XY is the year after your current year. If your current year is 2018, use 2019 for year 20XY).

Check Number	Date	Description of Transaction	Payment	Deposit	Balance
	12/31	*Check register balance*			*52,932.00*
4021	1/3	The Business Store (Select Account 15000, Furniture and Equipment) for computer furniture[2]	500.00		52,432.00
4022	1/4	The Office Supply Store (Account 13000, Supplies)	100.00		52,332.00

---

[2]If a Set Check Reminder window appears, read it. Put a checkmark in the box "Do not display this message automatically in the future" > click <OK> to close.

Record the following vendor and customer transactions for the month of January.

Date	Description of Transaction
1/05	Enter bill (Invoice No. 201) for items received from Podcast Ltd. for the purchase of 30 audio files, $15 each, for a total of $450. (*Reminder:* Type **Invoice No. 201** in the Ref. No. field. Select the Items tab.)
1/05	Enter bill (Invoice No. 150eB) for items received from eBooks Express for the purchase of 32 PDF files, $25 each, for a total of $800. (*Reminder:* Type **Invoice No. 150eB** in the Ref. No. field.)
1/05	Enter bill (Invoice No. 400TV) received from TV Flix for the purchase of 30 video files, $30 each, for a total of $900.
1/10	Returned two PDF files to eBooks Express Credit Memo No. CM3, $50.
1/15	Create invoice to sell 10 eBooks (PDF files) on account to iPrint Design for a total credit sale of $500, Invoice # 9.
1/15	Create invoice to sell 30 Podcasts (audio files) on account to Audio Answers for a total credit sale of $900, Invoice # 10.
1/15	Sold 16 TV Programs (video files) on account to Video Solutions for a total credit sale of $960, Invoice # 11.
1/17	Audio Answers returned 2 Podcasts (audio files), $60, Credit No. 12. Apply to 1/15 invoice.
1/18	Create sales receipt (Sale No. 3) for credit card sales for 10 eBooks for $500; 1 Podcasts for $30; and 12 TV Programs for $720; for total credit card sales of $1,250.
1/20	Received a $600 check from Video Solutions in payment of 12/24 credit sale less return.

1/20	Your Name Retailers Inc. pays all outstanding December and January vendor bills less any returns for a total of $2,250. (*Hint:* eBooks Express $50 credit)
1/21	Enter bill to purchase computer furniture on account from The Business Store, Invoice No. BOS80, for a total of $800, terms Net 30 days. (Account No. 15000 Furniture and Equipment)
1/23	Received a check in full payment of Audio Answers' account less return, $840.
1/24	Received a check in full payment of iPrint Design's account, $500.
1/24	Received a check in full payment of Video Solution's account, $960.
1/25	Enter bill (Invoice No. 175eB) received from eBooks Express for the purchase of 8 PDF files, $25 each, for a total of $200.
1/25	Invoice No. 425TV received from TV Flix for the purchase of 11 video files, $30 each, for a total of $330.
1/25	Invoice No. 230 received from Podcast Ltd. for the purchase of 6 audio files, $15 each, for a total of $90.
1/26	Returned two audio files to Podcast Ltd., CM4, $30.
1/27	Create invoice to sell 16 eBooks (PDF files) on account to iPrint Design for a total credit sale of $800, Invoice # 13.
1/27	Sold 5 Podcasts (audio files) on account to Audio Answers for a total credit sale of $150 Invoice # 14.
1/27	Sold 6 TV Programs (video files) on account to Video Solutions for a total credit sale of $360, Invoice # 15.
1/27	Enter sales receipt for credit card sales. Sold 2 eBooks for $100; 1 Podcasts for $30; and 6 TV Programs for $360; for total credit card sales of $490, Sale No. 4.
1/28	Video Solutions returned 1 TV Programs (video files), Credit No. 16. Apply $60 credit to 1/27 invoice.

1/29	Received a check in full payment of Audio Answers' account, $150.
1/29	Received a check in full payment of iPrint Design's account, $800.
1/29	Your Name Retailers Inc. pays all outstanding vendor bills less any returns for a total of $1,390. (*Hint:* Podcast Ltd. $30 credit.)

Record the following compound entry for the month of January: (*Hint:* Company > Make General Journal Entries. If necessary, uncheck Adjusting Entry.)

| 1/30 | Pay the note payable in the amount of $800.00. The account distribution is shown below. |

Acct. No.	Account	Debit	Credit
26000	Your Name Notes Payable	555.00	
63400	Interest Expense	245.00	
10000	Home State Bank		800.00

Write checks for these additional January transactions.

1/30	Issue Check No. 4031 to Mobile One in the amount of $80 for cellular service. (Account No. 68100 Telephone Expense)
1/30	Issue Check No. 4032 to ISP in the amount of $50 for Internet service. (Account No. 61700 Computer and Internet Expense)
1/30	Issue Check No. 4033 to Everywhere Telephone in the amount of $68 for telephone service. (Account No. 68100 Telephone Expense)
1/30	Issue Check No. 4034 to Reno Water/Garbage Utilities the amount of $111 for Electricity/Gas. (Account No. 68600 Utilities Expense.)

| 1/30 | Issue Check No. 4035 to Reno Water/Garbage for $74 for Water/ Garbage service. (Account No. 68600 Utilities Expense). |
| 1/30 | View the Check Register. Select Check 4034, then click ⬛ Edit Transaction . The Write Checks window appears for the disbursement. Check No. 4034 should be written to Regional Utilities, not Reno Water/Garbage. Write the check correctly to Regional Utilities to pay $111 electricity bill. (*Hint:* Use Pay To The Order Of down arrow.) Close the Write Checks window and the Check Register. |

MAKE DEPOSIT

| 1/30 | Record 8 deposits in the amount of $5,590. This includes payments received from customers and credit card sales. |

CHECK REGISTER

Display the check register to see Account No. 10000, Home State Bank activity for January. If necessary, select the check that needs to be changed, then select ⬛ Edit Transaction to go to the Write Checks window.

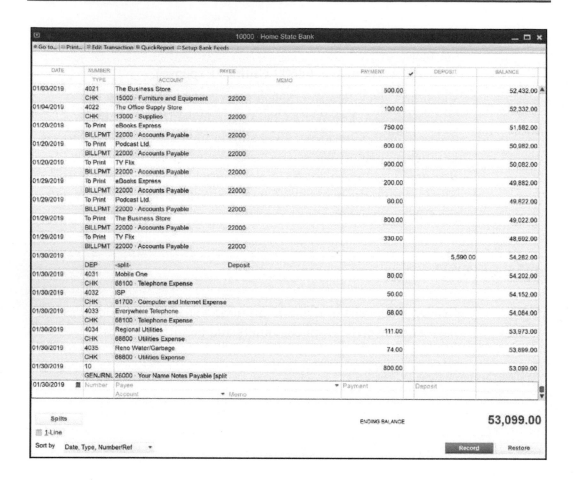

Backup. The suggested file name is **Your Name Chapter 6 January Check Register. QBB.** (If a screen appears that says number of backup copies has been exceeded, click No, don't delete.)

ACCOUNT RECONCILIATION

Use the January bank statement on the next page to reconcile the Home State Bank account. Check numbers are shown on the following bank statement. Depending on whether you recorded a check number for each vendor payment, check numbers may or may not be included on the Reconcile window.

Statement of Account Home State Bank January 1 to January 31, 20XY		Account #923-121379	Your Name Retailers Inc. Your Address Reno, NV	
REGULAR CHECKING				
Previous Balance	12/31	52,932.00		
Deposits		5,590.00		
Checks (−)		5,423.00		
Service Charges (−)	1/31	10.00		
Ending Balance	1/31	**$53,089.00**		
DEPOSITS				
	1/18	1,250.00	Credit Card	
	1/27	490.00	Credit Card	
	1/30	600.00	Video Solutions	
	1/30	840.00	Audio Answers	
	1/30	500.00	iPrint Design	
	1/30	960.00	Video Solutions	
	1/30	150.00	Audio Answers	
	1/30	800.00	iPrint Design	
CHECKS				
	1/4	500.00	4021	
	1/4	100.00	4022	
	1/22	750.00	4023	
	1/22	600.00	4024	*Continued*

Statement of Account Home State Bank January 1 to January 31, 20XY		Account #923-121379	Your Name Retailers Inc. Your Address Reno, NV	
	1/22	900.00	4025	
	1/30	800.00	4026	
	1/30	200.00	4027	
	1/30	60.00	4028	
	1/30	330.00	4029	
	1/31	800.00	4030	
	1/31	80.00	4031	
	1/31	50.00	4032	
	1/31	68.00	4033	
	1/31	111.00	4034	
	1/31	74.00	4035	

Once the $10 Service Charge is deducted from the account register balance, the bank statement and account register agree.

Check Register Balance:	$53,099.00
Bank Service Charge:	10.00
Bank Statement Balance:	$53,089.00

1. Prepare the account reconciliation for January. (*Hint:* Your Reconcile window may not show all of the check numbers. That is okay.)
2. Compare your Reconciliation Detail to the one shown.

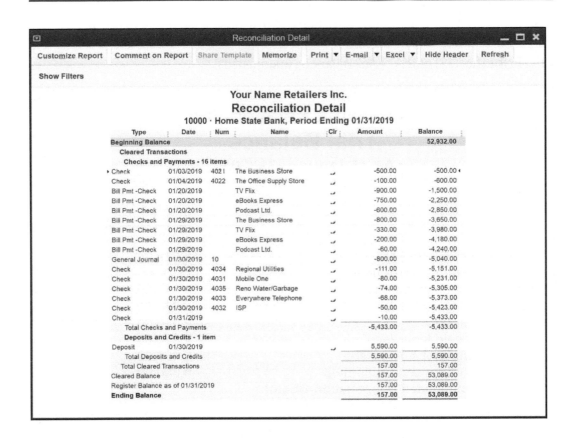

3. Compare your Reconciliation Summary the one shown.

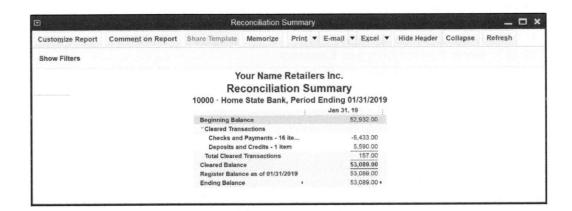

4. Close the Reconciliation Detail and Reconciliation Summary reports.

UNADJUSTED TRIAL BALANCE

1. Print the 1/31/20XY Trial Balance (unadjusted).

Your Name Retailers Inc.
Trial Balance
As of January 31, 2019

	Jan 31, 19	
	Debit	Credit
10000 · Home State Bank	53,089.00	
11000 · Accounts Receivable	300.00	
12000 · Undeposited Funds	0.00	
12100 · Inventory Asset	985.00	
13000 · Supplies	2,500.00	
18000 · Prepaid Insurance	2,350.00	
14000 · Computer Equipment	2,400.00	
15000 · Furniture and Equipment	5,300.00	
16000 · Accumulated Depreciation-CEqmt.		120.00
17000 · Accumulated Depreciation-F&E		200.00
22000 · Accounts Payable	0.00	
26000 · Your Name Notes Payable		18,903.00
30000 · Common Stock		45,500.00
30200 · Dividends	0.00	
32000 · Retained Earnings		194.00
46000 · Sales		5,290.00
50000 · Cost of Goods Sold	2,645.00	
60400 · Bank Service Charges Expense	10.00	
61700 · Computer and Internet Expenses	50.00	
63400 · Interest Expense	245.00	
68100 · Telephone Expense	148.00	
68600 · Utilities Expense	185.00	
TOTAL	70,207.00	70,207.00

2. Backup. The suggested file name is **Your Name Chapter 6 UTB.QBB.**

END-OF-MONTH ADJUSTING ENTRIES

Your Name Retailers Inc. changed their adjusting entry policy for the new fiscal year. The new policy is to record adjusting entries at the end of each month to properly reflect all the month's business activities. Make the following adjusting entries for the month of January on 01/31/20XY. (*Hint:* On the Make General Journal Entries window, put check mark next to Adjusting Entry–☑ ADJUSTING ENTRY.)

1. Supplies on hand are $2,300.00. (This is Entry No. 11.)

Acct. #	Account Name	Debit	Credit
64900	Supplies Expense	200.00	
13000	Supplies		200.00

Computation:	Supplies	$2,500.00
	Office supplies on hand	−2,300.00
	Adjustment	$ 200.00

2. Adjust one month of prepaid insurance ($50/month). (Entry No. 12.)

Acct. #	Account Name	Debit	Credit
63300	Insurance Expense	50.00	
18000	Prepaid Insurance		50.00

3. Use straight-line depreciation for your computer equipment. Your computer equipment has a five-year service life and no salvage value. (Entry No. 13.)

   To depreciate computer equipment for the month, use this calculation:
   $2,400 ÷ 5 years X 1/12 months = $40.00

Acct. #	Account Name	Debit	Credit
62400	Depreciation Expense	40.00	
16000	Accumulated Depreciation-CEqmt.		40.00

4. Use straight-line depreciation to depreciate furniture. The furniture has a 5-year service life and no salvage value. (Entry No. 14.) To depreciate furniture for the month, use this calculation:

$4,000 \div 5$ years X $1/12$ month $= \$67.00$

Acct. #	Account Name	Debit	Credit
62400	Depreciation Expense	67.00	
17000	Accumulated Depreciation-F&E		67.00

5. You purchased new furniture during the month. Use straight-line depreciation to depreciate your furniture. The furniture has a 5-year service life and a $100 salvage value.

Use the following adjusting entry. (Entry No. 15.) The computation is:

$(\$500 + \$800 - \$100) \div 5$ years X $1/12$ month $= \$20.00$

Acct. #	Account Name	Debit	Credit
62400	Depreciation Expense	20.00	
17000	Accumulated Depreciation-F&E		20.00

6. After journalizing and posting the adjusting entries, close the Make General Journal Entries window, then display or print the Adjusting Journal Entries as of 01/31/20XY.

Comment: If your unadjusted and adjusted trial balances *do not agree* with the textbook illustration, drill-down to the appropriate entries. Edit the entries, then reprint your reports.

Your Name Retailers Inc.
Adjusting Journal Entries
January 31, 2019

Accrual Basis

Date	Num	Name	Memo	Account	Debit	Credit
01/31/2019	11			64900 · Supplies Expense	200.00	
				13000 · Supplies		200.00
					200.00	200.00
01/31/2019	12			63300 · Insurance Expense	50.00	
				18000 · Prepaid Insurance		50.00
					50.00	50.00
01/31/2019	13			62400 · Depreciation Expense	40.00	
				16000 · Accumulated Depreciation-CEqmt.		40.00
					40.00	40.00
01/31/2019	14			62400 · Depreciation Expense	67.00	
				17000 · Accumulated Depreciation-F&E		67.00
					67.00	67.00
01/31/2019	15			62400 · Depreciation Expense	20.00	
				17000 · Accumulated Depreciation-F&E		20.00
					20.00	20.00
TOTAL					377.00	377.00

ADJUSTED TRIAL BALANCE

1. Print the 1/31/20XY Adjusted Trial Balance.

	Your Name Retailers Inc.					
	Adjusted Trial Balance					
Accrual Basis	January 31, 2019					

	Unadjusted Balance		Adjustments		Adjusted Balance	
	Debit	Credit	Debit	Credit	Debit	Credit
10000 · Home State Bank	53,089.00				53,089.00	
11000 · Accounts Receivable	300.00				300.00	
12000 · Undeposited Funds	0.00				0.00	
12100 · Inventory Asset	985.00				985.00	
13000 · Supplies	2,500.00			200.00	2,300.00	
18000 · Prepaid Insurance	2,350.00			50.00	2,300.00	
14000 · Computer Equipment	2,400.00				2,400.00	
15000 · Furniture and Equipment	5,300.00				5,300.00	
16000 · Accumulated Depreciation-CEqmt.		120.00		40.00		160.00
17000 · Accumulated Depreciation-F&E		200.00		87.00		287.00
22000 · Accounts Payable	0.00				0.00	
26000 · Your Name Notes Payable		18,903.00				18,903.00
30000 · Common Stock		45,500.00				45,500.00
30200 · Dividends	0.00				0.00	
32000 · Retained Earnings		194.00				194.00
46000 · Sales		5,290.00				5,290.00
50000 · Cost of Goods Sold	2,645.00				2,645.00	
60400 · Bank Service Charges Expense	10.00				10.00	
61700 · Computer and Internet Expenses	50.00				50.00	
62400 · Depreciation Expense			127.00		127.00	
63300 · Insurance Expense			50.00		50.00	
63400 · Interest Expense	245.00				245.00	
64900 · Supplies Expense			200.00		200.00	
68100 · Telephone Expense	148.00				148.00	
68600 · Utilities Expense	185.00				185.00	
TOTAL	70,207.00	70,207.00	377.00	377.00	70,334.00	70,334.00

2. Close reports, then backup. The suggested file name is **Your Name Chapter 6 January Financial Statements.QBB.**

3. Exit QuickBooks or continue with the next section.

SUMMARY AND REVIEW

Additional resources are on the textbook's Online Learning Center (OLC) at www.mhhe.com/qbd2018. The OLC includes Student Edition links and Information Center links. When you link to the Student Edition, choose a chapter to populate more resources.

RESOURCEFUL QUICKBOOKS

1. From the menu bar, select Help > Year-End Guide.

   What are the three task areas that must be addressed at year-end?
   List them.

2. From the Year-End page > link to Print financial reports. Answer these
   questions.

   a. What does the Trial Balance tell you? (Click More. . .)

   b. What does the Profit & Loss Standard report tell you?

   c. What does the Balance Sheet Standard tell you?

Multiple Choice Questions: The Online Learning Center includes the
multiple-choice questions at www.mhhe.com/qbd2018 > Student Edition,
Chapter 6 > Multiple Choice.

_____ 1. The January 1, 20XY Trial Balance contains:

   a. The same accounts as the 12/31/20XX postclosing trial balance.

   b. No revenue, expense, or dividend accounts.

   c. Both of the above.

   d. None of the above.

_____ 2. In Chapter 6, you enter transactions for:

   a. The first month of the new fiscal year.

   b. January.

   c. Both of the above.

   d. None of the above.

_____ 3. In Chapter 6, you complete which steps in the Accounting Cycle?

    a.   Steps 1.-9.

    b.   Steps 2.-8.

    c.   Steps 3.-7.

    d.   All the steps.

_____ 4. In Chapter 6, all the following Banking section icons are used *except:*

    a.   Reconcile.

    b.   Check register.

    c.   Write checks.

    d.   Enter bills.

_____ 5. In Chapter 6, all the following Customers section icons are used *except:*

    a.   Create invoices.

    b.   Estimates.

    c.   Create sales receipts.

    d.   Receive payments.

_____ 6. In Chapter 6, the following Vendors section icon was used:

    a.   Pay bills.

    b.   Purchase Orders.

    c.   Enter bills against inventory.

    d.   Write bills.

_____ 7. In Chapter 6, the Company section icon used was:

    a.   Chart of accounts.

    b.   Items and services.

    c.   Both of the above.

    d.   None of the above.

_____ 8. The Year-End Guide checklist includes all of the following *except:*

    a.   Reconcile all bank and credit card accounts.

    b.   Print financial reports.

    c.   Back up company file access.

    d.   Access to the QuickBooks Knowledge Base.

_____ 9. The work flow for invoicing is:

    a.   Create invoice, Receive payment, Record deposit.

    b.   Create sales receipt, record deposit.

    c.   Enter bill, Pay bill.

    d.   Receive invoice, Pay bill.

_____ 10. The QuickBooks menu bar Help selection includes:

    a.   Ask Intuit.

    b.   Support.

    c.   Year-end guide.

    d.   All of the above.

Short-answer and True/make true questions: To answer these questions, go online to www.mhhe.com/qbd2018 > Student Edition > Chapter 6 > QA Templates. The analysis question at the end of the chapter is also included.

1. Your Name Retailers Inc. fiscal year begins on January 1.

2. Step 4 of the accounting cycle is reconciling the bank statement.

3. The check register's balance does *not* show the bank service charge.

4. Your check register and bank statement are used as source documents for recording entries.

5. In this chapter, Your Name Retailers Inc. makes adjusting journal entries on a quarterly basis.

6. In this chapter, accounting records are completed for January 1 - March 31, 20XY.

7. Your Name Retailers Inc. makes closing journal entries on a monthly basis.

8. For the period of January 1 to January 31, 20XY, Your Name Retailers Inc. net income (loss) is $_____.

9. At the end of the month, Your Name Retailers Inc. total assets are $_____.

10. At the end of the month, Your Name Retailers Inc. total liabilities are $_____.

11. At the end of the month, Your Name Retailers Inc. had generated cash flow from/for operating activities of $_____.

12. At the end of the month, Your Name Retailers Inc. had generated cash flow from/for financing activities of $_____.

Exercise 6-1: Follow the instructions below to complete Exercise 6-1.

1. If necessary, start QB and open Your Name Retailers Inc.

2. If necessary, restore the Your Name Chapter 6 January Financial Statements file. This backup was made on page 252.

3. Back up the file as a portable company file. (*Hint:* File > Create Copy > Portable Company File.) The suggested file name is **Your Name Exercise 6-1 (Portable).QBM.**

4. Print the 01/01/20XY to 01/31/20XY Journal.

5. Print the 01/31/20XY trial balance.

6. Print the financial statements:

   a. Profit & Loss-Standard from 01/01/20XY to 01/31/20XY).

   b. Balance Sheet-Standard as of 01/31/20XY.

   c. Statement of Cash Flows from 01/01/20XY to 01/31/20XY.

7. Print the Audit Trail for all dates.

Read Me: Save reports as PDF Files

Your instructor may want you to email reports as PDF attachments. To do that, follow these steps:

1. Display the report.

2. Select Print > Save as PDF. *Or,* select E-mail > Send reports as PDF.

3. The suggested file name is **Exercise 6-1 Journal.pdf**, etc.

You need Adobe Reader to save as PDF files. If download the free Adobe Reader, https://get.adobe.com/reader/.

Exercise 6-2: Send an e-mail to your professor and attach a copy of Your Name Exercise 6-1 (Portable).QBM file. (*Hint:* Follow the Accountant Transfer steps 1–5 in Chapter 5.

ANALYSIS QUESTION:

Why did Your Name Retailers Inc. generate more cash from operating activities than net income for January?

In Project 1, you complete the business processes for Your Name Hardware Store, a merchandising business. Your Name Hardware Store sells shovels, wagons, and wheel barrows. It is organized as a corporation. The purpose of Project 1 is to review what you have learned about merchandising businesses and use their typical source documents.

Source documents that generate transaction analysis for accounts payable, inventory, accounts receivable, and cash are included in this project. You will also complete account reconciliation. At the end of Project 1, a checklist is shown listing the printed reports that should be completed. The step-by-step instructions also remind you to print reports and backup at regular intervals.

GETTING STARTED

Follow these steps to open Your Name Hardware Store:

Step 1: Start QuickBooks 2018. From the menu bar, select File > Close Company.

Step 2: The No Company Open window appears. Restore the backup file, Your Name Hardware Store.QBB. You created this company and backed it up in Exercises 1-1 and 1-2. If the Your Name Hardware Store.QBB backup file does <u>not</u> exist, complete Exercises 1-1 and 1-2 on pages 24-27.

When the Save Company File as window appears, rename the company file Your Name Project 1 Begin.QBW.

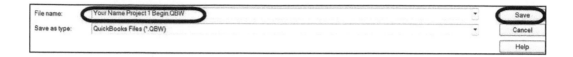

Hint: If an Update Company window appears, read the information; click <Yes>.

Step 3: Confirm company information. Select . The My Company window shows information about Your Name Hardware Store. (*Hint:* Your first and last name should be shown before Hardware Store.)

Step 4: If needed, edit the Company Information and Legal Information by selecting [image]. When satisfied that the company information is correct, close the My Company window.

COMPANY PREFERENCES

Step 5: From the menu bar, select Edit > Preferences. Click on Company Preferences tab > select Accounting.

Step 6: Click on the box next to Use account numbers. Make sure boxes next to Date warnings are unchecked.

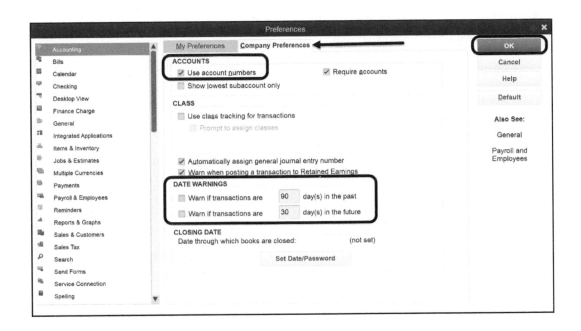

To save selections, click <OK >.

Step 7: From the menu bar, select Edit > Preferences > My Preferences tab and select Checking. In the Open the Write Checks form with account field, add Account 10000, Home State Bank. Accept the default for B/S-Assets: Cash.

- Check marks are next to Open the Write Check Form with . . . account,

- Open the Pay Bills form with . . . account,

- Open the make deposits form with . . . account.

For each of these selections, choose Home State Bank account.

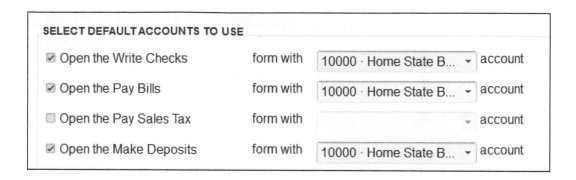

Click <OK> to save selections.

Step 8: From the menu bar, select Edit > Preferences > My Preferences > Send Forms. Uncheck box next to Auto-check the Email Later checkbox if customer's Preferred Delivery Method is e-mail. In the e-mail using area, select Web Mail. (*Hint:* If you use Outlook, it is shown.)

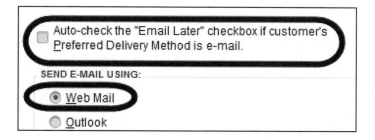

To save preferences, click <OK>. If a Warning window says that QuickBooks must close all its open windows to change this preference, click <OK>.

Step 9: From the menu bar, select Edit > Preferences > Items & Inventory > Company Preferences. Put a check mark next to Inventory and purchase orders are active.

> PURCHASE ORDERS AND INVENTORY
>
> ☑ Inventory and purchase orders are active.

To save preferences, click <OK >. To see the Home page, click

.

CHART OF ACCOUNTS

Step 10: Delete the following accounts:

48300 Sales Discounts
51800 Merchant Account Fees
80000 Ask My Accountant

Step 11: Edit the following accounts and delete what currently displays as the Description.

Account	New Name	Type	Tax Line Mapping
18700 Security Deposits Asset	**Prepaid Insurance**	**Other Current Asset**	**B/S-Assets: Other Current Assets**
30100 Capital Stock	**Paid in Capital**	**Equity**	**B/S-Liabs/Eq.: Paid in or Capital Surplus**
30200 Dividends Paid	**Dividends**	**Equity**	**Unassigned**
30000 Opening Balance Equity	**Common Stock**	**Equity**	**B/S-Liabs/Eq.: Capital Stock -Common Stk.**
68600 Utilities	**Utilities Expense**	**Expense**	**Other Deductions: Utilities**

Step 12: Add Account No. 26000.

New Account	Description	Type	Income Tax Line
26000 Your Name Notes Payable	None	**Long Term Liability**	**B/S-Liabs/Eq.: Loans from stockholders**

Step 13: Make a backup to your USB drive. Use **Your Name Hardware Store Chart of Accounts (Portable).QBM.** (*Hint:* Backups in Project 1 are portable files: File > Create Copy > Portable company file.)

Step 14: You purchased Your Name Hardware Store in December of last year. (*Hint:* Use 12/31/last year to enter opening balances. If you notice an account description when entering beginning balances, delete it.) Use this Balance Sheet to record the beginning balances. Then display the chart of accounts.

Your Name Hardware Store Balance Sheet January 1, 20XX (Your current year)		
ASSETS		
Current Assets		
Home State Bank	$ 84,000.00	
Prepaid Insurance	2,900.00	
Total Current Assets		$86,900.00
Fixed Assets		
Furniture and Equipment	6,000.00	
Total Fixed Assets		6,000.00
Total Assets		$92,900.00

LIABILITIES AND STOCKHOLDERS' EQUITY		
Your Name Notes Payable	9,500.00	
Total Liabilities		$9,500.00
Common Stock		83,400.00
Total Liabilities and Equity		$92,900.00

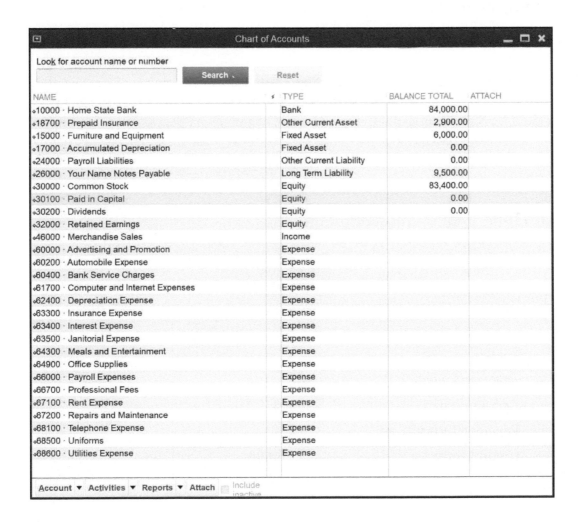

NAME	TYPE	BALANCE TOTAL	ATTACH
10000 · Home State Bank	Bank	84,000.00	
18700 · Prepaid Insurance	Other Current Asset	2,900.00	
15000 · Furniture and Equipment	Fixed Asset	6,000.00	
17000 · Accumulated Depreciation	Fixed Asset	0.00	
24000 · Payroll Liabilities	Other Current Liability	0.00	
26000 · Your Name Notes Payable	Long Term Liability	9,500.00	
30000 · Common Stock	Equity	83,400.00	
30100 · Paid in Capital	Equity	0.00	
30200 · Dividends	Equity	0.00	
32000 · Retained Earnings	Equity		
46000 · Merchandise Sales	Income		
60000 · Advertising and Promotion	Expense		
60200 · Automobile Expense	Expense		
60400 · Bank Service Charges	Expense		
61700 · Computer and Internet Expenses	Expense		
62400 · Depreciation Expense	Expense		
63300 · Insurance Expense	Expense		
63400 · Interest Expense	Expense		
63500 · Janitorial Expense	Expense		
64300 · Meals and Entertainment	Expense		
64900 · Office Supplies	Expense		
66000 · Payroll Expenses	Expense		
66700 · Professional Fees	Expense		
67100 · Rent Expense	Expense		
67200 · Repairs and Maintenance	Expense		
68100 · Telephone Expense	Expense		
68500 · Uniforms	Expense		
68600 · Utilities Expense	Expense		

Chart of Accounts

Look for account name or number

Search   Reset

Account ▼   Activities ▼   Reports ▼   Attach   Include inactive

BACKUP

Step 15: Make a backup to your USB drive. Use **Your Name Hardware Store Beginning Balances (Portable).QBM.** (*Hint:* To check that your beginning balances were entered for 12/31/last year, display the 12/31 balance sheet and compare to the one shown on pages 264-265.)

VENDORS

Step 16: Go to the Vendor Center and add the following vendors.

Vendor name:	**AAA Shovels**
Opening Balance.	**0.00**
As of:	**1/1/current year**
Company Name:	**AAA Shovels**
Full Name:	**Tim Nelson**
Address:	**300 First Avenue**
	Santa Cruz, CA 95061
Work Phone:	**831-555-2243**
Fax:	**831-555-2245**
Main Email:	**tim@aaa.biz**
Website:	**www.aaashovels.biz**
Payment Settings:	
Account No.	**20000**
Payment Terms:	**Net 30**
Credit Limit:	**15,000.00**

Additional Info:

Vendor Type:	**Suppliers**

Vendor name:	**BBB Wheel Barrows**
Opening Balance:	**0.00**
As of:	**1/1/current year**
Company Name:	**BBB Wheel Barrows**
Full Name:	**Betsy Benson**
Address:	**6012 Mesquite Street**
	El Paso, TX 79901
Work Phone:	**915-555-3000**
Fax:	**915-555-3100**
Main Email:	**betsy@BBB.com**
Website:	**www.BBBwheel.com**

Payment Settings:

Account No.	**20000**
Payment Terms:	**Net 30**
Credit Limit:	**15,000.00**

Additional Info:

Vendor Type:	**Suppliers**

Vendor name:	**CCC Wagons**
Opening Balance:	**0.00**
As of:	**1/1/current year**
Company Name:	**CCC Wagons**
Full Name:	**Caitlin Carson**
Address:	**2301 Dugout Road**
	Chandler, AZ 85226

Work Phone:	**480-555-2288**
Fax:	**480-555-2299**
Main Email:	**caitlin@CCC.net**
Website:	**www.CCCwagons.net**

Payment Settings:

Account No.	**20000**
Payment Terms:	**Net 30**
Credit Limit:	**15,000.00**

Additional Info:

Vendor Type:	**Suppliers**

INVENTORY ITEMS

Step 17: Go to the Inventory Center to add these inventory parts:

Item Name/Number:	**Shovels**
Purchase Description:	**Shovels**
Purchase Cost:	**15.00**
COGS Account:	50000, Cost of Goods Sold
Preferred Vendor:	**AAA Shovels**
Sales Description:	Shovels
Sales Price:	**30.00**
Income Account:	**46000, Merchandise Sales**
Asset Account:	12100, Inventory Asset
On Hand:	0.00
Total Value:	0.00
As of:	01/01/20XX

Item Name/Number:	**Wheel barrows**
Purchase Description:	**Wheel barrows**
Purchase Cost:	**75.00**
COGS Account:	50000, Cost of Goods Sold
Preferred Vendor:	BBB Wheel Barrows
Sales Description:	Wheel barrows
Sales Price:	**100.00**
Income Account:	46000, Merchandise Sales
Asset Account:	12100, Inventory Asset
On Hand:	0.00
Total Value:	0.00
As of:	01/01/20XX

Item Name/Number:	**Wagons**
Purchase Description:	**Wagons**
Purchase Cost:	**20.00**
COGS Account:	Cost of Goods Sold
Preferred Vendor:	CCC Wagons
Sales Description:	Wagons
Sales Price:	**50.00**
Income Account:	46000, Merchandise Sales
Asset Account:	12100, Inventory Asset
On Hand:	0.00
Total Value:	0.00
As of:	01/01/20XX

CUSTOMERS

Step 18: Go to the Customer Center and add the following retail Customers:

Customer Name:	**Dawn Bright**
Opening Balance:	**0.00**
As of:	**1/1/20XX**
Full Name:	**Dawn Bright**
Address:	**1800 W. Peoria Avenue**
	Reno, NV 92731
Main Phone:	**503-555-8630**
Main Email:	**db@myemail.com**

Payment Settings:

Account No.:	**DB1**
Payment Terms:	**Net 30**
Preferred Delivery Method:	**Mail**
Preferred Payment Method:	**Check**
Credit Limit:	**10,000.00**

Additional Info:

Customer Type:	**Retail**

Customer Name:	**Roy Lars**
Opening Balance:	**0.00**
As of:	**1/1/20XX**
Full Name:	**Roy Lars**
Address:	**603 Nature Drive**
	Reno, NV 97401
Main Phone:	**541-555-7845**
Main E-mail:	**roy@mail.biz**

Payment Settings:

Account No.:	**RL2**

Payment Terms:	**Net 30**
Preferred Delivery Method:	**Mail**
Preferred Payment Method:	**Check**
Credit Limit:	**10,000.00**

Additional Info:

Customer Type:	**Retail**

Customer Name:	**Shar Watsonville**
Opening Balance:	**0.00**
As of:	**1/1/20XX**
Full Name:	**Shar Watsonville**
Address:	**3455 West 20th Avenue**
	Reno, NV 97402
Main Phone:	**541-555-9233**
Main E-mail:	**shar@email.com**

Payment Settings:

Account No.:	**SW3**
Payment Terms:	**Net 30**
Preferred Delivery Method:	**Mail**
Preferred Payment Method:	**Check**
Credit Limit:	**10,000.00**

Additional Info:

Customer Type:	**Retail**

Customer Name:	**Credit Card Sales**
Opening Balance:	**0.00**
As of:	**1/1/20XX**
Additional Info > Customer Type:	**Retail**

BACKUP

Step 19: Make a backup to your USB drive. Use **Your Name Hardware Store Vendors Inventory Customers (Portable).QBM** as the filename.

TRANSACTIONS FROM SOURCE DOCUMENT ANALYSIS

Step 20: After analyzing the source documents, record the appropriate transactions. All transactions occur during January of your current year.

AAA Shovels   **INVOICE # 74A**

TO   Your Name Hardware Store   **Date: January 6**
Your address
Reno, NV 89557   Due Date: February 5

QTY	DESCRIPTION	UNIT PRICE	LINE TOTAL
25	Shovels	15.00	$375.00
		Total	$375.00

Make all checks payable to AAA Shovels
Thank you for your business!

CCC Wagons   **INVOICE # 801**

TO	Your Name Hardware Store Your address Reno, NV 89557	Date: January 6 Due Date: February 5

QTY	DESCRIPTION	UNIT PRICE	LINE TOTAL
30	Wagons	20.00	$600.00
		Total	$600.00

Make all checks payable to CCC Wagons

Thank you for your business!

 BBB Wheel Barrows   **INVOICE # ER555**

TO	Your Name Hardware Store Your address Reno, NV 89557	Date: January 6 Due Date: February 5

QTY	DESCRIPTION	UNIT PRICE	LINE TOTAL
32	Wheel barrows	75.00	$2,400.00
		Total	$2,400.00

Make all checks payable to BBB Wheel Barrows

Thank you for your business!

Your Name Hardware Store			SALES RECEIPT

Your address
Reno, NV 89557

	SALES NUMBER	1
SOLD TO:	SALES DATE	January 10

Credit Card Sales

Quantity	Description	Unit Price	Amount
4	Shovels		120.00
5	Wheel barrows		500.00
8	Wagons		400.00
Direct All Inquiries To:		SUBTOTAL	1,020.00
Your name		TAX	
Your phone number		TOTAL	$1,020.00
Your email			

Your Name Hardware Store			SALES RECEIPT

Your address
Reno, NV 89557

	SALES NUMBER	2
SOLD TO:	SALES DATE	January 12

Credit Card Sales

Quantity	Description	Unit Price	Amount
3	Shovels		90.00
4	Wheel barrows		400.00
5	Wagons		250.00
Direct All Inquiries To:		SUBTOTAL	740.00
Your name		TAX	
Your phone number		TOTAL	$ 740.00
Your email			

Your Name Hardware Store			INVOICE	
Your address				
Reno, NV 89557				
		Invoice Number	1	
SOLD TO:		**Invoice Date**	January 12	
Dawn Bright				
1800 W. Peoria Avenue				
Reno, NV 92731				
Quantity	**Description**	**Unit Price**	**Amount**	
1	Shovel		30.00	
Direct All Inquiries To:		SUBTOTAL	30.00	
Your name		TAX		
Your phone number		TOTAL	$30.00	
Your email				

Your Name Hardware Store			SALES RECEIPT	
Your address				
Reno, NV 89557				
		SALES NUMBER	3	
SOLD TO:		SALES DATE	January 17	
Credit Card Sales				
Quantity	**Description**	**Unit Price**	**Amount**	
2	Shovels		60.00	
7	Wheel barrows		700.00	
3	Wagons		150.00	
Direct All Inquiries To:		SUBTOTAL	910.00	
Your name		TAX		
Your phone number		TOTAL	$910.00	
Your email				

Memo

Date: 1/20 current year

Re: Vendor Payments

Your Name Hardware Store pays all outstanding vendor bills for a total of $3,375.00 (*Hint:* The required payment method is Check from Home State Bank; assign check numbers 1 - 3 automatically.) Refer to the remittances that follow.

AAA Shovels	$ 375.00
BBB Wheel Barrows	2,400.00
CCC Wagons	600.00
TOTAL	$3,375.00

Note: On the Pay Bills window, select Assign check number. In the Check No. field, type **1, 2, 3.**

REMITTANCE	
Invoice #	74A
Customer ID	Your Name Hardware Store
Date	January 20
Amount Enclosed	375.00

	AAA Shovels	PHONE	(310) 555-2243
	3000 First Avenue	FAX	(310) 555-2245
	Santa Cruz, CA 90036	E-mail	tim@aaa.biz

REMITTANCE	
Invoice #	ER555
Customer ID	Your Name Hardware Store
Date	January 20
Amount Enclosed	2,400.00

	BBB Wheel Barrows	PHONE	(915) 555-3000
	46011 Mesquite St.	FAX	(915) 555-3100
	El Paso, TX 76315	E-mail	Baker@BBB.com

REMITTANCE	
Invoice #	801
Customer ID	Your Name Hardware Store
Date	January 20
Amount Enclosed	600.00

	CCC Wagons	PHONE	(928) 555-2288
	2301 Dirt Road	FAX	(928) 555-2299
	Dugout, AZ 860035	E-mail	Caitlin@CCC.com

Your Name Hardware Store   **SALES RECEIPT**

Your address
Reno, NV 89557

SOLD TO: SALES NUMBER   4
Credit Card Sales   SALES DATE   January 21

Quantity	Description	Unit Price	Amount
6	Shovels		180.00
8	Wheel barrows		800.00
9	Wagons		450.00

Direct All Inquiries To: SUBTOTAL $1,430.00
Your name   TAX
Your phone number   TOTAL $1,430.00
Your email

McGraw-Hill Education, *Computer Accounting Essentials with QuickBooks 2018, 9e*

Memo

**Your Name
Hardware Store**

Date: 1/21 current year

Re: Rent

Write Check No. 4 to vendor, Stevens Rentals, for $1,350 in payment of rent. (*Hint:* Add vendor as needed, uncheck To be printed. Account: Rent Expense.)

Your Name Hardware Store			INVOICE
Your address			
Reno, NV 89557			
		Invoice Number	2
SOLD TO:		**Invoice Date**	January 22
Shar Watsonville			
3455 West 20th Avenue			
Reno, NV 94702			

Quantity	Description	Unit Price	Amount
1	Wagon		50.00

Direct All Inquiries To:	SUBTOTAL	50.00
Your name	TAX	
Your phone number	TOTAL	$50.00
Your email		

AAA Shovels

INVOICE # 88A

TO   Your Name Hardware Store
     Your address
     Reno, NV 89557

Date: January   24

Due Date: February 23

QTY	DESCRIPTION	UNIT PRICE	LINE TOTAL
15	Shovels	15.00	225.00
		Total	**$225.00**

Make all checks payable to AAA Shovels

Thank you for your business!

CCC Wagons

INVOICE # 962

TO   Your Name Hardware Store
     Your address
     Reno, NV 89557

Date: January 24

Due Date: February 23

QTY	DESCRIPTION	UNIT PRICE	LINE TOTAL
18	Wagons	20.00	360.00
		Total	**$360.00**

Make all checks payable to CCC Wagons

Thank you for your business!

McGraw-Hill Education, *Computer Accounting Essentials with QuickBooks 2018, 9e*

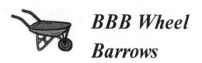

BBB Wheel Barrows

INVOICE # ER702

TO   Your Name Hardware Store
Your address
Reno, NV 89557

Date: January 24

Due Date: February 23

QTY	DESCRIPTION	UNIT PRICE	LINE TOTAL
20	Wheel barrows	75.00	1,500.00
		Total	**$1,500.00**

Make all checks payable to BBB Wheel Barrows

Thank you for your business!

Your Name Hardware Store			SALES RECEIPT

Your address
Reno, NV 89557

SALES NUMBER   5

SOLD TO: SALES DATE   January 26

Credit Card Sales

Quantity	Description	Unit Price	Amount
6	Shovels		180.00
6	Wheel barrows		600.00
6	Wagons		300.00

Direct All Inquiries To:		SUBTOTAL	1,080.00
Your name		TAX	
Your phone number		TOTAL	$1,080.00
Your email			

Memo

Your Name
Hardware Store

Date: 1/27 current year

Re: Your Name Notes Payable

Write Check No. 5 to Your Name for $420.80 in payment of Your Name Notes Payable. (*Hint:* For Your Name Notes Payable, Add New > Other) Use the following Expense distribution.

Account	Debit	Credit
Your Name Notes Payable	340.00	
Interest Expense	80.80	
Home State Bank		420.80

Memo

Your Name
Hardware Store

Date: 1/27 current year

Re: Utilities

Write Check No. 6 to Rainer Utilities for $225.65 in payment of electricity and gas expenses. (*Hint:* Add new vendor, Utilities Expense.)

Your Name Hardware Store			SALES RECEIPT

Your address
Reno, NV 89557

| | | SALES NUMBER | 6 |
| SOLD TO: | | SALES DATE | January 29 |

Credit Card Sales

Quantity	Description	Unit Price	Amount
4	Shovels		120.00
5	Wheel barrows		500.00
8	Wagons		400.00
Direct All Inquiries To:		SUBTOTAL	1,020.00
Your name		TAX	
Your phone number		TOTAL	$1,020.00
Your email			

Memo

Your Name Hardware Store

Date: 1/30 current year

Re: Customer Payments

Received check for two customer accounts.

1. Received a check in full payment of Dawn Bright's account, $30.
2. Received a check in full payment of Shar Watsonville's account, $50.

Memo

Your Name
Hardware Store

Date: 1/30 current year

Re: Credit Card Receipts

Record the deposit to Home State Bank in the Amount of $6,280 ($6,200 from credit card sales; $30 and $50 from customer sales).

Date: January 30

List of Deposits

Coins		Totals
Quarters		$
Dimes		$
Nickels		$
Pennies		$
Total		$
Cash		Totals
$1		$
$5		$
$10		$
$20		$
$50		$
$100		$
	Total	$
	Total Cash	$

Home State Bank
Your Name Hardware Store
Your Address
Reno, NV 89557

Checks	Description	Amount
1	Credit cards	$6,200.00
2	D. Bright	$ 30.00
3	S. Watsonville	$ 50.00
4		
5		
6		
7		
8		
	Total Deposit	$6,280.00

Below is a list of the transactions recorded during January:

Your Name Hardware Store
Transaction List by Date
January 2015

Type	Date	Num	Adj	Name	Memo	Account		Split	Debit	Credit
Jan 15										
Bill	01/06/2015	Invoice No. 74A		AAA Shovels		20000 · Accounts Payable		12100 · Inventory Asset		375.00 •
Bill	01/06/2015	Invoice No. 801		CCC Wagons		20000 · Accounts Payable		12100 · Inventory Asset		600.00
Bill	01/06/2015	Invoice No. ER555		BBB Wheel barr...		20000 · Accounts Payable		12100 · Inventory Asset		2,400.00
Sales Receipt	01/10/2015	1		Credit Card Sales		12000 · Undeposited Funds	✓	-SPLIT-	1,020.00	
Sales Receipt	01/12/2015	2		Credit Card Sales		12000 · Undeposited Funds	✓	-SPLIT-	740.00	
Invoice	01/12/2015	1		Dawn Bright		11000 · Accounts Receivable		46000 · Merchandise Sales	30.00	
Sales Receipt	01/17/2015	3		Credit Card Sales		12000 · Undeposited Funds	✓	-SPLIT-	910.00	
Bill Pmt -Check	01/20/2015	1		AAA Shovels	20000	10000 · Home State Bank		20000 · Accounts Payable		375.00
Bill Pmt -Check	01/20/2015	2		BBB Wheel barr...	20000	10000 · Home State Bank		20000 · Accounts Payable		2,400.00
Bill Pmt -Check	01/20/2015	3		CCC Wagons	20000	10000 · Home State Bank		20000 · Accounts Payable		600.00
Sales Receipt	01/21/2015	4		Credit Card Sales		12000 · Undeposited Funds	✓	-SPLIT-	1,430.00	
Check	01/21/2015	4		Stevens Rentals		10000 · Home State Bank		67100 · Rent Expense		1,350.00
Invoice	01/22/2015	2		Shar Watsonvile		11000 · Accounts Receivable		46000 · Merchandise Sales	50.00	
Bill	01/24/2015	Invoice No. 88A		AAA Shovels		20000 · Accounts Payable		12100 · Inventory Asset		225.00
Bill	01/24/2015	Invoice No. 962		CCC Wagons		20000 · Accounts Payable		12100 · Inventory Asset		360.00
Bill	01/24/2015	Invoice No. ER702		BBB Wheel barr...		20000 · Accounts Payable		12100 · Inventory Asset		1,500.00
Sales Receipt	01/26/2015	5		Credit Card Sales		12000 · Undeposited Funds	✓	-SPLIT-	1,080.00	
Check	01/27/2015	5		Your Name		10000 · Home State Bank		-SPLIT-		420.80
Check	01/27/2015	6		Rainer Utilities		10000 · Home State Bank		68600 · Utilities Expense		225.65
Sales Receipt	01/29/2015	6		Credit Card Sales		12000 · Undeposited Funds	✓	-SPLIT-	1,020.00	
Payment	01/30/2015			Dawn Bright		12000 · Undeposited Funds	✓	11000 · Accounts Receivable	30.00	
Payment	01/30/2015			Shar Watsonvile		12000 · Undeposited Funds	✓	11000 · Accounts Receivable	50.00	
Deposit	01/30/2015				Deposit	10000 · Home State Bank		-SPLIT-	6,280.00	
Jan 15										

BACKUP

Step 21: Back up to your USB drive. The suggested filename is **Your Name Hardware Store January (Portable).QBM.**

ACCOUNT RECONCILIATION

Step 22: Complete account reconciliation for Account No. 10000, Home State Bank on 01/31/20XX. Use the bank statement shown on the next page. (*Hint:* Remember to enter the $25.00 for Bank Service Charges.)

Statement of Account			Your Name Hardware Store	
Home State Bank			Your Address	
January 1 to January 31		Account No. 415-331	Reno, NV 89557	
REGULAR CHECKING				
Previous Balance	12/31	$84,000.00		
Deposits		6,280.00		
Checks (−)		5,371.45		
Service Charges (−)	1/31	25.00		
Ending Balance	1/31	**$84,883.55**		
DEPOSITS				
	1/30	30.00	Dawn Bright	
	1/30	50.00	Shar Watsonville	
		6,200.00	Credit Card	
CHECKS				
	1/20	375.00	1	
	1/20	2,400.00	2	
	1/20	600.00	3	
	1/21	1,350.00	4	
	1/27	420.80	5	
	1/28	225.65	6	

REPORTS

Step 23: Print the Reconciliation Summary and Reconciliation Detail reports.

Step 24: Print the journal (all dates).

Step 25: Print the trial balance (01/31/20XX).

Step 26: Print the vendor balance detail, customer balance detail, and inventory stock status by item.

Step 27: Print the income and expense graph by account and expenses (01/01/20XX to 01/31/20XX).

Step 28: Print the January financial statements: Profit & Loss-Standard, Balance Sheet-Standard, and Statement of Cash Flows.

Step 29: Print the audit trail (all dates).

BACKUP AND E-MAIL

Step 30: Make a backup of Project 1, Your Name Hardware Store to your USB drive. Use **Your Name Hardware Store Complete (Portable).QBM** as the file name.

Step 31: Send an e-mail message to your professor and to yourself with the Your Name Hardware Store Complete (Portable) file attached. Type **Your Name Hardware Store Complete** in the Subject line of the e-mail. If PDF files are the preferred format for saving reports, email those to your instructor.

Step 32: Receive the Your Name Hardware Store Complete e-mail with the correct company file attached. Print it.

Step 33: Turn in completed Check Your Progress: Project 1 and required printouts to your professor.

Student Name_____ **Date**_____

CHECK YOUR PROGRESS: PROJECT 1, Your Name Hardware Store

1. What are the total debit and credit balances on the
   Trial Balance?   _____

2. What are the total assets on January 31?   _____

3. What is the balance in the Home State Bank
   account on January 31?   _____

4. How much is total income on January 31?   _____

5. How much net income (net loss) is reported on
   January 31?   _____

6. What is the balance in the Inventory-Shovels
   account on January 31?   _____

7. What is the balance in the Inventory-Wheel barrows
   account on January 31?   _____

8. What is the balance in the Inventory-Wagons
   account on January 31?   _____

9. During January sales per week for shovels were?   _____

McGraw-Hill Education, *Computer Accounting Essentials with QuickBooks 2018, 9e*

10. What is the balance in the Common Stock account on
     January 31?   _____

11. What is the total cost of goods sold on
     January 31?   _____

12. Were any Accounts Payable incurred during the month
     of January? (Circle your answer.)   YES   NO

Project 2

Student-Designed Merchandising Business

You have learned how to complete the accounting cycle for merchandising businesses. Project 2 gives you a chance to create a merchandising business of your own.

You select retail as the business type, edit your business's Chart of Accounts, create beginning balances and transactions, and complete QuickBooks' computer accounting cycle. Project 2 also gives you an opportunity to review the software features learned so far.

Before you begin, you should design your business. You will need the following:

1. Company information that includes business name, address, and telephone number.
2. Select retail as the business type.
3. A Chart of Accounts
4. A beginning Balance Sheet for your business.
5. One month's transactions for your business. These transactions must include accounts receivable, accounts payable, inventory, sales, and dividends. You should have a minimum of 25 transactions; a maximum of 35 transactions. these transactions should result in a net income.
6. Complete another month of transactions that result in a net loss.

A suggested checklist of printouts is shown on the next page.

	PROJECT 2 CHECKLIST OF PRINTOUTS *Ask your professor how these should be turned in.*	
	Chart of Accounts	
	Check Register	
	Vendor List	
	Item List	
	Customer List	
	Reconciliation-Summary and Detail	
	Journal	
	Trial Balance	
	Profit & Loss-Standard	
	Balance Sheet-Standard	
	Statement of Cash Flows	
	Audit Trail	

Appendix A
Review of Accounting Principles

Appendix A is a review of basic accounting principles and procedures. Standard accounting procedures are based on the double-entry system. This means that each business transaction is expressed with one or more debits and one or more credits in a journal entry and then posted to the ledger. The debits in each transaction must equal the credits. The double-entry accounting system is based on the following premise: each account has two sides–a debit (left) side and credit (right) side. This is stated in the *accounting equation* as:

$$\text{Assets} = \text{Liabilities} + \text{Equities}$$

Assets are the organization's resources that have a future or potential value. Asset accounts include: Cash, Marketable Securities, Accounts Receivable, Supplies, Prepaids, Inventory, Investments, Equipment, Land, Buildings, etc.

Liabilities are the organization's responsibilities to others. Liability accounts include: Accounts Payable, Notes Payable, Unearned Rent, etc.

Equities are the difference between the organization's assets and liabilities. Equity accounts for organizations that are sole proprietorships or partnerships include: Capital and Withdrawals. Equity accounts for organizations that are corporations include contributed capital accounts like Common Stock which represent external ownership and Retained Earnings which represent internal ownership interests. Temporary equity-related accounts known as revenue and expense accounts recognize an organization's income producing activities and the related costs consumed or expired during the period.

Since assets are on the left side of the accounting equation, the left side of the account increases. This is the usual balance, too; assets increase on the left side and have a debit balance. Liabilities and Equities accounts are on the right side of the equation. Therefore, they increase on the right side and normally carry credit balances. Another way to show the accounting equation and double-entry is illustrated below.

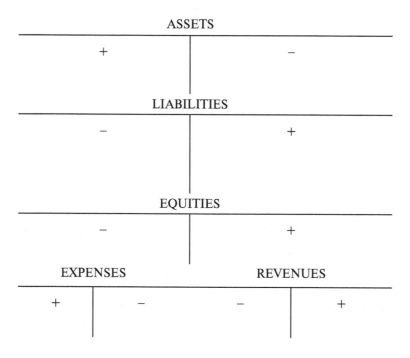

Each element of the accounting equation, Assets, Liabilities, and Equities, behaves similarly to their placement in the equation. Assets have debit balances; Liabilities have credit balances; Equities have credit balances; Expenses have debit balances because they decrease equity; and Revenues have credit balances because they increase equity.

The Chart of Accounts is a listing of all the general ledger accounts. The QuickBooks chart of accounts shows the account number and name, Type (this classified the accounts for financial statements) and Balance Total. To view the chart of accounts, go to the QuickBooks Home page's Chart of Accounts icon. The Your Name Retailers Inc. chart of accounts is shown as an example of a typical merchandising business's chart of accounts.

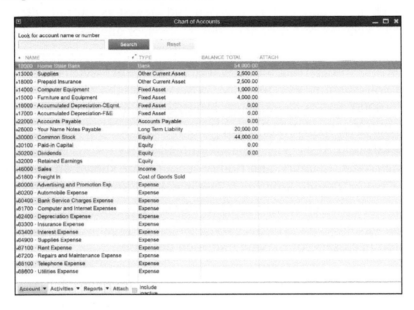

Report information in the form of financial statements is important to accounting. The Balance Sheet reports the financial position of the business on a specific date. It shows that assets are equal to liabilities plus equities—the accounting equation. The Profit & Loss shows the difference between revenue and expenses for a specified period of time (month, quarter, or year). The Income Statement is another name for Profit & Loss. QuickBooks tracks revenue and expense data for an entire year. At the end of the year when all revenue and expense accounts are closed, the resulting net income or loss is moved into the equity account, Retained Earnings. The Statement of Cash Flows reports the operating, financial, and investing activities for the period. It shows the sources of cash coming into the business and the destination of the cash going out.

The most important task is accurately recording transactions into the appropriate accounts. QuickBooks helps you by organizing the software into Home,

Vendors, Customers, Employees, Company, Banking, and Report Centers. By selecting the appropriate Center and/or icon, you can record transactions into the right place. Once transactions are entered, QuickBooks keeps this information in a database. Then the data can be accessed and viewed as journal entries or transaction listings, account or ledger activities, reports, or analysis.

Recording and categorizing business transactions will determine how QuickBooks uses that information. For instance, observe that the chart of accounts shows Account 10000 Home State Bank classified as a Bank Type; Account 13000 Supplies classified as Other Current Asset; Account 14000 Computer Equipment classified as Fixed Asset. The Type column classifies the account for the financial statements—Asset, Liability, and Equity accounts are shown on the Balance Sheet; Income, Cost of Goods Sold, and Expense accounts are shown on the Profit & Loss Statement. As you work with QuickBooks, you see how the accounts, recording of transactions, and reports work together to provide your business with the information necessary for making informed decisions.

Another important aspect of accounting is determining whether the basis for recording transactions is cash or accrual. In the cash basis method, revenues and expenses are recognized when cash changes hands. In other words, when the customer pays for their purchase, the transaction is recorded. When the resource or expense is paid for by the business, the transaction is recorded. In the accrual method of accounting, revenues and expenses are recognized when they occur. In other words, if the company purchases inventory on April 1, the transaction is recorded on April 1. If inventory is sold on account on April 15, the transaction is recorded on April 15 *not* when cash is received from customers. Accrual basis accounting is seen as more accurate because assets, liabilities, revenues, and expenses are recorded when they actually happen. The chart on the next two pages summarizes Appendix A, Review of Accounting Principles.

ACCOUNTING EQUATION:	Assets =	Liabilities +	Owners Equities +	Revenues −	Expenses
Definition:	Something that has future or potential value "Resources"	Responsibilities to others "Payables" "Unearned"	Internal and External ownership	Recognition of value creation	Expired, used, or consumed costs or resources
Debit Rules: DR	Increase	Decrease	Decrease	Decrease	Increase
Credit Rules:CR	Decrease	Increase	Increase	Increase	Decrease
Account Types and Examples	**Current Assets:** Cash, Marketable Securities, Accounts Receivable, Inventory, Prepaids **Plant Assets:** Land, Buildings, Equipment, Accumulated Depreciation **Noncurrent Assets:** Investments, Intangibles	**Current Liabilities:** Accounts Payable, Unearned Revenue, Advances from Customer **Noncurrent or Long-term Liabilities:** Bonds Payable, Notes Payables, Mortgage Payable	**Sole Proprietor:** (both internal and external) Name, Capital; Name, Withdrawals **Partnership:** (both internal and external) Partner A, Capital; Partner A, Withdrawals, etc. **Corporation:** External: Common Stock, Preferred Stock, Paid-in Capital Internal: Retained Earnings, Dividends	**Operating Revenue:** Sales, Fees Earned, Rent Income, Contract Revenue **Other Revenue:** Interest Income	**Product/Services Expenses:** Cost of Goods Sold, Cost of Sales **Operating Expenses:** Selling Expenses, Administrative Expense, General Expense, Salary Expense, Rent Expense, Depreciation Expense, Insurance Expense **Other Expenses:** Interest Expense

T-Account Rules	Assets		Liabilities		Owners Equities		Revenues		Expenses
	Acquire resources	Consume resources	Pay bills Recognize earnings	Buy on credit Receive cash or other assets before earning it	Internal: Net Loss External: Owners reduce ownership thru withdrawals or dividends	Internal: Net Income External: Investment made by owners in company	Sales returns Sales discount given	Sales Earned Income	Resources consumed expired or used
	increase	*decrease*	*decrease*	*increase*	*decrease*	*increase*	*decrease*	*increase*	*Increase* *decrease*

Basic Financial Statements:

Income Statement

Revenue – Expense = Net Income (NI) or
Net Loss (NL)

(Prepare first)

Statement of Equity

Beginning* + NI (or –NL) – (Dividends or Withdrawals) = Ending*

*for Sole Proprietors and Partnerships use "Capital" and Withdrawals
for Corporations use "Retained Earnings" and Dividends

(Prepare second)

Balance Sheet

Assets = Liabilities + Equities

(Prepare third)

Statement of Cash Flows

Operating +/– Investing +/– Financing + Beginning Cash = Ending Cash

(Prepare last)

Appendix B Troubleshooting

Appendix B, Troubleshooting

McGraw-Hill Education, *Computer Accounting Essentials with QuickBooks 2018, 9e*

14. Update QuickBooks, pages 313–314
    ○ Update Company During Restore, page 314
    ○ Update Company and Security Warning During Restore, pages 315–316
15. QuickBooks Support From Intuit, page 316
16. Help Windows, pages 316–317

QUICKBOOKS FOR THE MAC

Every new Mac lets you install and run Microsoft Windows using a built-in utility called <u>Boot Camp.</u> Boot Camp helps you install Windows on our Mac. After you install, restart your Mac to switch between macOS and Windows. How to install Windows on your Mac with Boot Camp is explained at <u>https://support.apple.com/en-us/HT201468</u>.

If you want to run Windows and Mac applications at the same time, without rebooting, you can install Windows using VMware Fusion (<u>http://www.vmware.com/products/fusion/</u>) or Parallels software (<u>http://www.parallels.com/products/desktop/</u>).

INSTALLATON AND ACTIVATION

The QuickBooks 2018 software include with this textbook is a 5-month single user copy for desktop installation. To download and activate QuickBooks 2018, refer to Chapter 1, pages 3 through 15.

Note to instructors: For the classroom site license information, go to <u>www.mhhe.com/qbd2018</u> > Site License. Intuit offers free Educator Registration and classroom site licenses.

DEFAULT FILE LOCATIONS

Company Files

The default location for company files with qbw extensions is C:\Users\Public\Public Documents\Intuit\ QuickBooks\ Company Files

Recommended Backup Routine: .QBB and .QBM Extensions

Back up your company file at the end of each classroom session or each day to a network drive; external hard drive; removable storage device such as a CD, USB flash drive, or to a remote site over the Internet. Do not store backups on your computer's hard drive where you store your working data—if your computer's hard disk fails, you may lose your backup files as well as your working data.

Set Default Location for Backups

When you first use the backup feature, you need to enter the default location where you want to store your backups. You can set or change this default using these instructions.

1. Go to the File menu and click Backup Copy > Create Local Backup (for backup files ending in the extension .QBB).
2. On the Create Backup window, the radio button next to Local backup should be selected. Click on the <Options> button.
3. Click Browse to find the location where you want to store your backups. The directory you choose remains your default until you change it.

For backup files ending in the extension .QBM, select File > Create Copy > Portable company file. On the Save Portable Company File window in the Save in field, select the backup location. (*Hint:* File > Create Copy also includes the selection Backup copy for .QBB backups.)

SET UP FOLDERS FOR DATA MANAGEMENT

You may want to organize QuickBooks' file types in separate folders. QuickBooks' file types include portable backup files (.QBM extensions) and company files (.QBW extensions).

How Do I Show File Extensions?

To show files extensions, follow these steps.

1. Go to File Explorer. (Right-click the start button > left-click File Explorer.)
2. Click on the View tab. A check mark should be next to File name extensions ☑ File name extensions.
3. Close File Explorer.

QuickBooks Company Files Folder

You may want to set up a folder for QuickBooks' company files. QuickBooks' company files end in the extension .QBW. Before restoring files, set up a folder labeled QuickBooks Company Files_QBW.

QuickBooks Company Files_QBW
File folder

When you restore files in QuickBooks, a Save Company File as window appears. In the Save in field, select the QuickBooks Company Files_QBW folder.

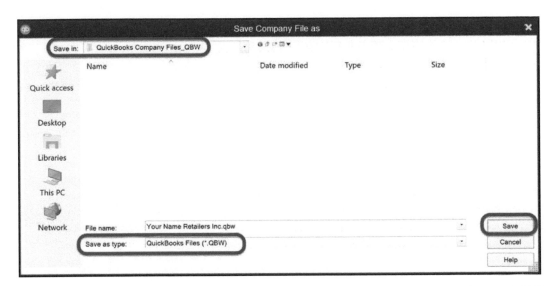

By saving the company files to its own folder, you store the company files (.QBW files) in a different location than the backed up files (.QBM or .QBB extensions).

When a company is opened in QuickBooks, the following file extensions are associated with that company file:

1. .QBW: QuickBooks working file or company file
2. .DSN: Database source name
3. .ND: network data file
4. .TLG: transaction logs

Your Name QB Backups Folder

After completing work, you are instructed to save the backed up files to a separate folder labeled Your Name QB Backups [use your first and last name].

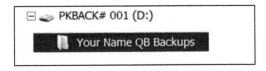

☐ Name		Type
⬜ sample_product-based business (Portable).QBM		QuickBooks Portable Company File
⬜ Your Name Accounting Beginning Balances (Portable).QBM		QuickBooks Portable Company File
⬜ Your Name Accounting Chart of Accounts (Portable).QBM		QuickBooks Portable Company File
⬜ Your Name Accounting December (Portable).QBM		QuickBooks Portable Company File
⬜ Your Name Accounting EOY (Portable).QBM		QuickBooks Portable Company File
⬜ Your Name Accounting Financial Statements (Portable).QBM		QuickBooks Portable Company File
⬜ Your Name Accounting UTB (Portable).QBM		QuickBooks Portable Company File
⬜ Your Name Chapter 2 End (Portable).QBM		QuickBooks Portable Company File
⬜ Your Name Chapter 3 October 1.QBB		QuickBooks Company Backup File
⬜ Your Name Chapter 3 October Check Register.QBB		QuickBooks Company Backup File
⬜ Your Name Chapter 3 October End.QBB		QuickBooks Company Backup File
⬜ Your Name Chapter 4 End.QBB		QuickBooks Company Backup File
⬜ Your Name Chapter 4 November.QBB		QuickBooks Company Backup File
⬜ Your Name Chapter 4 Vendors and Inventory.QBB		QuickBooks Company Backup File
⬜ Your Name Chapter 4 Vendors.QBB		QuickBooks Company Backup File
⬜ Your Name Chapter 5 December Financial Statements.QBB		QuickBooks Company Backup File
⬜ Your Name Chapter 5 December UTB.QBB		QuickBooks Company Backup File
⬜ Your Name Chapter 5 EOY (Portable).QBM		QuickBooks Portable Company File
⬜ Your Name Chapter 6 January Check Register.QBB		QuickBooks Company Backup File
⬜ Your Name Chapter 6 January Financial Statements.QBB		QuickBooks Company Backup File
⬜ Your Name Chapter 6 UTB.QBB		QuickBooks Company Backup File
⬜ Your Name Exercise 4-2 December.QBB		QuickBooks Company Backup File
⬜ Your Name Exercise 6-1 (Portable).QBM		QuickBooks Portable Company File
⬜ Your Name Hardware Store Beginning Balances (Portable).QBM		QuickBooks Portable Company File
⬜ Your Name Hardware Store Chart of Accounts (Portable).QBM		QuickBooks Portable Company File
⬜ Your Name Hardware Store Complete (Portable).QBM		QuickBooks Portable Company File
⬜ Your Name Hardware Store January (Portable).QBM		QuickBooks Portable Company File
⬜ Your Name Hardware Store Vendors Inventory Customers (Portable).QBM		QuickBooks Portable Company File
⬜ Your Name Hardware Store.QBB		QuickBooks Company Backup File
⬜ Your Name Retailers, Inc. (Backup Aug 31,2017 12 51 PM).QBB		QuickBooks Company Backup File
⬜ Your Name Retailers, Inc. Chapter 3 (Backup Oct 03,2017 02 55 PM).QBB		QuickBooks Company Backup File
⬜ Your Name sample_service-based business (Portable).QBM		QuickBooks Portable Company File
⬜ Your Name Sports End (Portable).QBM		QuickBooks Portable Company File
⬜ Your Name Sports January (Portable).QBM		QuickBooks Portable Company File
⬜ Your Name Sports Starting Balance Sheet (Portable).QBM		QuickBooks Portable Company File
⬜ Your Name Sports Vend Inv Cust (Portable).QBM		QuickBooks Portable Company File

Thirty-two backup files are shown. If Practice Set 2, Your Name Sports, is completed, 36 backups are listed. Two types of backups are shown – QuickBooks Portable Company Files (.QBM extensions) and QuickBooks Company Backup Files (.QBB extensions).

Types of Backup Files

QuickBooks includes three types of backup files:

1. Backup copy (.QBB extensions)
2. Portable company file (.QBM extensions)
3. Accountant's copy (.QBX or .QBA extensions)

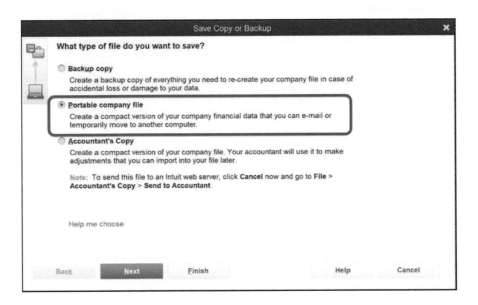

In *Computer Accounting Essentials with QuickBooks 2018, 9e,* the methods shown for backing up are the Portable company file (.QBM) selection or the Backup copy (.QBB) file. Portable company files are smaller than Backup copy files. For emailing a file, portable company files (.QBM) are recommended.

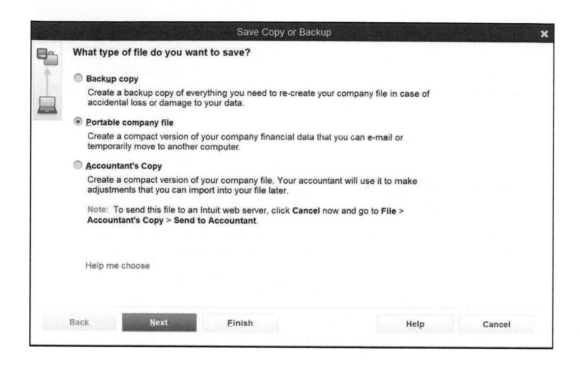

Backup Location No Longer Available

QuickBooks saves the location where files are backed up. If you decide to use another backup location, this Warning window will appear.

Click <OK>, then select the location where you want to back up. Type the file name, then save.

Restore Previous Local Backup

If you want to restore a file previously backed up with the company that is currently open, use the File > Open or Restore Company selection. On the Open or Restore Company window, restore the appropriate backup copy (.QBB) or portable file (.QBM).

TROUBLESHOOTING BACKUP AND RESTORE: USING USB DRIVES

USB drives use different file systems. To see your USB drive's file system, right-click on the drive letter, left-click Properties, then select the General tab. Some USB drives are more reliable than others. If you are experiencing difficulty using a USB drive when either restoring from or backing up to it, use your Desktop instead. In other words, backup to your desktop first, then copy the file to a USB drive. Do the same thing in reverse when you want to restore a file. Copy the file from the USB drive to your desktop, then restore the file from your desktop instead of from a USB drive.

Create Copy or Backup: Portable Company Files

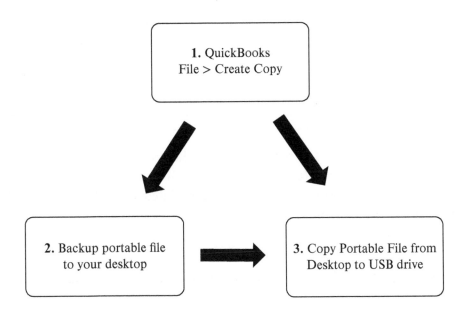

Restore a file

1. If the portable file resides on a USB drive, copy the file from the USB drive to your desktop.

2. Start QuickBooks. Open or restore the file from your desktop instead of the USB drive.

QBW File Already Exists

When restoring a file, if a screen prompts "[File name]. . .qbw already exists. Do you want to replace it?"

Click <No>. In the File name field, change the name slightly; for example, add your initials.

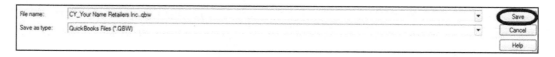

Now that you changed the file name, you can click <Save> to continue restoring your file. (*Hint:* Your Name Retailers Inc. is used in this example. Your file name may differ.) You could also delete the files associated with the company. Then, restore the file without changing its name.

QuickBooks Login Password

When opening a QB company, if a QuickBooks Login window appears, click <OK> to continue. (*Hint:* You do not need to type a password if a password has <u>not</u> been set up.)

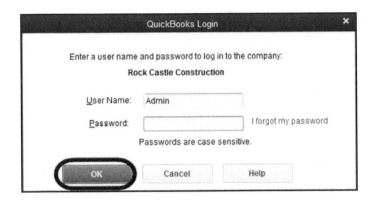

Or, if you set up a password, type it. In Chapter 2, the authors suggest that you do not type a password to avoid the need for typing one when restoring or opening company files.

USE EXCEL WITH QUICKBOOKS

Your instructor may want you to email QuickBooks assignments completed in *Computer Accounting Essentials with QuickBooks 2018.* QuickBooks includes a way to export reports to Excel.

1. Display the report for the appropriate date.

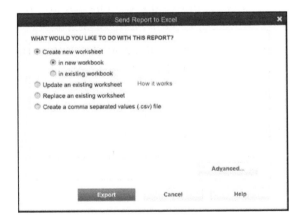

2. You have two choices: E-mail, then select Send report as Excel; *or,* select the Excel button. In these steps you click **Excel ▼** > Create New Worksheet. The Send Report to Excel window appears. Accept the default, in new workbook. The selection for in an existing workbook allows you to add worksheets to an existing file.

3. Click <Export>.

---

4. Excel opens. Save the workbook.

5. Close the QuickBooks report.

E-MAIL REPORT AS A PDF FILE

You can email reports as PDF files.

When you send a report as a PDF file, the report is attached to an email message. If you do not have Acrobat Reader, you can download it for free from https://get.adobe.com/reader/.

1. Display the report you want to email as a PDF file.

2. Click E-mail, Send report as PDF.

3. If an Email Security window appears, read the information. Then put a check mark in the Do not display this message in the future box. Click <OK>.

4. If a Choose Your Email Method window appears, select
    Setup my email now. The Preferences window appears. If using
    Outlook, select it. (If Web Mail is selected and that is how you are
    sending email, do not change it.)

5. Your email account opens. The report is an attached PDF file. Type
    the recipient's email address and send. Go to the
    File menu, and then click Save as PDF.

You can also display the report, select Print, then save as
PDF file. Then, email an attachment.

PRINTING AND FILTERING REPORTS

There are numerous ways to print or display reports. For example, you can filter reports for the type of transaction.

After completing an Exercise, let's say you want to look at the vendor bills paid. In this example, Project 1, Your Name Hardware Store is used.

1. From the Reports menu or Report Center, select Accountant & Taxes > Journal. In the From field, type the appropriate from and to dates.

    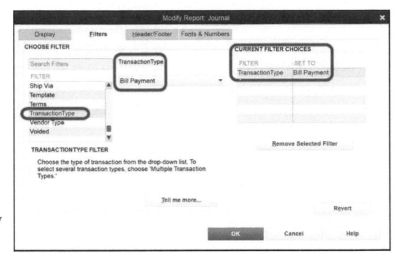

2. Select <Customize Report>. The Modify Report: Journal window appears. Select the Filters tab.

3. In the Filter list, select Transaction Type. In the Transaction Type field, select Bill Payment.

4. Click <OK>. The Journal appears with the vendor payments, Bill Pmt-Check, shown.

Your Name Hardware Store
Journal
January 2018

Trans #	Type	Date	Num	Adj	Name	Memo	Account	Debit	Credit
12	Bill Pmt -Check	01/20/2018	1		AAA Shovels	20000	10000 · Home State Bank		375.00
					AAA Shovels	20000	20000 · Accounts Payable	375.00	
								375.00	375.00
13	Bill Pmt -Check	01/20/2018	2		BBB Wheel Barrows	20000	10000 · Home State Bank		2,400.00
					BBB Wheel Barrows	20000	20000 · Accounts Payable	2,400.00	
								2,400.00	2,400.00
14	Bill Pmt -Check	01/20/2018	3		CCC Wagons	20000	10000 · Home State Bank		600.00
					CCC Wagons	20000	20000 · Accounts Payable	600.00	
								600.00	600.00
TOTAL								3,375.00	3,375.00

ADD SHORTCUTS TO THE ICON BAR

1. From the menu bar, select View > Customize Icon Bar > Add. You can also delete shortcuts that you do not want to appear on the Icon Bar.

2. The Add Icon Bar Item window appears. Select an item to add. Observe the Label and Description field identifies the item. You can also customize the label and description. Click <OK>.

3. The Customize Icon Bar window appears. To reorder the icons, drag an icon's diamond up or down to the position you want.

ICON BAR LOCATION

The Icon Bar can be located on the top, left, or it can be hidden. To change the location of the Icon Bar, from the menu bar, select View. The Left Icon Bar is selected. Other selections include Top Icon Bar or Hide Icon Bar.

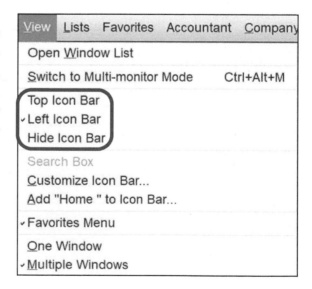

UNINSTALL QUICKBOOKS AND REMOVE ALL QUICKBOOKS FILES AND FOLDERS

It is sometimes necessary to uninstall QuickBooks, rename installation files left behind, and then reinstall QuickBooks. This may be required when a QuickBooks function is damaged or when simply reinstalling QuickBooks does not correct an issue. This process is called a **Clean Install** or **Clean Uninstall.**

Note: Be sure to have your QuickBooks download file and license and product numbers available before uninstalling QuickBooks. Read the instructions on this website to determine which uninstall method you prefer http://support.quickbooks.intuit.com/support/Articles/HOW12212.

TOGGLE QUICKBOOKS TO ANOTHER EDITION

The student trial version software, included with the textbook, can be used on one computer for 5 months.

1. From the menu bar, select File > Toggle to Another Edition. The Select QuickBooks Industry-Specific Edition window appears. Select QuickBooks Pro.

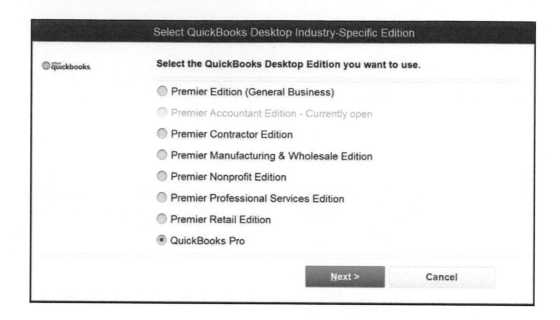

2. Click <Next> and the version of QuickBooks changes to the Pro.

QUICKBOOKS RELEASES

The screen images that appear in the textbook were done with QuickBooks Accountant 2018. If you are using your own laptop or PC, the author suggests updating the software. When you compare screen images with the textbook, you may notice some differences. For example, if you are using QuickBooks 2018 at school and the computer lab is <u>not</u> updating the software, this could result in some differences in screen images, *or* if you are not updating to the new release on your laptop or PC.

Periodically, updates to QuickBooks software are available for download. These updates improve program functionality and fix known issues with the software. Read this online support site information, http://support.quickbooks.intuit.com/support/Articles/HOW12418.

UPDATE QUICKBOOKS

Product updates, also called maintenance releases, prompt you to install the update when you first start QuickBooks. The updates are identified using release numbers such as R3, R4, etc. The authors suggest installing updates. This information is also shown on pages 84-85 (a.-e.).

1. If a QuickBooks Update Service window appears, read the information.

2. After selecting <Install Now>, the User Account Control window appears > click <Yes>. The update starts to install. Wait for the Update complete window to appear.

3. After clicking <OK>, QB starts.

If the QuickBooks Update Service window appears during restore, there are two types of pop-ups.

1. Update Company window.
2. Security Warning window.

Update Company During Restore

If an Update Company window appears during restore, click <Yes>. An Update Company window appears.

A Working window appears.

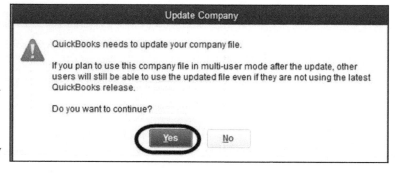

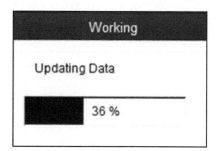

When the data is restored successfully window appears, select <OK>.

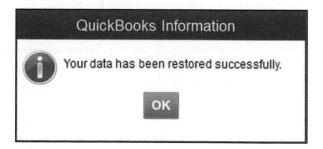

Depending on whether you are restoring a .QBB (backup file) or .QBM (portable file), your update screens may differ.

Update Company and Security Warning During Restore

QuickBooks updates automatically. If an Update Company window appears during restore, click <Yes>. An Update Company window appears.

If a Security Warning window appears, Click <Yes>.

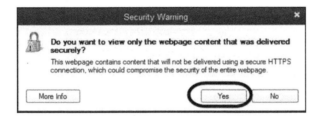

You can press the function key <F2> to see the QuickBooks release being used.

Your release number may differ. If some of your screen images look different when compared to the illustrations in the textbook, you or the computer lab may not have updated QuickBooks. For more information, refer to page 312, QuickBooks Releases.

QUICKBOOKS SUPPORT FROM INTUIT

QuickBooks support is available from Intuit, the publisher of QuickBooks software, at http://support.quickbooks.intuit.com/support/.

From the support website, you can:

- Ask a question.
- Browse Topics.
- Go to Top FAQs.
- Link to Announcements, Additional Resources, Connect via Twitter and facebook, and look at Other products.

HELP WINDOWS

Use the <F1> function key for Help from any QuickBooks window. When you press <F1>, a Have a Question window appears. In the example, <F1> was selected from the Home page.

You can search help, type a word in the Search field, Visit Support, or Ask Community. When Use Home page insights is selected, information is shown. Additional links can also be selected.

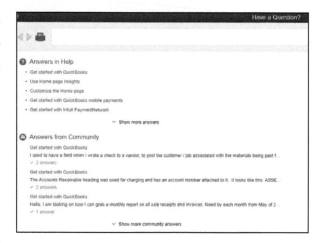

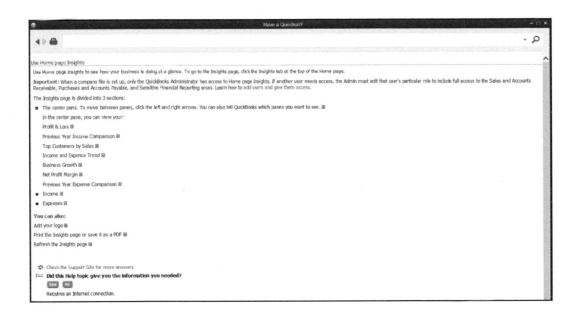

Appendix C

Glossary

Appendix C lists a glossary of terms used in *Computer Accounting Essentials with QuickBooks 2018, 9th Edition*. Appendix C is also included on the textbook website at www.mhhe.com/qbd2018.

accounting equation	The accounting equation is stated as assets = liabilities + equities. (p. 291)
accounts payable	A group of accounts that show the amounts owed to vendors or creditors for goods, supplies, or services purchased on account. (p. 137)
accounts payable ledger	On the accounts payable ledger, vendors and payable details are shown. The vendor balance detail report shows all the transactions related to each vendor. The totals shown in the Balance column are the company's unpaid balances. (p. 153)
accounts payable transactions	Purchases on account from vendors. (p. 137)
accounts receivable	Group of accounts that show the amounts customers owe for services or products sold on credit. (p. 166)

accounts receivable ledger   Customers and receivables accounts which are grouped together. The customer balance detail report shows all transactions related to customers, grouped by customer and job. The totals in the Balance column are the unpaid balances for each customer and job. (p. 166)

accounts receivable transactions   Credit transactions from customers. (p. 166)

account reconciliation   As you write checks, withdraw money, make deposits, and incur bank charges, each of these transactions is recorded in QuickBooks and then matched with the bank's records. This matching process is called reconciliation. (p. 115)

assets   The organization's resources that have future or potential value. (p. 291)

backing up   Saving your data to a hard drive, network drive, or external media. Backing up ensures that you can start where you left off the last time you used QB 2018. (p. 15)

balance sheet	Lists the types and amounts of assets, liabilities, and equity as of a specific date. (p. 97)
bill	A request for payment for products and services. Also called invoice. (p. 154)
chart of accounts	List of all the accounts in the company's general ledger. (p. 90)
closing the fiscal year	Moving expense and revenue accounts to retained earnings. (p. 226)
compound transaction	An entry that affects three or more accounts. (p. 209)
credit sales	Refers to sales made to customers that will be paid for later. (p. 174)
customer invoice	Request for payment to a customer for products or services sold. (p. 166)
desktop	Also called the Home page. (p. 43)

desktop software	Refers to software that is installed locally; for example, QuickBooks Accountant Desktop 2018 is installed on the hard-drive of the computer. (p. v)
equities	The difference between the company's assets and liabilities. (p. 291)
external media	Backing up to a drive other than the computer's hard drive or network drive. (p. 16)
general journal	The general journal shows the debits and credits of transactions and can be used to record any type of transaction. In this text, you use the general journal to record adjusting and closing entries. (p. 209)
home page	Displays information about the company. The QB Home page includes areas for vendors, customers, employees, company, banking and their accompanying workflow processes. The Home page is also called the desktop. (p. 43)

income statement	An income statement is where a business reports its revenues and expenses and determines its net income or loss for a period. QuickBooks refers to the income statements as the Profit & Loss. (p. 44)
icon bar	The icon bar contains shortcuts to the tasks and reports you use the most. You can place the Icon Bar to the left of the QB desktop, above it, or hide it. The Icon Bar can also be customized. (p. 42)
insights page	The insights page shows the company's financial information. (p. 44)
inventory items	A product that is purchased for sale and is tracked in the Inventory account on the balance sheet. (p. 143)
invoice	A request for payment for products and services. Also called bill. (p. 154)
liabilities	Liabilities are the organization's responsibilities to others. Liability accounts include accounts payable, notes payable, unearned rent, etc. (p. 291)

menu bar	Contains menus for File, Edit, View, Lists, Favorites, Accountant, Company, Customers, Vendors, Employees, Banking, Reports, Window and Help. (p. 43)
portable backups	To email or move your company data, create a portable backup. A portable file is a compact version of your company file, small enough to be sent by email or saved to portable media. Use a portable file whenever you need to copy your company data to another location or send it to another person. Portable backup files end in the extension QBM. (p. 33)
preferences	By setting preferences, you can customize QuickBooks to suit the needs of your business and personal style of working. Preferences allow you to configure the way in which some functions and keys work in QuickBooks. (p. 87)
profit & loss	This report is also known as an income statement. It summarizes income and expenses for the month, so you can tell whether you're operating at a profit or a loss. The report shows subtotals for each income or expense account in your chart of accounts. The last line shows your net income (or loss) for the month. (p. 44)

QuickBooks backups	To safeguard your QB data against accidental loss, create regular backups. The backup contains everything you need to recreate your company file. QuickBooks backup files end in the extension QBB. (p. 33)
restore	Previously backed up data can be restored or retrieved from the File menu's Restore Previous Local Backup selection. Files can also be restored from the No Company Open window; select the Open or restore an existing company. (p. 16)
separation of duties	Work is divided between different employees to ensure data integrity. Separation of duties is a basic internal control. For example, to keep employees from stealing customer payments, the tasks of opening the mail, recording customer payments, and making deposits at the bank are assigned to three different employees. (p. 188)
statement of financial position	Lists the types and amounts of assets, liabilities, and equity as of a specific date. Also called the balance sheet. (p. 97)

taskbar	In Windows 8/7/Vista, the Start button and taskbar are located at the bottom of the screen. (p. 42)
title bar	Contains company name and the program name. (p. 42)
trial balance	This report lists the ending debit and credit balances at the end of a reporting period. The trial balance shows that debits and credits are equal. (p. 121)
USB drive	USB is an abbreviation of Universal Serial Bus. USB drives are known as flash drives, pen drives, etc. USBs are used as storage media. (p. 2)
user interface (UI)	The general look of a program is called its user interface. (p. 29)
vendors	A person or company from which the company buys products or services. (p. 137)

Index